To Jim & Becky
July 18, 2015

Opa
Thomas A. Crawford

Resurrections...of an Obituary Writer

BY TOM CRAWFORD

RESURRECTIONS

of an Obituary Writer

By
TOM CRAWFORD

IN MEMORIAM

ENSIGN CHARLES C. MANTELL

(1919-1944)

TABLE OF CONTENTS

ENSIGN MANTELL OF WHITINSVILLE DIES IN SO. PACIFIC CRASH

1919-1944

WHITINSVILLE, July 4 – Ensign Charles C. Mantell, son of Mr. and Mrs. Cornelius Mantell of Sylvan road, pilot of a naval torpedo bomber, was killed while on duty in the South Pacific area June 8, according to a letter received by the family from an officer of his squadron who was an eyewitness to the crash in which the young man met his death.

In the letter was the memorial service program held on a carrier ship for Ensign Mantell and his crewmates. According to the letter, Ensign Mantell was on patrol duty and was taking off from the carrier when the plane failed to gain elevation, turned over and crashed into the sea.

Known as "Chick" Mantell

Known by a host of friends in this and surrounding sections as "Chick" Mantell, he entered the Naval Air service on Nov. 12, 1942, reporting at Chapel Hill, N.C. He was commissioned an ensign on graduation on Aug. 21, 1943, at Corpus Christi, Tex. He also took advanced training at Ft. Lauderdale, Fla., and Glen View, Ill., before being assigned to duty early this year in the South Pacific theater.

He was a graduate of Northbridge High School and prior to entering the service was employed at Heald Machine Co., Worcester.

A memorial service for Ensign Mantell will be held Sunday afternoon at the Methodist Church at a time to be announced. Rev. Glenn D. Glazier is in charge of arrangements.

Ensign Mantell was born in this town, son of Cornelius and Clara (Cnossen) Mantell. Besides his parents he leaves three sisters, Mrs. Dora Norman, Mrs. Thomas Crawford and Mrs. Joseph Johnston, this town; three brothers, Sidney and Andrew of this town and Cornelius of Mendon.

The (Worcester, Mass.) *Evening Gazette*   JULY 4, 1944

"CHICK"

My uncle Chick was 13 the day I was born.

I was 12 the day he died.

That was June 8, 1944.

His TBF, the same type of plane that George H. W. Bush, U.S. President No. 41, piloted during World War II, crashed into the Pacific on takeoff from the U.S.S. Cabot., a Navy carrier.

Word of the death was delivered at the Linwood Avenue playground in the Blackstone River Valley village of Whitinsville in the town of Northbridge in Central Massachusetts.

It was brought by my father, whom I'd never seen so somber.

We drove, mostly in silence, in Dad's 1940 Hudson up Fletcher Street to the house on Sylvan Road that Chick had helped my grandfather build.

Chick was the youngest of seven siblings, and seemingly the favorite of all.

Most of the clan was already gathered there, sitting in the green backyard.

It was the saddest day of my life, because the shortest of lives are the most difficult to celebrate.

But memories have been kinder.

Chick was the first person to take me to a golf course.

I must have been 6 or 7.

He even let me hit a couple of balls off the high tee, then the 9th at Edgewood Golf Club across the Douglas town line in Uxbridge.

The great Scot, golf architect Donald Ross, had brought golf to Whitinsville in 1925.

He had laid out the nine holes of the private Whitinsville Golf Club on rolling meadow next to the Mumford River, which remained a picturesque tributary of the Blackstone River despite having been befouled for years by the industrial waste from the textile factories above it.

There was only one house on the golf course at the time

At this writing, there remains only one, a colonial built in 1790, 12 years after the town of Northbridge was incorporated and 14 years after its owner, Colonel Fletcher, went to the Revolutionary War.

The colonel's daughter Betsy later married a Whitin, the founder of a textile dynasty, and after his death, honored him by having South Northbridge renamed Whitinsville. By the early 20th century, however, the Fletcher-Whitin homestead had passed through several families.

In 1910 it was called Parkis place, and was being rented out to new immigrants too poor to own their own horses and wagons but still willing to walk the mile into town for work, shopping, schooling and worship.

One of those immigrant families was the Mantells, who had come over to the United States from The Netherlands in 1907.

In 1910, they moved into Parkis place.

It was a wonderful place to grow up, according to all the members of the family. There was an orchard, old growth trees and plenty of room for gardening.

Then in the early '20s, the Whitin Machine Works, the principal industry, employer, landlord and retailer in town, decided to build a golf course near Parkis place.

Chick was only a 6-year-old boy when it was finished in 1925. My mother, nine years older, observed the whole process.

One day, as she sat on a stone wall at Parkis place watching the workmen grade the slopes for the fourth green a few yards away, a genial Scotsman approached her and asked her for a favor.

Apparently, the Whitin Machine Works had provided a tenement for Mr. and Mrs. Ross downtown, but the increasingly famous golf architect was worried that his wife might be lonely and could use some company.

He asked if my mother would be willing to pay her a visit.

She willingly did so and expressed the view 75 years later that that visit and subsequent ones brought a measure of companionship to the lonely woman.

The golf course had an immediate and lasting impact on the town, and in particular to the families on its immediate flanks.

Several of the Mantell boys became caddies and learned to play. Chick's older brother Andy joined the greenskeeping staff at the club, later attended Stockbridge, the agricultural arm of Massachusetts State College, now the University of Massachusetts. Andy later became head greenskeeper at Madison Country Club in Ohio where Arnie Palmer migrated north from Latrobe, Pa. for early experience in his pro career. And Andy eventually built his own course, Hidden Valley at nearby Thompson, Ohio, on Lake Erie.

On the other side of the Whitinsville course, just out of sight and around the bend from the clubhouse, lived the Youngs.

Pete Young worked in the shop, as the Whitin Machine Works, a producer of such textile preparatory machinery as spinning frames, was called locally. It employed more than 5,000 during good times. But during the summer, Pete worked more and more on the course, also on the greenskeeping staff.

His son Raymond, a later member of the caddie corps, eventually became president of the exclusive club, whose waiting list for years rose into the hundreds.

One of Ray's sons, Gary, also went into golf, and became the head professional at nearby Pleasant Valley Country Club in Sutton, for a lengthy period a stop on the Professional Golf Association and Ladies Golf Professional Association tours.

Three of the Ovian boys, sons of an Armenian refugee from the Ottoman persecution and purges of the late 19th and early 20th century, also rose from the caddie ranks to golf club ownership in Connecticut and Long Island. The Ovians also were neighbors of the Youngs and the golf course.

But Parkis place, now adjacent to a golf course, perhaps became too idyllic.

After serving as the Mantell home for 26 years, it was decided that the pastoral estate next to the fourth green of the prestigious Whitinsville Golf Club was just too much house for a now very well entrenched immigrant family.

Ownership was passed to Ralph E. Lincoln, a vice president of the Whitin Machine Works, who was also an avid golfer, and the Mantells were forced to move.

This is where history ends and memory begins.

My first recollections were these:

1.   My grandparents moved into a six-family tenement on Overlook Street in the New Village section built for recent immigrant factory workers at the "shop." My grandmother, a country girl born in the green farmland of Friesland east of what was then called the Zuider Zee (which was later to become through Dutch engineering the Ijsselmeer), was miserable in the small apartment.

2.   At about the same time, the Pierce family farm up the road from

Parkis place went into bankruptcy, and the farmhouse became vacant and rentable. The Mantells immediately moved back near their original home. My first vivid memory there is of the oak tree that came down during the September 1938 hurricane and crashed through the roof over the kitchen. The second was turning around while playing at the well in front of the farmhouse and discovering that my brother Bob, then 3, had disappeared. I ran frantically into the kitchen of Pierce's place yelling, "Bobby fell in the well, Bobby fell in the well." I had never seen my father, who was asthmatic and not very athletic, move so fast. He climbed down the slippery fieldstones of the well, and found Bob holding onto a pipe at the bottom, and carried him up to the dry light.

3.   Stuart Brown, my grandfather's employer at the Whitin Spinning Ring Co., an independent corporation that was nevertheless a satellite of the Whitin Machine Works, had recognized and understood the severe trauma caused by the family's displacement from Parkis place, and sought to remedy the matter. He suggested that my grandfather buy some property from the Pierce farmland, which was being parceled off as house lots. When my grandfather, just having raised seven children through the depression, acknowledged that he did not have the cash to buy any land, Mr. Brown suggested that he have the price of the land taken out of his weekly pay in installments The five dollars that was deducted from his pay for an undetermined number of months or years resulted in the purchase of several ultimately valuable acres of farmland.

4.   The next image is of my grandfather, then 63, and my Uncle Chick digging a cellar hole by hand, pick and shovel, removing the dirt and boulders in wheelbarrows trundled up from the cellar hole on planks. Not long after the house was finished, arrangements were made to sell the house to his youngest daughter, my Aunt Jennie, and her husband Joe, and build another for themselves. A third parcel was sold to the eldest daughter Dora and her husband so they could build a house. My parents were offered a contiguous parcel to the rear that faced on Fletcher Street, and that parcel

was bought for $100, which at that time was five times my father's weekly salary.

5.   I used to stand beside the refrigerator (ice boxes were just going out) and marvel how Uncle Chick could come in from his labors (he was now working on the second house with my grandfather) and gulp down an entire quart of milk. I was eventually to find out that that wasn't all that he drank. After he got his first car, he would volunteer to baby-sit.

We would go to the golf course, to the ice cream stand and to the quarry. The quarry in North Uxbridge, Mass. was a real adventure. Chick and his two older brothers, Andy and Connie, frequently swam at the quarry. Swimming there itself was illegal, which I am certain must have been compounded by the fact they were often in the buff. But what remains to this day even more discomforting was their habit of leaping from heights of 30 to 40 feet or perhaps even higher from the sheer rock cliffs above into the pristine quarry waters. Naked. It took years for me to get even to the high board at a pool, and then properly attired in swimming trunks.

6.   There was another place Chick took me – to a barroom. Not that I was ever taken inside. But I still remember which barroom, and recall only that the wait for him to come out seemed interminable, although I am certain he went in for only a beer or two.

Then came Pearl Harbor

Before entering the Navy less than a year later, Chick was feted at a family dinner at Ma Glockner's restaurant in Bellingham, Mass. It was a large and occasionally boisterous gathering, and may have been the last time that some of those who attended saw Chick.

As for me, I, as a pre-teen, now proudly had a pen pal. Our teacher in

Grammar School encouraged each of us to write, via V-Mail (letters that were photographed and miniatured for ease of handling) to our relatives and friends in military service.

The V-Mail correspondence was acknowledged in one of the last letters we received from Chick aboard the Cabot:

"Dear Gert, Tom and Kids," it begins, dated May 16, 1944.

"Hurray it happened! My mail has finally caught up to me and believe me it sure seemed good to hear from you all again.

Most of the letters were dated the first of April or thereabouts, yours being the third but from now on everything should be O.K.

Glad to hear you're all doing well and that the kids are fine. This makes me one ahead of you again, I believe. But I owe Tommy a few myself. Jackie (born on Feb. 24, 1943) must be quite a boy now and I imagine by this time he's keeping you on your toes. Glad to hear Bobby is the same as always. Don't worry, he'll do all right. I believe he's got the right attitude already. Tell Tommy I'm glad to get his V-mail letters and that I'll write to him before we shove off again if possible."

Much of the rest of the letter made inquiries about other members of the extended family, and remarked on the excellence of the Navy food even if it did not measure up to Ma Glockner's chicken. He also lamented about his writing skills, after having been assigned to censor the letters that were going out from the squadron.

And he was impressed at the romantic nature of much of the correspondence, although he did attribute some of this to what a lot of water (the Pacific) can do. He made specific reference to one unnamed steward from Georgia who was writing the same romantic letters and sending them to six girls. He mused about what it would be like when all six met him at the train station. There was one disturbing paragraph.

"Was supposed to go on a practice attack today but my plane started shooting oil before takeoff so I downed it and hit the sack again."

He ended the letter:

"Another letter to my girl (?) and off to the sack.

Always,
Chick"

The memorial service for Chick and his two crew members, ARM2c Milton Wartjes Helm and ACM2c General Lee Turner, Jr. was held aboard the Cabot on the 11th of June, 1944. The service at the Methodist Church in Whitinsville was four weeks later.

Sixty years later, my youngest brother Jack, who had never seen his youngest uncle, suggested we establish a memorial for Chick and began arrangements with the local veterans to establish the same at the corner of Fletcher Street and Country Club Drive, across from the 18th Century home where he grew up, now adjacent to the golf course. The ceremony was held on a rainy Saturday, June 10, 2006.

Members of the Crawford, Mantell, Johnston, Knebusch, Smith and Kennedy families joined to commemorate their uncle. A nephew of another victim of the crash, the aforementioned Milton Helm, also was located and attended the ceremony. All in attendance acknowledge the tributes of the state, county and town fathers who participated.

My brother Jack later managed to contact Chick's best friend on the carrier, who witnessed the crash and attributed it to a faulty catapult that did not give the plane enough airspeed. The plane rolled due to inadequate lift and hit the seas. The depth charges caused it to explode.

The Northbridge town manager, Michael Coughlin, who attended the commemoration, went that extra mile by establishing via the Internet that an article written by Ernie Pyle about aircraft carrier plane crews had actually been written after his visit to the U.S.S. Cabot, Chick's ship.

⌒

A clipping of that article, published by **The** (Worcester, Mass.) **Evening Gazette**, *remains in the family archives, and reads as follows:*

Ernie Pyle Says:
WATCHING CARRIER PILOTS LAND IS NERVE WRACKING. FLIERS COME IN FROM EVERY DIRECTION; SOME PLANES LOST

IN THE WESTERN PACIFIC (Delayed) The first time you see a plane land on a carrier, you almost die. At the end of the first day my muscles were sore just from being all tensed up while watching the planes come in.

It is all so fast, timing is so split-second, space is so small – well, somebody said that carrier pilots were the best in the world, and they must be or there wouldn't be any of them left alive.

Planes don't approach a carrier as they would on land – from way back and in a long glide. Instead, they almost seem to be sneaking up as if to surprise it. They're in such an awkward position and flying at such a crazy angle you don't see how they can ever land on anything.

But it's been worked out by years of experience, and it's the best way. Everything is straightened out in the last few seconds of flying. That is – if it works.

Anything can happen in those last few seconds. Once in a great while the plane loses its speed and spins into the water just behind the ship. And planes have been known to ram right into the stern of the ship.

The air currents are always bad. The ship's "island" distorts the currents, and makes the air rough. Even the wake of the ship – the waters churned up by the propellers – have an effect on the air through which the planes must pass.

If half a dozen planes come in successively without one getting a "wave off" from the signalman, you're doing pretty well. For landing on the deck of a small carrier in a rough sea is just like landing on half a block of Main Street while a combined hurricane and earthwake is going on.

You would call it a perfect landing if a plane came in and hit on both wheels at the same time, in the center of the deck headed straight forward, and caught about the third one of the cables stretched across the deck.

But very few of them are perfect. They come in a thousand different ways. If their approach is too bad, the signalman waves them around again.

They'll sometimes come in too fast and hit the deck so hard a tire blows. They'll come in half-sideways, and the cable will jerk them around in a tire-screeching circle.

They'll come in too close to the edge of the deck, and sometimes go right on over the catwalk. They'll come in so high they'll miss all the arresting gear and slam into the high cables stretched across mid-decks, called "The Barrier."

Sometimes they do a somersault over the barrier, and land on their backs. Sometimes they bounce all around and hit the "island." Sometimes they bounce 50 feet in the air and still get down all right. Sometimes they catch fire.

During the Tokyo strike, one of the big carriers running near us lost three planes in 10 minutes. One was shot up and had to "ditch" in the water alongside the ship.

The next one slammed into the "island," and was so wrecked they just heaved the wreckage over the side. The next one to come in crashed the "barrier" and burned up.

And on the other hand, you'll land planes for weeks without a bad crackup. We wrecked three planes our first three days out in crashes — and not a single one after that.

The first time I watched our boys land, they were pretty bad. They hadn't flown for about two weeks, and were a little rusty.

It's always that way after a ship has been in port for a while. Everybody dreads the first two or three days, until they get their hand in again.

As I was watching the first flight coming in one by one, my room-mate, Lt. Comdr. Al Masters, came up behind me and said, "Well, I see you've got the carrier stance already. I noticed you leaning way over to help pull them around into position."

When all the planes were back, I walked over to Comdr. Al Gurney, the air officer, and said, "If I'm going to watch this for the whole trip, you'll have to provide me with some heart-failure medicine."

And he replied, "Well, think of me. I've had to watch two thousand of them. It'll drive you nuts."

The previous skipper of this ship finally got so he refused to watch when the planes were coming in. He just stood on the bridge and kept looking forward.

And a friend of mine in the crew is almost as bad. He is Chief Bos'ns Mate George Rowe, from Fort Worth, Texas. His nickname is "Catfish."

"I was on this ship for a year before I ever saw an entire flight land," he said. "I just couldn't bear to look at them."

But as the trip wore on the boys improved and my own nerves hardened, and between us, we managed to get all our planes down for the rest of the trip without a single casualty either to them or to me.

DR. W. EDWARD BALMER
DECEASED ON THURSDAY

1873-1966

WHITINSVILLE – Dr. W. Edward Balmer, 92, of 40 Hill St., who was instrumental in the founding of the Whitinsville Hospital in 1913, died Thursday in his home.

He was born in Whitinsville, the son of the late William and Sarah (Rae) Balmer, and practiced medicine in this community 62 years. He was the dean of Blackstone Valley physicians.

A graduate of Northbridge High School in 1891 and of Williston (later Williston-Northampton Academy in Easthampton, Mass. Ed. Note) Academy in 1893, he attended Yale College (Class of 1897) and was graduated from Yale Medical School in 1900.

He began his practice in Boston in 1901. He came to this community a short time later. He served as the Northbridge Board of Health physician from 1909 to 1963. He was a member of the Northbridge School Committee from 1913 to 1928, acting for 14 years as chairman.

Dr. Balmer was named associate medical examiner for the Seventh District of Worcester County in 1906 and medical examiner in 1919. He became school physician in 1928 and served in that capacity 35 years.

Dr. Balmer served as chairman of the staff at Whitinsville Hospital from its founding until he became president in 1946, where (sic) that office was created.

In 1949, he was selected by the Worcester District Medical Society as their (sic) candidate for the General Practitioner's Award of the American Medical Society. The basis of the selection was his activity in the various branches of medicine and the respect held by his medical contemporaries for his skill and knowledge.

At a community gathering in Vail Field in 1951, he received tributes for his outstanding medical and civic service. He was given a scroll with the names of 1900 Northbridge persons whose births he attended.

Dr. Balmer was a corporate member of Whitinsville Savings Bank, a member of the Massachusetts Medical Legal Society, Granite Lodge of Masons St. Elmo Chapter, Royal Arch (Order) Masons, and a deacon of Village Congregational Church for 12 years.

He leaves his widow, Josephine (Clark) Balmer, a son Edward Balmer of Woodstock, N.Y., two daughters, Miss Elizabeth Balmer, at home, chairman of the English Department of Sutton High School, and Eleanor, wife of Victor Orsini of New York City, and four grandchildren.

Funeral services were held Saturday in the Village Congregational Church. Rev. Charles D. Myers, pastor, officiated. Burial was in Pine Grove Cemetery. The Carr Funeral Home was in charge of arrangements.

DR. W. EDWARD BALMER
1873-1966

Who delivered you?

Or to be accurate, who assisted your mother in that delivery.

For years, I thought "Doc" Balmer had assisted in mine.

For years I was wrong.

Our family was very fortunate.

We had two family doctors.

Dr. Harold Williams, mother's doctor, delivered me.

He had been her family doctor before she got married, so we retained the best of both medical worlds, two family doctors who made house calls.

And both continued to do so on a regular basis.

When Doc Balmer made a.call, he was thorough.

By the time he left, he had checked everybody and not only had made a diagnosis, invariably correct, of what was wrong, but knew enough about the five members of the family to predict what might go wrong in the future.

He concentrated on hygiene and nutrition.

Shortly before sitting down to write this piece, I asked Spaulding Ross (Sonny) Aldrich, a friend from adolescence and childhood and a member of the Northbridge Historical Society, if he could guess a particular feature of Doc Balmer that I had in mind.

No, he said, and asked me what it was.

"He was always washing his hands," I said.

The flash of nostalgic recognition rolled across Sonny's face, and his eyes shone.

And he remembered.

Bending over the kitchen or bathroom sinks at home. Leaning over the sinks in the schools where he examined pupils. In the Pythian Building where examinations were occasionally conducted and at his office in the Eagle Printing Building on Pine Street.

Washing, washing, washing.

One gains a greater appreciation of hygiene in medicine and Dr. Balmer's practicing of it by reading "The Cry and the Covenant" by Morton Thompson, himself a physician.

Dr. Thompson chronicled the life in novel form of the Hungarian obstetrician Dr. Ignaz Philipp Semmelweis, whose antiseptic practice of washing hands after performing autopsies and before delivering babies was not widely adopted in the medical field until after his death in the latter part of the 19th Century.

Thousands of mothers and their newborns had been dying in the lying-in hospitals and clinics throughout the world because of childbed (puerperal) fever passed on to them by their doctors and midwives.

Dr. Balmer began his practice only a decade after Semmelweis' methods began to be adopted and he was no doubt very much aware of them.

But Dr. Balmer was a devoted churchman as well as a physician, and it is also likely that he was very much aware of the important role of physical cleanliness outlined in the Biblical books of Leviticus 11:32-40 and Numbers 19:11-19 regarding contact with dead bodies.

And physicians, from the writing of the Torah on, who abided by these Bible principles were not only fulfilling God's law as revealed to the Israelites, and any others including Moslems and Christians who recognized it as such. They also were providing loving care to their patients.

The late Peter Hackett, who had recorded "Historic Sidelights", the title of his column, for the Blackstone Valley Tribune/Advertiser for a number of years, reported one incident of that loving care.

His column of March 25, 1981 was based on a letter he had received from a Mrs. Alixira Pouliot of Uxbridge, Mass., who regarded Dr. Balmer as not only the dean, but the saint of (Blackstone) valley physicians.

"I sincerely believe," she wrote, "that if records were gone through, they would reveal that my daughter Elizabeth, born April 13, 1961, was the last baby he delivered at the Whitinsville Hospital. I was 41 years old at the time, and she was my ninth child. I went into shock after her birth, and even though near death at the time, I can remember him standing at the foot of the bed weeping while Dr. (Henry) Sullivan, who had been called in, was tending to me, preparing me to be sent by ambulance to a specialist in St. Vincent's (Sic) (St. Vincent Hospital in Worcester Mass. Author's. Note).

"He called every day that I was in the hospital, and after I got home. I could almost write a book about the many kindnesses and personal consideration this saintly man did for my family and others."

Dr. Balmer was 88 at the time.

Mrs. Pouliot's letter evoked my curiosity as to how many babies he had delivered.

During my research, I encountered Eleanor (Balmer) Orsini, one of his two daughters who as a widow had returned to Whitinsville, her hometown, to care for her aging mother and older sister.

Mrs. Orsini, then 95, still driving and totally alert, was kind enough to invite me to her home.

There she advised me that her father had a birth book in which he recorded the particular details of each of the births at which he assisted.

There were 1,971 of them.

Mrs. Pouliot had been right.

The last recorded in the book, No. 1,971, was that of Elizabeth Pouliot.

Mrs. Orsini allowed me to leaf through the record.

There were my cousin Bill, No. 1051 on Aug. 23, 1927, my cousin

Marjorie on Sept. 13, 1928, Peter Pouliot, No. 1153 on Dec. 27, 1928, my cousin Charlotte, No. 1400, March 17, 1934, my cousin Scott No. 1565, May 5, 1937, my brother Jack (Dr. Williams must have been unavailable) No. 1720, Feb. 24, 1943.

The little booklet resolved another question.

Dr. Balmer was a little different from modern doctors.

He never sent a bill.

Patients paid, or they didn't pay.

It wasn't as though Dr. Balmer didn't know though.

My father told me about. the time he and Doc Balmer were engaged in a conversation in front of Flagg's drug store.

The conversation somehow got around to people paying their bills.

My father was perhaps curious how Doc Balmer kept track of his accounts.

Oh, I know, he averred. I'll show you.

In the next few minutes, Doc Balmer made reference to each of the pedestrians who passed by.

He's paid for, he would interject.

And she's paid for, he'd gesture.

Oh, he isn't paid for, he'd say. Neither are his kids.

My father got the idea.

And it was really no great revelation either.

For my father, as treasurer of the Whitin Community Association, the local gym (a combination boys and girls club), the Whitinsville Hospital, which Doc Balmer had helped found, and chairman of the town Board of Assessors, which recorded property assessments and collections, was well aware of those things.

Leafing through the birth book also produced another revelation.

Neatly penciled at the end of many entries was a four letter word, in red, –PAID.

It was gratifying to see that the Crawfords were all paid for. And sad to see that quite a few others never were.

The epitaph for Dr. W. Edward Balmer at Pine Grove Cemetery, Whitinsville, Mass. reads:

TO HEAL SOMETIMES
TO RELIEVE OFTEN
TO COMFORT ALWAYS

ARNOLD BANNING

1903-1991

NORTHBRIDGE – Arnold Banning, 88, of Whitin Avenue, a local florist, died Saturday in St. Vincent Hospital, Worcester, after he was stricken ill at his home.

He leaves his wife, Madeline (Visser) Banning; two sons, Harold R. and Willard L. Banning, both of Whitinsville; a daughter, Sylvia A. Baker of Uxbridge; a brother, Dr. Andrew Banning of Grand Rapids, Mich.; a sister, Dr. Fredericka Romiero of San Jose, Calif.; nine grandchildren; seven great-grandchildren; nephews and nieces. Mr. and Mrs. Banning were married Sept. 1, 1927. He was born in The Netherlands, son of Hermanus and Sietske (VanderSluis) Banning, and came to the United States at age 10. He later lived in Northbridge and Uxbridge, and many years in Whitinsville.

He and his wife started the florist business, now Banning's Flower Shop and Greenhouse Inc., in Whitinsville, in 1929. They owned and operated the business for many years, and he was still working part-time at the time of his death. A son, Willard L. Banning, is now president of the business. Before that, he worked for the late James Whitin of Uxbridge and Arthur F. Whitin of Whitinsville as grounds and greenhouse keeper of their estates.

Mr. Banning attended the former Boston School of Floral Design.

He was a member, elder and deacon of Pleasant Street Christian Reformed Church, and was instrumental in the building of the present church. He was a Sunday school teacher and leader of several parish Bible study groups. He was an active member of the former first Christian Reformed Church in Whitinsville. Mr. Banning was chaplain of the Blackstone Valley Chapter of Gideons International, and served for several years on the Whitinsville Christian School Board. He was a member of the Whitin Community Gym Bible class in Whitinsville.

Mr. Banning was a member of Worcester County Horticultural Society in Boylston. He was a bowler, winning many awards. He was a charter member of the former Kiwanis Club in Whitinsville. He was a longtime oil painter, and a charter member of the Blackstone Valley Art Association and a member of the North Shore Artists Association in Rockport.

Funeral services will be held at 2 p.m. tomorrow in Pleasant Street Christian Reformed Church, Pleasant Street, Whitinsville. The Rev. Robert W. Eckardt will officiate. Burial will be in Riverdale Cemetery. Calling hours at Buma Funeral Home, 480 Church St., Whitinsville, are 2 to 4 and 7 to 9 p.m. today. In Mr. Banning's memory, Banning's Flower Shop will be closed tomorrow afternoon. Memorial contributions may be made to Whitinsville Christian School, Linwood Avenue, Whitinsville, 01588, or Gideons International, 2900 Lebanon Road, Nashville, Tenn. 37214.

Died Oct. 5, 1991
Worcester (Mass.) **Telegram & Gazette**   *Oct. 7, 1991*

FROM WHITIN AVENUE TO EBBETTS FIELD

Arnold Banning was one of my favorite newspaper customers. And not just because of his tipping. Although at the beginning, that was huge.

For when the The (Worcester, Mass.) Evening Gazette raised its price from four cents to five cents, a potential for stagflation existed.

The newboys who operated out of Mame Sherlock's store on Prospect Street in the Blackstone Valley mill village of Whitinsville received a penny a paper. With a route of 80 customers, that amounted to 80 cents a day, for the six-day week, or $4.80, a tidy sum.

A majority of those customers did not wait for the penny change on Friday, collection day, which lifted the weekly take home pay to above $5.50. That was enough for two movie tickets, several sodas, a couple of comic books, the church collection and a few cents left over after the obligatory $2 deposit into the bank account.

The increase to five cents a copy brought an extra quarter of a cent, but a threat to that highly valued penny tip. How many customers would recognize how valuable that extra penny was, and how many would tip anything at all now that the weekly price had been raised to 30 cents, an even number?

It turned out to be more than a dozen, including Arnold Banning.

When I arrived at the Banning floral shop, located in the old carriage house of the Arthur Whitin estate, for my first collection, I received 35 cents, a five cent tip. Mr. Banning, and several other customers, had helped me defeat inflation.

But there was something more important waiting for me at the floral shop, near the end of the route. It was one of the last innings or half innings of the Red Sox game.

My five years delivering newspapers was concurrent with the return of the war veterans to the Major Leagues.

For me, every summer from 1946 through 1949 had been a wonderful adventure. One of the best chronicles of those years was provided by David Halberstam is his "Summer of '49'.

It seemed that all the best tippers on the paper route were Boston Red Sox fans. And all of them had their radios on for the afternoon games, whether they were being played at Fenway Park in Boston or in faraway St. Louis.

So a newsboy could be working in the afternoon and still sted au courant with the ball game as one worked from customer to customer, house to house, fan to fan.

The game was usually in the late innings by the time I got to Whitin Avenue, where the Banning florist shop was. And the radio in the shop was always on. It was a great place to relax, listen to a half inning, and dash off during the between-innings commercial to the next customer with a radio.

Mr. Banning got a kick out of me and my enthusiasm.

It was a healthy era. The "Curse of the Bambino" had been conceived in the 1920s with the shipping of Babe Ruth from Boston to the Yankees, but it had not yet developed into a festering wound among the Fenway faithful.

In fact, the postwar Bronx Bombers had been in relative decline.

After all, the St. Louis Browns had won the American League pennant in 1944, the Detroit Tigers in '45, and the Red Sox, with Williams, Doerr, Pesky, Dom DiMaggio, Tex Hughson, "Boo" (Who?) Ferriss and Joe Dobson, had swept to an easy victory in the 1946 pennant race.

There was a hiccup in 1947, but the Sox had bounced back in 1948 to tie the Indians and force a playoff with a sweep of the Yankees in the last two days of the season. And in 1949, the Red Sox were 12 games back when they started a stirring comeback which cascaded them into a one-game lead with two games to play against the rival Yankees in Yankee Stadium.

Of course, they lost both and the pennant.

Mr. Banning observed my adolescent enthusiasm during those last excruciating days of the pennant race, and saw my pain. He walked up to me in the florist shop after the regular season had ended, and asked me if I wanted to go to the World Series.

He said he had two tickets, and that I could take my father. My father hadn't been to a World Series game since the days of John McGraw's Giants, and may have been as thrilled as I.

We sat in the upper deck of Ebbetts Field that autumn day, and my principal memory, without going back to read the game story and the box score, is of big Don Newcomb on the mound against the Brown Bombers. But the pervading memory overall is of Arnold Banning's perceptiveness and his kindness.

Worship has been described as the activity you devote the most energy and time to. The half century was when idolatry to baseball began to yield. Ted Williams broke his elbow in an All-Star collision with the wall in the 1950 game. I had left the paper route to my brother Bob to earn more college money in a summer construction job, and then went off to school in Western Pennsylvania, where the idols were either the downtrodden Pittsburgh Pirates or the rejuvenated Cleveland Indians.

Over the next four decades, I only occasionally was back home during the Memorial Day season for the obligatory visit to the florist shop and the decorating of graves at Pine Grove Cemetery. The welcomes were always warm.

But in the late 1980s, I was making more frequent visits to an aging mother who was living alone Although my middle brother Bob made fortnightly visits to handle her finances, and my youngest brother lived only a couple of blocks away in the same hometown, all of us felt it incumbent to pay more than close attention to her.

I would drive down from Western Massachusetts in the morning, and frequently find not only the doors locked, but the screen door locked so that I could not get in. The choice was to knock down the screen door so I could use my key to get in the kitchen door, or go down town for breakfast and wait for her to get up.

On one of those mornings, I entered Friendly's. There was Arnold, now in his mid-80s, sitting with his morning coffee. We both perked up. I joined him, and one of the first things I did was thank him again for the World Series tickets. We reminisced, and the conversation eventually found its way to religion.

He had become a pillar of one of the two Christian Reformed Churches that had flourished in Whitinsville. His brother was on the faculty of Bangor Theological School in Maine, and both were Christian scholars.

I, after a 14-year absence from organized religion, had conducted a seven-year study of the tenets of the faith as presented by the Watchtower Bible and Tracy Society.

I acknowledged to Arnold that I, raised a United Presbyterian, eventually had become a baptized Jehovah's Witness.

Arnold launched into a friendly inquiry analogous to the one I had experienced at the hands of elders in the South Congregation of the Witnesses in Springfield, Mass., and a bonus inquisitor, Bob Suder, a circuit overseer.

Arnold asked question after question, whether I accepted Jesus as the Messiah, whether I believed in the resurrection, my understanding of the ransom sacrifice.

The longer the discussion proceeded, the more satisfied was the look on Arnold's face. I was able to dwell at more length on my current understanding of Scripture based on the prophecies of Daniel and Jesus as disclosed to John and chronicled in the Revelation.

Arnold concluded that I was as enthusiastic about my faith as he had always been, as reflected by his works and his kindnesses. When we looked at the clock that morning, we discovered we had been talking in the booth for more than two and a quarter hours.

We took our leave. As for the preaching and teaching work we discussed, Arnold said, "Keep doing what you are doing."

PROFESSOR ELIZABETH NIXON

1913 - 1956

(The following obituary was compiled by the author from reports by several newspapers after Miss Nixon's death in an automobile collision on January 17, 1956 and from a subsequent eulogy by a colleague)

BEDFORD, Iowa — Two women, a professor of journalism at a Pennsylvania college and her sister-in-law, a resident of Omaha, Neb., were killed yesterday in a two-car collision on Highway 2 one-half mile east of here.

The women, Prof. Elizabeth Nixon, 42, most recently of New Wilmington, Pa., and Mrs. Florence Nixon, 54, were en route to Pennsylvania for the ordination of a niece as a deaconess in the Methodist Church at Buckhill Falls, Pa.

Two other persons were injured in the crash, Glenn C. Nixon, the brother and husband respectively of the deceased, and H. F. Ferguson, 64, a farmer near Bedford and the driver of the other car.

Police told reporters that the cars were traveling in opposite directions when they collided on a small rise where there were patches of snow.

Mr. Nixon, the proprietor of a hardware store in north Omaha, was admitted to a hospital at Clarinda and later was transferred to an Omaha hospital for treatment of multiple facial fractures.

Mr. Ferguson suffered a broken hip, facial lacerations and a bruised chest. He was also treated at the Clarinda hospital.

The Youngstown, (Ohio) Vindicator reported that Miss Nixon had resigned last week from her post as professor of journalism at Westminster College in New Wilmington. She had served on the Westminster faculty since 1946. The resignation was effective on Feb. 1.

The Sioux City (Iowa) Journal reported that Miss Nixon had spent the past week visiting members of her family in the area. The Columbia Missourian added that she had been summoned from Columbia, where she had just completed a special project at the University of Missouri, by the illness of her mother.

The members of her family include her mother, Mrs. Lulu Nixon, and two sisters, Mrs. S. M. Hickman and Mrs. William Earlich, of Sioux City; another sister, Mrs. Floyd Becker of LeMars, Iowa, and a brother, Cecil of Norfolk, Neb.

Miss Nixon was born in Schaller, Iowa on June 20, 1913, the daughter of the late Rev. Frederick (Butler) and Lulu (Cole) Nixon, and received her early schooling in LeMars and Sioux City.

She graduated from East High School in Sioux City and studied at Morningside College and at Iowa State College, where she specialized in medical illustration.

During this depression period, she also joined the staff of the Sioux City Journal, became a social worker, commercial artist and later served as a secretary of the First Methodist Church in Modesto, Calif.

After winning a national competition for a scholarship in medical illustration, she attended Vanderbilt University. However, her career in that field was cut short by an operating room accident which resulted in paralysis on one side of her body. Although two operations relieved the paralysis, she was never able to regain the complete control of her right hand necessary in drawing.

She then decided on journalism as a career alternative and entered Northwestern University in Evanston, Ill., where she was awarded bachelor and master's degrees.

At Northwestern, she also served on the staff of the Christian Advocate, and after graduation, with the Friendship Press in New York.

She joined the faculty at Westminster in 1946 as assistant professor of journalism and assistant in the news bureau. She headed both the department and the news bureau after the untimely death of its chairman, George Collins, in 1952.

In 1955, she took a leave of absence from Westminster to supervise a U.S. State Department project providing instruction to foreign radio and television specialists at the University of Missouri in Columbia.

She had served as an assistant professor of journalism at that university since June of 1955, and had just completed that program under the State Department contract.

Miss Nixon's body was taken to Morningside at Sioux City, where the W. Harry Christy Funeral Home was in charge of arrangements. The Revs. M. L. Metcalf and E. F. Broberg were to officiate at services at the funeral home on Friday, Jan. 19, with burial in Graceland Park Cemetery. The pallbearers were listed as Glen Knipfer, John Weisensee, Milton Delzell, Lloyd Pippen, Dwight Sanford and Lloyd Eastling.

Died Jan. 17, 1956

(The above obituary was compiled from reports from the Omaha {Nebraska} World-Herald, the Sioux City {Iowa} Journal, The {Youngstown, Ohio} Vindicator, The Columbia Missourian and The Holcad, a student-produced weekly at Westminster College, and from a eulogy written by one of her colleagues at Westminster, Dr. Amy Charles, a member of the English Department)

⤳

LIZ, WE HARDLY KNEW YE

How do you say thank you to an old, i.e. (former) teacher who dies young?

We were her next to last journalism class at Westminster.

There were eleven of us, counting Shirley Musgrave, who transferred to Penn State after two years, and Bruce Godfrey, who transferred in from Washington and Lee.

The rest were Marie Aboulian (later Barber), Ron Wolk, Bob Pellett, Bob Chidester, George Benaman, Gordie Arndt, George Lindow, Vic Wanty and myself.

The bond we felt crossed the lines of gender, nationality, religion, but unfortunately not yet race, not that early, from 1950 to 1954.

And that bond was reflected admirably by members of her last class, the authors of the editorial published in the January 6, 1956 edition of TheHolcad, the student newspaper at Westminster.

The lead paragraph read, under the headline, Miss Nixon Resigns:

"We were going to print the following notice as an obituary with a black border on the front page, but we changed our minds."

'Died, suddenly, on January 5, at Westminster college, the journalism department due to the resignation of Miss Elizabeth Nixon.

Survivors include three seniors, nine juniors and a number of sophomore and freshmen journalism majors who are now faced with the problem of what to do next in their major field.

Seldom do you find a professor who was admired more by her graduates. They are almost unanimous in their respect, admiration and praise for the guidance she gave them in the journalism field."

The editorial continued with a plea for the continuation of the journalism department at the school and the hiring of a capable and competent full-time journalism professor to lead it.

Little did the writers realize how prophetic they were.

Ten days later, Miss Nixon was dead, the victim of a winter crash on an Iowa highway,

And journalism, as an independent, observant discipline, disappeared from the Westminster curriculum, although vestiges revived and remained under various other academic titles.

This piece in itself is not a paean to academic journalism as such, although it has its merits.

One of my employers was kind enough to send me to a two-week news and managing editor seminar at Columbia, and the experience was among the most exhilarating of my career.

But the teaching of principles and training under Liz Nixon remained useful throughout a career, training listed in a eulogy written by a colleague. That colleague, Dr. Amy Charles, made me cognizant years later of the courage and pluck required for Elizabeth Nixon to provide that training despite physical handicap and illness.

I am grateful that Dr. Charles shared this intimate knowledge with us in her articulate and heartfelt eulogy, dated June 12, 1962.

It follows:

ELIZABETH NIXON (1913 – 1956)

BY DR. AMY M. CHARLES

Mary Elizabeth Nixon was born in Schaller, Iowa, on 20 June 1913, the youngest of the seven children of the Reverend Frederick Butler Nixon and Lulu Cole Nixon. She received most of her early schooling in LeMars and Sioux City, Iowa. Following her graduation from East High School in Sioux City, she attended Morningside College and studied art at the Iowa State College at Ames. During the depression she became a commercial artist, a social worker, a member of the staff of the Sioux City Journal, and a free-lance writer. Later, in California, she served as secretary at the First Methodist Church in Modesto and worked with several boards of the Methodist Church in San Francisco.

After winning a national competition for a scholarship in medical illustration, she attended Vanderbilt University. Her new career was cut short, however, by an accident in an operating room which left one side of her body paralyzed; and she returned to California. When, after two operations, she recovered from the paralysis, she found that she would never regain the complete control of her right hand necessary in drawing. It was at this point that she decided to follow her earlier interest in journalism and to take her degree in journalism at Northwestern University.

While she was working for her bachelor's degree at Northwestern, she served on the staff of the Christian Advocate as feature writer and as news editor of the fifth edition and completed her academic work with such distinction that she was elected to membership in Theta Sigma Phi, the journalism honorary. From Evanston she went to New York, where she became an editor for the Friendship Press.

Asked to prepare to go to India to help establish courses in journalism at several colleges, she returned to Northwestern to take her master's degree and to write her thesis on the development of the Indian press, at the same time carrying a full-time job in advertising with Montgomery Ward. Conditions in India in 1946 were uncertain, however, and the plans were postponed (and later, after Mohandas Gandhi's assassination, cancelled). In the meantime Miss Nixon began her career at Westminster College as assistant professor of journalism and assistant in the news bureau.

Students and colleagues who knew her during her years at Westminster need not be reminded of the influence of her work there as the journalism courses were expanded to provide a full major and Miss Nixon character-istically turned her energies to developing her courses in reporting and copy-editing, history of journalism, advertising, typography, specialized press, feature writing and senior seminar. The students will long remember the specialized press projects that carried them into internships on the magazines of such firms as Hamilton Watch, Armstrong Cork, Norwich Pharmacal, Prudential Life, Bell Telephone and Westinghouse; the journalism shows that enabled the college to install a United Press wire machine; the Lawrie radio series in the history of journalism; or the invaluable instruction and advice they were given as they worked on layout for Scrawl or Argo or on plans for Seed and Silo or the Journalistocrat.

To all her work in journalism Miss Nixon brought both her own wide knowledge and her respect for a job well done. She was never satisfied merely to fill the class period, to fall back on last year's notes, to teach any two classes in exactly the same way. She set high standards for her students and for herself; and though her students might joke about "No Late Papers" and complain of being overworked in their courses, they went out from her classes well grounded in their field, prepared to undertake the work for which she had trained them. They knew that they could write her about their work or stop by to talk over the problems they found on the job, that she was always eager to hear what they were discovering as practicing journalists or as graduate students, that she would never fail to remind them of their responsibilities as ethical journalists when they were tempted to follow the easy way of compromise. As with any good teacher, it is impossible to estimate the extent of her influence — but Miss Nixon's accomplishment may be judged in some measure by the subsequent accomplishments of her students.

The same interest and enthusiasm and knowledge Miss Nixon conveyed to her students at Westminster proved invaluable when in 1955 she was chosen by the University of Missouri to direct the first program for foreign radio and television specialists sponsored by the International Educational Exchange Service of the Department of State. On leave of absence from her position as associate professor of journalism at Westminster, she was appointed assistant professor of journalism at Missouri. During the six months of this project she taught classes, arranged special lectures and tours, supervised the work of the fifteen foreign visitors as they came to know our country and to work in radio and television stations in various states, and conducted the group on a month-long tour. The report she wrote about this project, which she finished only two weeks before her death, was selected as a model for subsequent projects sponsored by the Department of State.

Elizabeth Nixon and her sister-in-law, Florence Price Nixon, were killed in an automobile accident near Bedford, Iowa, on 17 January 1956.

Any account of Miss Nixon's life would be incomplete without some attempt to present her character and her temperament as well as a survey of her professional achievement. Perhaps her dominant characteristic – and one reason she was able to transmit such idealism to her students – was her own deep and abiding faith in life and in the fundamental decency of human beings. Rarely discouraged for long, she met her own problems with courage and good cheer and encouraged others to do the same. She allowed no one the luxury of excuses, but her patience, her kindliness, her quiet "We'll work it out somehow" surmounted difficulties for herself and for others.

An intelligent woman with an alert, keen mind, she followed a bewildering variety of interests. In her spare time one might find her reading, listening to records, developing film, planning a new course or a trip, popping corn, talking with friends, etching a copper tray, laying out a magazine, building a fire, painting (a landscape or a kitchen wall!), criticizing the latest television newscaster, writing a feature article, or building a bookcase. She was almost literally never idle, and often visitors found themselves drawn into the current activity – anything from refinishing an old table or painting a watercolor to re-reading Emerson's "Self-Reliance," an essay that always had special meaning for her. She loved the outdoors, whether in Whitman's "Song of the Open Road" or in long walks at Cook's Forest. Having come to know her own country well in her travels as a journalist and in her residence in Iowa, California, Tennessee, Mississippi, New York and Pennsylvania, she remembered these places vividly and joyfully returned from time to time to visit such favorite spots as the bluffs near Missouri Valley, Gulf towns like Biloxi and Pass Christian, Yosemite, Niagara Falls, and San Francisco. She was eager to see more of her own country, to meet new people, and to know other countries as well. Her trip abroad in 1951 enabled her to observe the press in England, France, and Germany first-hand and to continue the interest in the international press she had developed in earlier work with the press in India, her assignment to cover the first United Nations meeting in San Francisco, and her concern for the United Nations commission on freedom of the press.

Miss Nixon had a rare gift for making friends. She loved people, and she was always ready to welcome a new friend into her life. In every place she lived, in every period of her life she found friends she cherished always – people she had known as a girl in Sioux City, students and teachers at Northwestern, co-workers in many places – people of all ages, from many walks of life. She could talk as readily to a visiting ambassador as to a child or to an elderly neighbor; and though she was shy by nature, she forgot her shyness in putting others at their ease. People responded to her instinctively, believed in themselves because she believed in them, and were often surprised to find that they were better than they had thought before they knew her. Generous herself, she had reason to be grateful to the many friends who had stood by her in adversity, and helped her in her education and in her profession – and though she never embarrassed them with outpourings of gratitude, she never forgot their kindness and their encouragement, nor did she neglect to thank them simply and honestly. Invariably she tried to turn her gratitude into action, to transmit the benefits to others.

She knew well the uses of laughter. All who knew her remember her spontaneous wit, her impatience with sham, her instinctive reaction to incongruity, her rich laughter. "Laughter," she wrote, "is the handmaid of wisdom; in her touch there is healing for the wounds of yesterday, and there is courage for the battles of tomorrow." Her sense of humor was both lively and kindly; and she loved best of all to tell a joke on herself.

All her responses were quick and instinctive: if her laughter was quick and her sympathy ready, her indignation could come just as quickly.

Nothing aroused this indignation more swiftly than injustice in any form, and she became indignant over an injustice to a student or to a colleague more readily than over one to herself. She learned to bear her own trials and disappointments with patience, but she never learned to ignore unfairness. Her honesty demanded that she speak when remaining silent would have been expedient. (But her friends knew her utter scorn for expedience.)

With all this vivid, outgoing warmth, there was always an underlying sense of strength. She knew the beauty of quietness and conveyed a sense of serenity to others even when she did not feel it herself. There was about her a depth, a sense of repose, at times almost a spiritual aloofness. This quality, which replenished the rich springs of her giving, came to her only because in illness and isolation and loneliness she had had to learn patience and calm. Only her family and her close friends knew that she lived this busy, consuming life despite ill health which had dogged her from childhood; but few among them realized the extent to which her health might have limited her activity, or her firm resolve never to let her health limit her life. Though she was fond of emphasizing that no Nixon had ever died of overwork except her father, she usually undertook more work than people of sounder health would consider. Throughout her work at Northwestern she carried full-time jobs and made up the time by sacrificing sleep – until in her final quarter there her brother and her friends forced her to agree to carry only the normal load of a graduate student. Few people knew that she lived with the almost constant pain of a chronic lung condition, because she simply would not use her health as an excuse or consider the possible ill effects of the rigorous winters in western Pennsylvania. At a time when her own health was in precarious state after an operation for cancer, her colleague George Collins died, and she carried his classes as well as her own simply because the job was there to be done. Although her refusal to submit to physical limitation undoubtedly intensified her efforts to excel in all she undertook, her experience of illness developed her patience, her sympathy, and the depth of her understanding. She played the role of neither saint nor martyr, however; and as her friend Virginia Ellison pointed out, she was absolutely without self-pity.

In any memorial it is difficult to avoid the extremes of praise made hackneyed and ineffectual by repetition; yet the simple truth is that Elizabeth Nixon ¬¬¬WAS a rare human being. She would reject our praise could she read these words, because she never considered her gifts unusual; yet she gave richly to us all, and we are immeasurably the better for having known her.

Amy M. Charles

12 June, 1962

(Dr. Charles, a native of Pittsburgh, graduated from Westminster College, and received master and doctoral degrees from the University of Pennsylvania. She joined the English faculty of the University of North Carolina at Greensboro in 1956 after 10 years on the Westminster faculty. Published works included "A Life of George Herbert," a 17th Century English poet. She died in Winston-Salem, N.C. on March 24, 1985 at the age of 62.)

VERNON WANTY, COLLEGE PRESIDENT

1918 - 1996

Vernon Wanty, 78, a retired college president who lived at 300 Willow Valley Lakes Drive, died Saturday morning at Willow Valley Lakes Health Center. He had lived in the retirement community for the past eight years.

Born in Sheffield, Yorkshire, England, he was a son of the late Harry and Emma Bennett Wanty.

He was a newspaper reporter and editor in New Wilmington, and taught journalism, English and speech at Westminster College and Towson State University in Maryland.

Dean of faculty at Middlesex County College in New Jersey, he later became president of Essex Community College in Baltimore County, Maryland. Upon his retirement in 1982, he was named president emeritus at Essex Community College.

He was a member of First Presbyterian Church, Sigma Delta Chi, Phi Delta Kappa, the Professional Newspaper Society, St. George's Society and Rotary International.

He also served on the session of the Chestnut Grove and Towson Presbyterian churches.

During World War II Wanty served in the Royal Engineers and Royal

Artillery of the British Army in the French, African and Italian campaigns.

He is survived by his wife, Mary Blackwood Wanty of Lancaster, and one daughter, Margaret B. W. Graham of Little Deer Isle, Maine.

Died June 1, 1996   *Lancaster* (Pa.) *Intelligencer, June 3, 1996*

THE SILENT GENERATION

England experienced a beautiful summer in 1965.

Meteorologists may look back on it as one of the finest of that century.

And it was on one of those fine summer days in early August that I chose to make my pilgrimage to Canterbury.

It was a very comfortable ride by British Rail, from Bromley, a large suburban city that bordered on the Greater London metropolis to the northwest.

That had been our home for more than a year, and we were beginning to broaden out after extensive explorations of London.

Canterbury Cathedral, described as the mother church of English Christendom, is imposing.

A woman I recognized, but could not place, was admiring it from the outside, and like many of us, was awestruck.

Many of you have had a similar such experience.

You recognize a face, but not only cannot remember the name, or where or when you last saw the face.

What to do?

The decision was made to follow her.

It was unlikely she was here alone.

Perhaps she and her husband had separated so that each could slake his or her historical or spiritual thirst.

It took some slaking.

She circled the library and the cloisters. Minutes went by. She examined the nave.

A quarter hour. A half hour.

Finally, he showed.

It was Vic Wanty.

Vernon (Vic) Wanty was one of 10 journalism majors who had graduated from my alma mater, Westminster College, New Wilmington, Pa., in June of 1954, eleven years before.

We had not seen each other since. And I barely knew his wife, the former Mary Blackwood.

But I pretended I did, and failed to acknowledge that I had been conducting a surveillance of Mary for the past half hour.

We agreed to have lunch together across the street.

We appreciated the ecumenical welcome advertised at the café.

French spoken here. Spanish spoken here. Swedish spoken here. Italian spoken here.

It appeared all the major European languages were spoken in the café with two exceptions.

The first was German, which 11 years after the end of the war was still anathema in England.

We discovered the second unspoken language when we attempted to order inside the café.

It became very obvious that most if not all the wait staff had been enlisted from the continent.

And even more evident when it was nigh impossible to make any of them understand an order in English.

This was particularly perplexing for Vic, an Englishman who had been born in Sheffield, in Yorkshire.

But we howled at the incongruity, and with a mix of continental phrases and words made our orders comprehensible to our uncomprehending waitresses.

Vic had overcome gaps before, linguistic, geographic and generational.

He had served with the Royal Engineers and Royal Artillery of the British Army in the French, North African and Italian campaigns during

World War II, and by the time he emigrated to the United States and belatedly enrolled in college, was 15 years older than most of his classmates.

The class that entered college in the United States in the autumn of 1950 was the first which was almost entirely composed of high school and private school graduates with no other experience.

There was a sprinkling of veterans in the sophomore class, but most of them had entered service at or near the end of World War II.

But in the junior and senior classes, there were more veterans, some with combat experience, some married, a few with children. They warranted our respect.

Not only were they older and more experienced, but they were for the most part more dedicated students.

This was perhaps why our generation of college students was later labeled by succeeding and less mature classes as the silent generation.

Mislabeled in my view.

I regard it more and more as the respectful generation.

And Vic was the only one in our class who I regarded as deserving of that generational respect.

His wife Mary did also. She was an employee on the college staff while he completed his studies.

There is a large category of dedicated women who worked their husbands' way through college during the postwar and later years, and they also deserve such respect.

But I have to demur when it comes to bestowing particular and generic labels on any generation.

This became particularly evident during the 50th and 60th anniversary celebrations of the D-Day invasion of Europe on June 6, 1944.

Television anchor Tom Brokaw was inspired by such to write his "The Greatest Generation."

It is best to let members of that generation reflect on the results, an extravagance of patriotism, flag-waving and flawed interpretations of history.

One of them was Albert B. Southwick, a columnist for "The (Worcester, Mass.) Sunday Telegram, and a member of a Navy bomber squadron during World War II.

In his column of June 20, 2004, he criticized extravagant ceremonies and the overuse of the word "hero."

"I have talked to many World War II veterans over the years and never found one who thought of himself in those terms," Southwick wrote. "…If veterans use the term, they usually do it with wry, disparaging smiles. We know better."

Southwick argued later in his column that the descriptive word hero should be reserved for those who earned it, not to everyone who put on a uniform.

"The remarkable thing about our part in the war was that most of us in the service were not heroes but just ordinary Americans who achieved an extraordinary result," he concluded.

He quoted in his column another critic of the commemoration extravaganza, David Gelernter, writing in The Wall Street Journal.

He expressed agreement with Gelernter that a better way to honor veterans would be to learn what the war was all about.

He took issue with Gelernter's view that the patriotic excess was "especially intense among members of the 1960s generation who once chose to treat all present and future soldiers like dirt and are willing at long last to risk some friendly words about World War II veterans, now that most are safely underground and guaranteed not to talk back."

Carol Pogash, a former San Francisco Examiner reporter who covered much of the Patty Hearst kidnapping case in 1974, recently reviewed a documentary about members of that generation. Pogash acknowledges in the review, printed in The New York Times on Dec. 11, 2004, of being swept up by the story at the time.

Fortunately, the review of the documentary, "Guerrilla: The Taking of Patty Hearst," shows more balance, criticizing it for embracing its subjects and romanticizing their criminality. She interviewed one of those subjects, former Symbionese Liberation Army member Russell Little, a resident of Hawaii since his release from prison.

Pogash paraphrased Little.

"My generation," Pogash wrote, "which overhauled civil rights, shoved a president from office and stopped the war in Vietnam, was full of a sense of our own power."

An exaggerated sense, one would gather.

We never knew Vic Wanty as a hero when he was in college. He never talked about it. He already had the respect of his fellow students, and as the dean of one college and president of another, likely gained the respect of many more.

WILLIAM VANDER LUGT, FORMER HOPE COLLEGE DEAN

Former Hope College dean and chancellor William Vander Lugt died Tuesday at a local nursing home. He was 89.

Born in The Netherlands, Mr. Vander Lugt came to the United States with his family in 1905. He attended Calvin College and the University of Michigan.

Mr. Vander Lugt began his educational career as a professor of philosophy at Central College. He served as dean of Westminster College in New Wilmington, Pa., before returning to Michigan and Hope College.

At Hope, Mr. Vander Lugt served as professor in 1954, as dean from 1955 to 1966, as distinguished professor at large from 1966 to 1970 and as chancellor from 1970 to 72.

Mr. Vander Lugt is survived by his wife Paternell; three sons, Robert of Jacksonville, Fla., William of DeLand, Fla., and Karel, of Sioux Falls, S.D.; seven grandchildren, and one great-grandchild.

Other survivors include a brother, Arie Vander Lugt of Grand Rapids, and two sisters, Johanna De Graaf and Elisabeth Heslinga, both of Jenison.

Visitation is scheduled for 7 to 9 p.m. Friday at Dykstra Funeral Homes, downtown chapel, 29 E. Ninth St. A funeral will be at 11 a.m.

Saturday at Hope Church. Burial will be in Pilgrim Home Cemetery.

Died June 9, 1992   **The Grand Rapids Press** *June 11, 1992*

"SOLID FOOD"

Dr. Vander Lugt was disturbed.

One would like to use the adjectives angry, furious, or livid, but they would not fit the man and his Christian personality.

He and a colleague, Westminster (Pa.) College history professor Wallace Jamison, had just returned from a college seminar at Latrobe, Pa.

They had gone to hear the renowned French Roman Catholic theologian Jacques Maritain at St. Vincent College.

And they had found themselves, confessionally, alone.

Dr. Vander Lugt, a Dutch reformed clergyman and academic dean of a United Presbyterian-related college, told his classes on returning to New Wilmington that he and Jamison had been the only Protestant academics in the region to avail themselves of the opportunity for this truly ecumenical experience.

It was the only negative reaction I ever experienced from this gentle intellect in my three years of exposure to him, and it had a paradoxical result, a positive lesson in tolerance.

The college required chapel attendance in those years, the early 1950s, and in order to accommodate the entire student body of more than

1,000 students, two sessions were scheduled, one in the morning and one in the afternoon.

All of the faculty members took their turns in conducting these sessions. These consisted of a brief lecture, or in the case of the arts, performances, in the academic discipline of choice, after initial devotions.

Those who skipped chapel in the morning were able to make up their lapses in the afternoon, and often did if word of a particularly interesting program spread around the campus.

In the original draft of this vignette, I wrote that the chapel was generally packed when Dr. Vander Lugt, who was serving as academic dean as well as a professor of religion and philosophy, conducted the service.

I, like April in American-born poet T. S. Eliot's "The Waste Land," was mixing "memory with desire."

Carol Shiels Roark, a classmate and most likely the brightest of all Dr. Vander Lugt's students, was kind enough a half century later to share her memory of those college days, and suggested that many students consciously avoided Dr. Vander Lugt's appearances and the required plunge into what the apostle Paul called the "deep things of God." (1st Corinthians 2:10)

But his appearances did attract a coterie of discerning students taking advantage of the infrequent opportunity to sup at a combination spiritual and intellectual banquet.

Although Westminster was a church-related college, many of its students were of an age and mind similar to those Hebrews that the Apostle Paul was admonishing in the 5th chapter of that epistle:

"For whom by reason of the time ye ought to be teachers, ye have need again that some one teach you the rudiments of the first principles of the oracles of God; and are become such as have need of milk, and not of solid food. For every one that partaketh of milk is without experience of the word of righteousness; for he is a babe. But solid food is for full grown men, even those who by reason of use have their senses exercised to discern good and evil." Hebrews 5:12-14.

Several hours of academic Bible study were required for graduation for all students, including study of the Old and New Testaments for freshmen and two additional survey courses.

The milk on this menu satisfied most students other than pre-ministerial students preparing for theological school, but there were plenty of other choices on that menu, if one developed the appetite.

Dr. Vander Lugt offered a challenging cuisine.

How challenging?

As he told an interviewer from the "Hope College Anchor," a student publication, years later, "The Gospel is such a rich and all-inclusive truth that no one has fully fathomed it."

Dr. Vander Lugt invited all of his students to plunge deeply into that rich lode.

I took the plunge in my junior year, and was never sorry. Two particular veins he led me to explore have never run out.

One is from Paul's letter to the Galatians.

He wrote to the Christians there:

"There is neither Jew nor Greek, there is neither slave nor freeman, there is neither male nor female; for you are all one (person) in union with Christ Jesus. Moreover, if you belong to Christ, you are really Abraham's seed, heirs with reference to a promise." Galatians 3:28,29

Hard to swallow?

Not without chewing. One wishes that one, whether professed Christian, observant Jew, or believing Moslem, had a cud.

Another vein.

Paul's letter to the Philippians:.

"So then, my beloved, even as ye have always obeyed, not as in my presence only, but now much more in my absence, work out your own salvation with fear and trembling;"

"Furcht und Zittern," the German words for fear and trembling, leapt out at me from the schedule of courses offered at the University of Munich years later.

It was a seminar by that title, and also the title of a work by the Danish theologian and existentialist Sören Kierkegaard that served as a text.

It was a great lesson in understanding Kierkegaard's fears and recognizing my lack of them.

President Franklin Delano Roosevelt tried to teach an entire generation during the Depression of the 1930s in the United States that the greatest fear to overcome was fear itself.

But in the Biblical sense, there are two fears, morbid dread which destroys hope, and reverential awe that is the beginning of wisdom that allows it: "The fear of Jehovah is the beginning of wisdom." (Psalm 111:10).

This wisdom leads to the realization of hope expressed so succinctly in the King James translation of the Bible at Hebrews 11:1.

"Now faith is the substance of things hoped for, the evidence of things unseen."

A more literal, if less lyrical translation of the Greek is:

"Faith is the assured expectation of things hoped for, the evident demonstration of realities though not beheld."

That passage has become more meaningful with age, and the appreciation for the foundation laid by Dr. Vander Lugt on which I chose to build so late in my life.

I never saw Dr. Vander Lugt again after his resignation in 1953, the end of my junior year, when he refused to take a loyalty oath to the administration of college President Will W. Orr, whose energies were directed more to the physical development of the college than academics.

But in 1967, a consular official at the U.S. Embassy in Belgrade asked me, then a foreign correspondent with United Press International, whether I would be willing to brief a group of college students from Michigan.

Happily, it was a delegation from Hope College in Holland. Many of them knew Dr. Vander Lugt and some had studied with him.

I was gratified to be able to send back with them my greetings to Dr. Vander Lugt — and my thanks.

CHAPTER 7

RIDL DIES; COACHED WESTMINSTER, PITT

NEW WILMINGTON – Westminster College lost a true friend and coaching legend Friday when Charles Gerald "Buzz" Ridl died at Montefiore University Hospital in Pittsburgh. He was 75.

Ridl was a collegiate head basketball coach for 19 years, serving as head coach at Westminster from 1956 to 1968 before moving to the University of Pittsburgh from 1968 to 1975. He compiled an overall record of 313-174, including a 216-91 mark at Westminster and a 97-83 record at Pitt.

Ridl also served Westminster in other capacities, including as director of athletics from 1977 to 1985, director of Alumni Affairs from 1975-77, head baseball coach from 1950-68 and head golf coach from 1979-91.

Spot in history:

"A giant among the Towering Titans, Buzz Ridl has earned a prominent and permanent place in Westminster history," said Westminster President Dr. Oscar E. Remick. "He was a man who embodied in his life the ideals and values of this college."

"Buzz was a great Christian man who was very warm and wonderful with his family," recalled current Titans head basketball coach Ron Galbreath, who played for Ridl and Westminster from 1958-62. "Like Will Rogers, I've never heard anyone say a bad thing about him."

Began ties as student:

Ridl began a lifetime association with Westminster as a student in 1938, playing basketball for the Titans and coach Grover Washabaugh. During his college career, he was elected president of his class for three years, was a member of Sphinx, a men's honorary leadership society, and was co-captain of the basketball team.

After a four-year stint in the United States Army Ridl joined the staff at Westminster as assistant basketball coach to Washabaugh in 1949. He became head baseball coach the following year and took over the head basketball duties when Washabaugh retired in 1956.

Indelible mark:

Over the next 12 years he left an indelible mark, winning 216 games while leading the Titans to the NAIA Championship game twice. His teams advanced to the NAIA National Tournament on four other occasions, including two semifinal appearances.

His most famous team was the 1961-62 Titan squad, which finished 26-3 and was selected as the top small college team in the nation. Ridl was named National Coach of the Year by the NAIA following that season.

Ridl is survived by his wife, the former Elizabeth Rogers, two children, Elizabeth (Ridl) Baun of Brandford Woods and Jack Ridl of Holland, Mich., and three grandchildren.

Visitation hours will be held at the Richard D. Cole Funeral Home, 328 Beaver St., Sewickley from 2-4 and 7-9 p.m. Sunday and from 1-2 p.m. Monday. Funeral services will be held at Sewickley Presbyterian Church in Sewickley at 2:30 p.m. Monday

Died April 28, 1995   *The Vindicator,* Youngstown, Ohio, April 29, 1995

CHARLES RIDL (1920-1995)

Basketball was my first love.

Before girls.

Fortunately, when I finally got over my first love, the girls were still there.

Unfortunately, I only had one real coach during this decade-long love of playing the game.

He was "Buzz" Ridl.

But that is getting ahead of the tip-off.

The love of the game started in the dusty attic of the old Grammar School in Whitinsville, Mass., where two baskets had been set up.

That is the first place I ever scored a basket, during an informal recess game or practice.

But the real place to play was on the floor of the Whitin Community Association gymnasium across Hill Street.

But we kids were not sent there to play basketball, but to learn to swim.

"Join the gym, learn to swim, eat Farina," still rings from adolescent ears.

We didn't get to play basketball during the gymnastic exercises Harold Case put us through before taking a shower and heading for the pool for swimming lessons.

The facility had been built in the early 1920s by the Whitin family for the benefit of the residents of the town, most of whom were employed in one or another department of the Whitin Machine Works, the huge textile machine factory that straddled the Mumford River, a tributary of the Blackstone which flowed from Worcester into Narragansett Bay in Rhode Island.

Most of us kids had learned to swim and decided we did not want to become gymnasts before we were allowed onto the basketball courts.

Casey was a physical marvel, a product of the gymnastic team at Springfield College in the western part of Massachusetts. He was looking for gymnasts and swimmers to develop, not basketball players.

But the return of the veterans from World War II and the establishment of the industrial basketball league for them two evenings a week captivated many of his gym rats.

We wanted to play basketball.

There was another major draw.

The association had engaged one of the great basketball teams of that or any other era to come to Whitinsville to play an all-star team of local players.

That team, before the Harlem Globetrotters eclipsed them in fame if not ability, was the New York Rens.

The members of the Renaissance team, recognized later in the

Basketball Hall of Fame at Springfield, captured the imagination of young and old alike, and the moves they exhibited on the gym floor during their one-game exhibition in Whitinsville were repeated by basketball *aficionados* for years.

I finally got to play for a real team when I made the Northbridge High School jayvees as a sophomore in 1947-48.

Coach Leo Smith paid little attention to the jayvees, especially that year, because the varsity had steamrollered through the Blackstone Valley competition and had earned a berth in the Western Massachusetts high school championship tournament at Springfield College.

A bad beating at the hands of Westfield in the first round of the tournament closed the season on a somber note.

The general tragedy became personal the next fall.

Coach Smith cut me from the team the next year.

He apparently had little use for a skinny five-foot five kid who insisted on practicing most of his shots from the pivot position, and had declined to play football, which was Leo Smith's forte as coach.

Understanding adults who noticed the effect this rejection had on the skinny high school kid made room on one of the industrial league squad rosters for an occasional bench player. And there was also the church league to play in.

But by my senior year, Coach Smith was gone, and I had grown nearly seven inches and gained five pounds.

So I made the team as a now six-foot one-inch, 135-pound senior.

The new coach was interim, inexperienced and indifferent, and a respectable team floundered to an unimpressive 8-12 season.

This foundation provided few grounds for confidence that I would do any better in college.

But the first place I headed after arriving on the Westminster College campus in New Wilmington, Pa. in September of 1950 was the college gym.

I was disappointed in the gym, a bandbox ultimately labeled "Old 77" for the consective home victories once achieved there. But I was not disappointed with the players I found on it on my first visit.

There were Don "Bandy" Myers, Jerry Neff and Ron Tranter, and a number of other varsity and freshmen scholarship players scrimmaging.

Bandy paid the kindest compliment of all when he said "Grover will be glad to see you" after we finished off a fast break together with a layup.

He was referring to Grover Washabaugh, the legendary coach of the Westminster Titans. Westminster had distinguished itself during the first college doubleheader at Madison Square Garden in New York in 1934, and had established valid small college basketball credentials over the seasons since.

It turned out that there were six scholarship players in the freshman class that year, one of the last during which freshmen were not allowed to play on the varsity roster.

The 1950-51 season was the last that the Westminster team played in

Old 77. Big teams such as Duquesne and Pitt refused to play there any more.

Another baseball scholarship player also tried out for basketball, and I was one of four others who tried out and made it as walk-ons.

That was no great achievement.

There were no cuts that year at Westminster.

Players just left the squad periodically if there were no prospect of a scholarship, no prospect of playing time, and just a future of very long and grueling practices.

But there was so much more.

We received brand new basketball shoes, much better than the Converse All-Stars a few of us graduated to in high school.

There were warm-up jackets and satiny pants.

And then there were road trips, to Pittsburgh, to Philadelphia, to Buffalo. And the whole team went in a big, comfortable bus, as many as 35 players and coaches and managers.

And there was a semblance of a training table, if only on game days.

"Buzz," a member of one of the pre-war Westminster teams that had played in Madison Square Garden, was coaching the freshman team that year.

He was expected to bring as many of the freshmen along to varsity level in one year, and if possible to the first string.

Westminster had a policy of recruiting six players in one year and one or two the next, so there was usually a strong corps of players starting in their junior and senior years.

Grover Washabaugh, the veteran varsity coach, was a devotee of racehorse basketball.

The running drills that he taught were designed to build both speed and endurance. His backward running drills were as effective as the backward skating drills in hockey.

And despite being a player of the game for a decade and a fan for nearly half a century, I failed to truly understand the motive behind that style of basketball until reading a basketball column in The New York Times the month of January, 2005.

The column compared the number of shots taken by the National Basketball League champion Boston Celtics during the early 1960s with those taken by several of the so-called fast break teams in the 2004-05 season.

The statistics revealed that the Celtics of those years consistently averaged more than 20 shots more per game than the modern run-and-gunners.

There are about four aspects to this.

1. Tight defense forces poor shots.

2. Poor shots provide opportunities for defensive rebounds.

3. Command of the defensive board plus good outlet passing opens up the fast break.

4. The fast break leads to more two on ones, three on twos and four on threes.

And as Hall of Famer Bill Russell answered so simply when queried on television as to how he would handle the giant centers of the 21st century: "I'd run them into the ground."

That makes five on four.

The columnist had not calculated in his analysis how many of the shots that the Boston Celtics took during their dominance of the league were layups or high percentage shots close to the hoop, but that is a logical corollary of the style of play.

I bought into that concept having been brought up not far from Kingston, R.I. and the run and gun philosophy of Frank Keating and his Rhode Island Rams with Ernie Calverly.

"Buzz" brought in another aspect of the game.

If you did not have the rebounding of Bill Russell, the passing of Bob Cousy and the speed of "Tiny" Archibald or their equivalents, you would have to develop a style which would avoid turnovers and score in a half-court set.

As Grover Washabaugh finished his great career, "Buzz" Ridl prepared for a change of style at the college without in any way denigrating the career or type of ball taught by his predecessor.

By the time he took over the helm in 1956, he was well prepared for the start of a head coaching career that would bring him and two schools national distinction.

His record at Westminster was 216-91, including two NAIA championship game appearances and selection as the top small college team in the nation in 1961-62.

At Pitt, his record from 1968 to 1975 was 97-83.

He had taken a 4-20 team and brought it to over .500 in four years. During the next four, he took it to the NCAA round of eight before being defeated by eventual national champion North Carolina State and to the NIT the following year.

Pittsburgh Post-Gazette sports columnist Bob Smizik described "Buzz" best in a column he wrote at his death.

"There was a time when almost no one cared about Pitt basketball, when crowds at Fitzgerald (Field House) were regularly less than 1,000, when televising a game was the rarest of occurrences, when the Big East wasn't even a dream and when the NCAA tournament was a once-every-other-decade kind of thing.

"Buzz Ridl changed all that," Smizik wrote in a column published on May 3, 1995.

He concluded the column with an explanation why Buzz walked away from the job after having built a citywide interest in the program at Pitt.

He quoted Dean Billick, later Pitt's associate athletic director.

"He (Buzz) was comfortable that he had won on the NAIA level and he wanted to see what it took at the next level," said Billick. "Once he had done that, he felt he had satisfied himself. He also felt, I think, uncomfortable with some of the pressures he saw. He wasn't comfortable either with what he saw in the recruiting rat race."

He was a small, quiet man who was a basketball giant, Smizik concluded in his column. And as others pointed out in his obituary, he was a kind, Christian man.

I was proud to have played for him for two years.

The first year, I was a walk-on player who was the second or third player off the bench on a strong freshman team.

I got some minutes here and there, and was grateful for them.

But never more so than against the Pitt freshmen at the old, cold Pitt field house next to the old football stadium.

The parents of my roommate George Lindow were from the North Side of Pittsburgh, and they had been generous to their son's lonely friend from New England by inviting me up to their summer camp on the Venango River in northwestern Pennsylvania.

They were also persuaded to attend the Pitt-Westminster game that winter in Pittsburgh.

It was the only time in college that I ever played in front of someone I knew. It was as though my own parents, 600 miles away, were in attendance.

For some reason, Buzz put me in quite early, and I stayed out on the floor, having picked up a couple of rebounds, scored several points (an anomaly) and also provided some assists for the star scorer and eventual Westminster Hall of Famer from Chester, W Va., Jerry Neff.

It was one of those very few games I ever played that were in the category described by Bill Russell in his book , co-written with Taylor Branch, "Second Wind, The Memoirs of an Opinionated Man."

Russell averred that achieving a high level of play on both sides was a more satisfying and exhilarating experience than championships, and an exhilaration experienced too seldom in his long career.

That spring,.no offer of a scholarship forthcoming, I requested a job as a waiter in one of the college dormitories for the following academic year.

I received it, without any realization that I had earned it because of either my academic or athletic record.

But it was the best news that my parents could receive, because at that time, board was the most expensive share of the financial burden for a college education.

That offer was combined with my decision to work the summer in the outside yard of the Whitin Machine Works with the hope of building myself up physically from a now 150-pound string bean spread over six feet two.

The job entailed stacking lumber, emptying sand cars by shovel and wheel barrow, unloading bags of cement, emptying coke cars inside the plant foundry, and enduring the smirks and sneers of the rough factory workers directed toward the skinny college kid.

One reflects now how there was enough time or energy to play summer basketball in Worcester with the likes of contemporaries such as Slim Stairs, the 1948 high school center who went on to Rhode Island State, Harry Brown, an earlier vintage high school player who went on to star with Worcester Polytechnic Institute, Herman "Pinky" Roche, a former Northbridge teammate who went to UMass, and Hank Spence, the Worcester North star who played at Boston University.

We were lucky to get the Worcester city dweller Hank on our Blackstone Valley studded squad. It may have happened because Hank's older brother George was an institution in Whitinsville. He was perhaps the first black man to work in the town, taking his huge frame into the foundry as a molder as had hundreds of immigrant laborers before him. And he earned their respect as a worker and a man.

In any event, that hard scrabble summer of work and the next academic year combined to build me up.

As a waiter at Browne Hall, one of the dormitories for freshman girls, one had not only the opportunity to monitor a major portion of the new female freshman class, but opportunities to eat double portions and extra desserts under the approving gaze of the cooks and bakers at the dining hall.

There were disappointments.

A couple of the six fellow freshmen who had athletic scholarships graduated to the varsity that year, but I was kept on the freshman team, the lone upperclassman there.

And although I had the dining room job, I was not given the special dispensation that all the other athletes on scholarship received, excuse from the job during the playing season.

But I started and played for Buzz all year under what were becoming changing conditions in college basketball. We were on the brink of the abolition of freshman basketball at the collegiate level and the waiving of the ban on freshmen playing at a varsity level.

The following fall, having retained a job on campus providing my board, I informed Buzz before the start of the next season that I had decided to concentrate on my academic work the last two years at school and give up basketball.

One could read in his eyes that he understood I didn't really want to quit. But there was also the understanding look on his face that it was probably for the best.

The desire exceeded the talent.

And, it must be acknowledged, the junior year at school was one of the richest ever periods of academic application and study.

After leaving Pitt in 1975, Buzz Ridl returned to Westminster, his first academic love, and took over as athletic director.

I would see him occasionally at alumni tours or at reunions, or at a Titan golf outing.

Always the kind smile, the welcome greeting, the acknowledgement of a shared past.

And one of the most amazing things.

In going through the Ridl file in my office, a collection of handwritten notes of thanks for my very modest gifts to the college's athletic program over the years. One wonders how many such personal notes he wrote.

Thanks primarily to Buzz, the modest gifts continue.

JEROME C. NEFF

1932 - 2007

Jerome (Jerry) Caton Neff was born on Thanksgiving Day, Nov. 24, 1932, in Crooksville, OH, to Hannah Marle and Rufus Gladstone Neff.

Jerry attended grade school and high school in Chester, WV, participating in band, student council, theater and student government. He played basketball, football and baseball, receiving All-State honors in basketball as a junior and senior.

Jerry attended Westminster College in New Wilmington, PA., on a basketball scholarship. He was named NAIA All-American and captained the team his senior year. He majored in business administration and minored in education and was a member of Sigma Nu fraternity.

On graduation, he entered the U.S. Army, where his honors as a basketball player included MVP at the Armed Forces International Tournament, Army All Star at the National AAU Tournament and an Olympics tryout in 1956.

Jerry started with Penton Publishing in 1963 as a salesman on New Equipment Digest and rose through the ranks at Penton to executive vice president. As international VP, he developed business in the major countries in Europe and the Far East.

Jerry was married to Gretchen Schulte of Kenosha, WI. Their family included several children and eleven grandchildren. Andrew and Laurie

Neff, San Carlos, CA; Beth and Mike Woznica, Encino, CA; Nancy Neff, Chicago, IL; Peter and Jean Chojnacki, Hudson, OH; Mary and Mike Rea, Twinsburg, OH; and Stephen and Shelly Neff, Twinsburg, OH; and Sarah Ellen (with the Lord). Jerry's sister Judith lives in Chester, WV.

On retirement in 1998, Jerry and Gretchen moved to Hilton Head, SC, where they enjoyed playing golf and tennis and walking on the beach. They traveled frequently, especially to visit family. Jerry served on a number of boards, including two terms on the board of trustees of Westminster College. He was inducted into the Westminster College Basketball Hall of Fame and co-founded the Towering Titans Organization, dedicated to supporting athletics at the college. One of his joys was playing basketball in the Senior Olympics alongside his college teammate Dick Black.

A memorial service will be held at the First Presbyterian Church, 950 William Hilton Parkway, Hilton Head, SC, at 4 o'clock in the afternoon on Friday, Oct. 5. A reception will follow at the Golf Club at Indigo Run.

In lieu of flowers, memorial contributions may be made to Westminster College Towering Titan Organization, 319 South Market Street, New Wilmington, PA, 16172.

The Island Funeral Home and Crematory is in charge of arrangements.

Died Oct. 2, 2007   **The Island Packet**, *Hilton Head, S.C. Oct. 5, 2007*

JERRY

I first saw Jerry Neff on the floor of "Old 77."

It wasn't even called that then, in the fall of 1950.

It was the gymnasium on the campus of Westminster College in New Wilmington, Pa., and frankly, at first sight, I was disappointed.

It was a bandbox, smaller than the Whitin Community Association gymnasium that I had grown up on and played high school basketball at in the Blackstone Valley town of Northbridge, Mass.

And there was every justification why Duquesne had decided to refuse to play there any longer. The home and away games played between the two rivals that year were played at Duquesne Gardens in Pittsburgh and at the Farrell High School Auditorium in that Western Pennsylvania steel town next to Youngstown, Ohio.

But "Old 77" was the first place I went to after my arrival in New Wilmington that September of 1950. I was hoping to try out for the basketball team.

When I got there, there was already a pickup scrimmage going on, and before too long, I was invited to participate.

Jerry Neff was playing along with a couple of other freshmen who I later determined had been granted basketball scholarships at Westminster.

I fit right in, enjoyed the play and got the biggest boost of all when Don "Bandy" Meyers yelled at me after a successful fast break that "Grover is going to be glad to see you ." "Bandy" was a sophomore and was to get considerable playing time as the sixth or seventh man on the varsity that year.

Grover was Grover Washabaugh, the legendary coach of the Westminster Titans, who achieved their initial fame by participating in the first collegiate basketball double header at the old Madison Square Garden in 1934. The four teams were Notre Dame, New York University, St. John's and Westminster.

I subsequently learned that Jerry, an all-state selection from Chester, W. Va., was one of six basketball scholarship freshmen that year. That meant there was considerable competition for any walk-ons, of which I was one.

But this was the next to last year that freshmen were barred from varsity competition, so there was a freshman team schedule and an opportunity to make one's mark.

There were 10 to 12 players on that squad.

Jerry was certainly its leader.

He was about 6' 3", was a great ball handler and had an accurate jump shot. But one of the things that impressed me most was his defense. I watched carefully how he stalked dribblers and managed to reach behind them and tap the ball back to himself or to another teammate as the start of a fast break down the other end of the floor.

I tried to emulate him and we teammates on the defense learned to cover and double team when he went ball-hawking.

As the 7th or 8th player on that freshman team, I didn't get many minutes. So it was a surprise when Coach Charles "Buzz" inserted me into the game against the Pitt freshmen at the old, and cold, Pitt Stadium.

I even scored a few points, but the greatest pleasure was serving as a feeder to Jerry who was the most capable member of the team to convert those feeds into buckets. One of the finest moments after the game came from Jim Brill, another member of the freshman team, when he approached me afterwards with a sincere "Nice game."

Years later, when reading Boston Celtics Hall of Famer Bill Russell's book "Second Wind, the Memoirs of an Opinionated Man," I learned we had shared an experience. Russell had contended that the infrequent occasions when two teams were both playing at the top of their form, and had created a ballet-like choreography on the court were more exhilarating experiences than even championships.

Three particular instances came to mind, beating rival Uxbridge High School in my senior year, helping Jerry Neff beat Pitt in the Steel City, and playing with Hall of Famer Frank Selvy on a U.S. Army regimental team in Straubing, Germany, defeating all comers and then having our application to play in the divisional championships rejected because we were too small a unit.

Jerry Neff went straight to the varsity and the starting five of the Westminster College Titans as a sophomore in a successful season marred only by the tragic death of senior Jerry Sybert in a car crash on a trip to his home town to obtain an engagement ring for his girlfriend.

Our sophomore year started in the new Memorial Field House, a monstrous facility in that era for a small college basketball team. It seated as many as 3,500 fans at a time when recent NCAA winner Holy Cross was playing at the small Worcester Auditorium which seated approximately 1,500.

Jerry became a Hall of Famer in his own right during those next three years at Westminster, and then continued that career with his Army basketball and the participation in the senior Olympics.

I saw him infrequently after graduation, at class reunions that took place every five years on the campus. During later reunions, I learned that both Jerry and his wife Gretchen, and Carol Shiels Roark, a fellow classmate and top scholar, had moved to Hilton Head Island in their retirement years.

Both Carol and Jerry suggested that I visit the resort island. I am indebted to both that I did so.

Carol, by then widowed, was active in the religious, historical and cultural life of the Lowcountry of South Carolina and Georgia. She took a particular interest in the Gullah people, the descendants of slaves transported to the coastal area from Angola, Sierra Leone and other parts of West Africa. They developed a significant, independent culture after the civil war on the sparsely populated islands and coastal marshland before the construction of bridges, highways and airports transformed it from an agricultural backwater to a tourist and retirement haven.

Jerry and Gretchen were wonderful hosts to any who arrived on the island, particularly if there was a connection to Westminster. He had become a co-founder of the Towering Titans, an athletic financial booster organization, and was named to the Westminster College Basketball Hall of Fame immediately after his nomination by Dick Black, who achieved considerable athletic notoriety himself as a high school basketball and baseball coach in Cleveland and at Mount Lebanon, Pa. high school, outside Pittsburgh.

Jerry and I did a lot of nostalgic reminiscing, particularly on the golf course, at dinners at their home in the Indigo Run Plantation, and at lunches around the island.

After Jerry's funeral, Dick and I discussed the Neff personality, one that made him known throughout the island of Hilton Head, no matter where one went. Dick related how Jerry had always expressed his envy of Dick, having a career teaching young students (Dick taught mathematics, not basket-weaving) and young athletes. We reflected on Jerry's very successful career in trade magazine marketing.

I responded that Jerry frequently expressed the same feelings regarding my years spent abroad in study, as a foreign correspondent and as a news editor. I had to remind Jerry of his world travels and successful business ventures.

He frequently thanked me for getting him more active in developing his own genealogical studies. Actually, he had visited the home of his forebears in Switzerland, the Naeffenhaus, before I got to County Down in Northern Ireland, to research mine.

Jerry and Gretchen and Phyllis Pitzer, another classmate of ours, and I had lunch at Boathouse II on Hilton Head in June, 2007, just before my flight to Belfast. Jerry died the day after my return to the island in October of a fast-developing and virulent lung cancer.

LAWRENCE R. PITZER

1927 - 2004

Lawrence R. Pitzer, 76, of Highland Beach, Fla., passed away on Friday, Sept. 10, 2004.

Formerly of Norwich, N.Y., he had been a full-time resident of Highland Beach since 1999. At the time of his death, Mr. Pitzer served as treasurer of the Bel Lido Property Owners Association and was also a member of the town of Highland Beach Public Safety Committee.

He spent the early years of his life in New Castle, Pa., and graduated from New Castle High School in the January class of 1946.

After service in the Army he graduated from Westminster College, New Wilmington, Pa.

He was associated with Norwich (N.Y.) Eaton Pharmaceuticals, which became a division of Procter and Gamble, and retired in 1990 after 35 years of service.

He is survived by his loving wife of 50 years, Phyllis M. Pitzer of Highland Beach, a son, David A. Pitzer and his wife Stephanie of Clifton Park, N.Y., and a daughter, Carol P. Bridges and her husband Bryan of Exeter, N.H. Also surviving are his grandchildren Kurt R. Pitzer, Kathryn E. Pitzer, Christopher L. Bridges and Andrew D. Bridges. He was predeceased by a son, Kurt L. Pitzer.

A memorial service will be held at 2 p.m. on Saturday, Sept. 18, 2004 at the Kraeer Funeral Home and Cremation Center, 1353 North Federal Highway, Boca Raton, Fla., 33432

Died Sept. 10, 2004

*This obituary was provided by the family for publication by **The Evening Sun** (Norwich, N.Y.) , the **New Castle News** (Pa.) and the **Sun-Sentinel** (Fort Lauderdale, Fla.)*

LARRY

A friend tells you that you have body odor.

A good friend, acknowledging you've made progress in this regard, agrees to become your college roommate.

A best friend invites you to be an usher at his wedding, assured you will not stink up the ceremony.

Larry was all of these.

That is why I kept track of him and his lovely wife Phyllis George Pitzer after college.

Everything went smoothly until the honeymoon.

We received a telephone call in early evening from up the Taconic Parkway that the newlyweds were like an emperor and empress, without clothes.

Someone had failed to put the honeymoon couple's suitcases in the trunk of the car.

Phyl's sister Doris and I were assigned the task of delivering the goods, which we did in a memorable trip.

Larry and Phyl didn't find how memorable for another 40 years.

In the summer of 1956, after completing a year of studying Ukrainian at the Army Language School in Monterey, Calif., I decided to use some of my 30 days travel time traversing the country overland.

Interim stops on the way included Flagstaff, Ariz., Denver, Chicago. and Cleveland. It took me about two weeks to get to the latter city and a stopover a few miles to the east at Madison, where my uncle Andy Mantell was greenskeeper at the Madison Country Club.

Larry and Phyl had set up housekeeping in Youngstown, an hour and a half south of Madison, and when I expressed my desire to drop down and visit them, Uncle Andy immediately offered his Model T.

Just be sure to watch the water level, he cautioned. You probably won't have to stop for gas, but check the water every once in a while.

I must make a confession here.

If I had ever been an adventurous uncle who owned a Model T, I would never have been willing to lend it to an inexperienced nephew just passing through.

Andy was more than generous.

The Pitzers in Youngstown were warned that I was coming, but not how.

They broke up when I drove up in the Model T, and I gushingly related how crowds of motorists stopped for gasoline at every service station between Madison and Youngstown where I stopped for water.

The following decade, after having spent four years in Europe, I tracked them down again, this time at Cherry Hill, N.J.

I had taken a modest step up by this time, and arrived in Cherry Hill in a standard Volkswagen, circa 1956, which had no chrome, idiot sticks for directional signals, a non-synchronized transmission, nominal heat, minimal comfort, and somewhere between 26 and 28 horsepower.

It became a standing joke that my mode of arrival would be more interesting than the arrival itself.

Another assignment to Europe intervened, and by this time, the Pitzers were residents of Norwich, N.Y., where Larry was associated with Norwich Eaton Pharmaceuticals, later a division of Procter & Gamble.

By this time, Larry and Phyl knew that I had become associated with the Jehovah's Witnesses, and there had been a series of exchanges of correspondence and literature in this regard.

I think Phyl thought that there was something more afoot.

Apparently, every time the Pitzers moved, the Witnesses proceeded to build one of their houses of worship, a Kingdom Hall, if not next door, very close.

It took some persuasion to convince them that I had nothing to do with it.

And perhaps that conviction that I was innocent of this took another blow after the Pitzers moved to Boca Raton, Fla., to assist in taking care of Phyl's mother, who lived to a very active age of 96.

Another friend from Longmeadow, Mass., had a summer home in West Palm Beach, and he began sending me clippings from the Florida newspapers about the controversy over the administration building at West Palm.

It seems that the corporate entity of the Watchtower Bible and Tract Society was interested in purchasing the facility to turn it into an assembly hall so congregations in that circuit and district could gather for their thrice-annual sessions.

I advised the Pitzers in advance that I had nothing to do with this latest incursion, but I am not sure that I was ever successful in persuading them.

In any event, it did not prevent them from welcoming me for a visit in South Florida near the end of the 1990s.

And this despite the shocking revelation that I had made at one of the class reunions back in Western Pennsylvania in the late '80s.

Larry and Phyl were sitting across the table of eight during very lively discussions that evening, probably at the Radisson in Sharon, Pa.

Suddenly, I started to describe the wonderful weekend I had spent with Phyl's sister Doris during the late summer of 1956.

Two mouths across the table went agape.

I ignored the two shocked physiognomies and proceeded with my tale.

About the wonderful trip to New York before flying to San Diego and my assignment to Monterey.

About how Doris and I went into Manhattan and enjoyed a Broadway show, watching a youthful and vigorous Paul Newman cavort about the stage in Joseph Hayes' play "Desperate Hours," about a home invasion.

About swimming at Jones Beach with Doris and then flying to San Diego and swimming at Pacific Beach in San Diego with hometown friends Terry and Valerie Conlin less than 24 hours later.

The most shocking thing as far as Larry and Phyl were concerned was that neither of them had ever heard a word about that weekend before.

They looked and acted like college house mothers and dorm proctors.

They needn't have been concerned. I had been invited to stay for the weekend at the George home, then in Darien, Conn., before my flight out to San Diego.

It had all been very platonic, an innocent and fun-filled time.

But I'll never forget the look on their faces.

FRANK MURPHY DIES
EX-MANAGING EDITOR

1873-1966

Francis P. (Frank) Murphy of 291 Beverly Road, retired managing editor of The Worcester Telegram, died yesterday at Cape Cod Hospital in Hyannis. He was stricken ill Tuesday while vacationing in Harwich Port.

He had observed his 77th birthday Sunday.

Associated with the Telegram for 49 years before retiring at 70 in 1966, Mr. Murphy remained a working newspaperman until his death. He had kept active in recent years working as a copy editor for The Catholic Free Press, leaving his desk three weeks ago to vacation on Cape Cod.

He had been managing editor of the Telegram from 1945 to 1966.

A man of few but telling words, Mr. Murphy was renowned in journalism as a teacher of young reporters and for his ability to organize a newspaper staff for coverage of fast-breaking news.

Mr. Murphy's harnessing of men and machines to assess and accurately report the June 9, 1953 tornado was an outstanding example of his talents.

Never one to seek personal credit, Mr. Murphy did say when retiring from the Telegram in 1966 that he considered his greatest accomplishment in journalism to be "making newspapermen out of suitable college graduates." In that regard, he added modestly, "I have had a prideful success."

Of the hundreds of writers who began their careers under Mr. Murphy, at least four were later Pulitzer Prize winners –Leland Stowe, the late Joseph A Keblinsky, James S. Doyle and Sanche de Gramont.

Joseph McGinnis, author of the best seller, "Making of the President, '68", started as a newspaperman under Mr. Murphy, as did Noah Gordon, author of several books, including the best seller, "The Rabbi."

A veteran reporter recalled when Mr. Murphy retired in 1966 that "he brought me up in the newspaper business almost like a father brings up a son."

Maybe that fatherly interest developed because Mr. Murphy began what he called "his newspaper life" on a weekly operated by his father, Peter B. Murphy, later city clerk of Marlboro.

Started on Weekly

In 1914, when Mr. Murphy was graduated from Boston High School of Commerce, he went to work for the Marlboro Times, which his father published weekly while also running a print shop.

Mr. Murphy had studied journalism at Boston University, taking night courses in 1913 and 1914 while going to high school days.

In April, 1917, he joined the Worcester Telegram as a correspondent in Clinton. The big news out of Clinton that month was the story about male members of St. Mary's parish keeping the pastor, Rev. Thoepold Blum * out of the church because he had fired the organist.

*A check of parish records at St. Mary's to determine whether the letters "o" and "e" in the priest's name had been transposed in the Murphy obituary produced only more confusion. A parish secretary reported that the name of the first parish priest at St. Mary's was Theo Suk. The name of the second was listed as an L. Blum. I shall leave it to future historians to determine who fired whom.

A thin man, with craggy features, coal-black hair parted in the middle, Mr. Murphy in his days as a reporter was nothing like Hollywood's boisterous, press card-in-hat reporters. Old timers mourning his passing last night could not recall him ever wearing a hat.

They remembered him always with sleeves rolled up, bony elbows against the desk wielding a copy editor's pencil.

Mr. Murphy served with the American Expeditionary Forces in France during World War I. He was with the 33rd Engineers.

The day after he retired from the Telegram, the Catholic Free Press said of him:

"Did he 'manage' the news? Of course he did. No newspaperman, especially one who has been an editor as long as he has, would ever profess that journalism is a completely objective science. But there is a difference between 'managing' and 'distorting' or 'sensationalizing'. The latter words are not part of his vocabulary.

The Free Press concluded, "Mr. Murphy's insight and talent will be missed. But more so will be his integrity and interest."

Following service in World War I, he returned to the Telegram, moving into the city room from Clinton in 1921 and becoming county news editor.

During the Roaring Twenties and Depression 1930s, he served as state editor, city editor, wire editor, and news editor under the late Mose H. Williams, whom he succeeded as managing editor in 1945.

Mr. Murphy once recalled he did a short stint as editorial writer under Roland F. "Cap" Andrews, a legendary editor of old Worcester newspaper days.

When Mr. Murphy joined the Telegram in 1917, the newspaper was owned by Austin Cristy and had been for 35 years. In 1919, Theodore T. Ellis bought the Telegram. Later, Ellis purchased The Evening Gazette from the late George F. Booth.

In 1925, the present organization was founded when Booth and the late Harry G. Stoddard combined to purchase both the Telegram and The Evening Gazette from Ellis. Mr. Murphy directed coverage of the 1938 hurricane, yearly blizzards and the 1955 floods.

When the world gloried at Charles A. Lindbergh's solo flight across the Atlantic in 1927, Mr. Murphy's charges already were writing of Robert H. Goddard's first pioneering rocket firings in a cow pasture in Auburn.

For more than 40 years, Mr. Murphy loved to vacation at Cape Cod. But he was a newspaperman 24 hours a day, which led in 1963 to a Telegram "scoop" of the national press with a story that there would be a new summer White House on Squaw Island in Hyannis Port.

In developing the copyrighted story, Mr. Murphy had learned the wife of President John F. Kennedy was interested in acquiring a home owned by singer Morton Downey. The White House later confirmed the Murphy story, and in that summer of 1963, shortly before his death, President Kennedy did locate his White House on Squaw Island.

In recalling his own career, Mr. Murphy noted he had "covered spot and breaking news stories in every town and city in the Telegram's circulation area, except Phillipston and Royalston, where apparently nothing ever happened in my day."

At one time, whistling was said to have bothered the oldtime telegraphers and was long a newsroom taboo. One of the first lessons of journalism experienced by a cub reporter was to hear Mr. Murphy thunder, "Who's whistling?"

Mr. Murphy, however, always looked as though he was whistling inside. "He was happy with every story he worked on, every paper he ever turned out. It was his whole life. And…he did a good job," said his widow, Mrs. Callie M. (Clifford) Murphy.

Richard C. Steele, president and publisher of the Telegram and The Evening Gazette, Inc., said, "I am terribly grieved. Frank Murphy was a dear friend as well as a professional colleague for years."

"Frank Murphy was one of the most competent and professional newspapermen it was my privilege to know and to work with," said Steele, recalling that reporters who had worked with and for him "have gone all over the world" in the field of journalism and related fields. "Their achievements serve to illustrate the professionalism Frank Murphy instilled in his reporters," Steele said.

Mr. Murphy had but one professional interest in life — newspapering. He loved it. He lived it.

It was the same with his feeling for railroads. He once recalled, "I preferred travel by rail to any other known method tried. And I tried them all from hoss back to jet and back to canoe."

Three of his seven children served as reporters on the Telegram, E. Jean (Murphy) Dennehy, Sarah A. (Murphy) Healey and Philip F. Murphy, who later worked for the Associated Press in Boston and the Cape Cod Standard Times.

Mentioned in the current edition of Who's Who in America, Mr. Murphy for many years belonged to the American Society of Newspaper Editors, Associated Press Managing Editors Association, the New England Society of Newspaper Editors and the New England Associated Press News Executives Association.

He also was a member of the Boston Veterans Journalists, the Academy of Political Science, the American Academy of Political and Social Science and the Holy Name Society of Our Lady of the Rosary Church.

In addition to his work at the Catholic Free Press, Mr. Murphy had served for a time in 1969 as a typographical and editorial consultant to the Marlboro Enterprise and the Hudson Sun.

He was born in Marlboro, July 1, 1896, the son of the late Peter B. and Ellen Agnes (Dacey) Murphy.

He leaves his wife, Callie M. (Clifford) Murphy; three sons, Philip F., Peter B. and Charles M. Murphy, all of Harwich Port; four daughters, E. Jean, wife of Paul J. Dennehy of Cypress, Calif.; Frances P., wife of Richard T. Shea, and Callie, wife of David W. Murphy, all of Worcester, Sarah A., wife of Dr. James Healey of Sudbury; one sister, Mrs. Eleanor Tobin of Maynard, and 16 grandchildren.

The funeral will be Saturday at 10 a.m. at Our Lady of the Rosary Church. Burial will be in St. John's Cemetery. Calling hours at the Callahan Brothers Funeral Home, Seven Hills Plaza, are Friday 2 to 4 and 7 to 9 p.m.

Died July 4, 1973   ***The Worcester*** (Mass.) ***Telegram,*** *July 5, 1973*

THE TORNADO

I got the call from Mom on June 10, 1953.

I had stayed on campus to see some of my friends a year ahead of me graduate and was scheduled to start a summer stint as a reporter at The Worcester (Mass.) Telegram at mid-month.

Mom said there had been a tornado in Worcester and that Frank Murphy had called, asking if I could start immediately.

That is indicative of the detail the managing editor of The Telegram immersed himself in as he marshaled every possible resource to cover the biggest storm story in Central Massachusetts since the 1938 hurricane.

I told Mom to call Mr. Murphy and tell him I was on my way, packed an overnight bag and grabbed a plane from Youngstown, Ohio to Newark.

I was home that day and was at work the next night.

Our beat from then until I went back to school for my senior year at Westminster College in New Wilmington, Pa. was the tornado.

The death toll kept rising during the summer as some who had been critically injured in the tornado died and their deaths were attributed to the storm. I recall writing an obituary just before returning to school in September that was No. 93. The official toll cited in the record books is 94.

The Telegram, 50 years later, listed the 25 deadliest tornadoes in the United States as calculated by the Storm Prediction Center back to 1840.

Worcester, with 94 deaths, ranked No. 19.

On June 18, nine days after the storm, The (morning) Telegram and its companion paper, The Evening Gazette, published a special 40-page edition on the Tornado.

Fifty years later, on June 8, 2003, the Sunday Telegram published a commemorative edition that put the storm in historical perspective.

Both are fascinating reading for the historian, the journalist and the storm buff.

After the coverage of the death, injury, damage to infrastructure and business and residential property, the coverage became even more personal.

Hundreds of families had had their personal items blown away, diaries, memoirs, photos, the things people hold so close.

The Telegram set up a system of recording and cataloguing these items as fishermen and boaters began to gather them from Cape Cod Bay and the Atlantic Ocean, up to 80 miles away, where the tornado had deposited them.

The newspaper assisted in the return of these prized mementoes to shattered families for the entire summer and beyond.

The significance of this service was not lost to me at the time, and became even more so as I grew older.

Reporter Chris Sinacola wrote a fine lead for one of his stories in the June 8, 2003 anniversary edition of the Telegram:

It ran as follows:

"NORTHBRIDGE — The killer tornado that struck Worcester and surrounding towns on June 9, 1953, had a nasty younger cousin."

His article described a companion twister that bounced across the hilltops of Sutton and Northbridge 15 miles south of Worcester and parallel to the path of the Worcester tornado.

The nasty cousin caused up to a $1 million in damage to farm buildings and residences in the two towns, including the brick factory of the Kupfer Brothers paper mill in the Riverdale section of Northbridge.

Included in the damage was the destruction of the chicken barn of my Uncle Bill and cousin Bill Crawford on Hill Street in Whitinsville.

All the chickens were lost, but insurance and persistence led my cousin to build a cow barn and dairy herd on the site, which prospered until taxes and residential encroachment forced him out of Massachusetts and redeployment to the pastureland of Schoharie County in upper New York State two decades later.

Unreclaimed were the family heirlooms that were in the attic of the farmstead.

The family Bible, passports, letters, photos and records had been blown away, possibly out to sea..

Nothing was ever found.

It was four decades later that my youngest brother Jack made contact with a distant cousin in St. Catherines, Ontario who had emigrated from Northern Ireland, and could provide us with some information.

When this cousin, also named Bill Crawford, came down to visit us, he brought a genealogical record which enabled us to fill a huge heritage gap.

There was another service performed for the public by the editorial staff under the direction of Frank Murphy.

The editors of the newspapers and the city fathers had quickly noted the languorous response of many of the traditional purveyors of emergency assistance in cases of disaster.

As a result, three groups, the Roman Catholic diocese, the Worcester area Council of Churches and the United Jewish Appeal had convened and immediately opened a joint disaster relief appeal.

Within 48 hours, the joint appeal had collected and distributed more than $2 million to those in immediate need, and had concluded that it could continue doing so as long as the need existed.

News of this successful response to need was shared by the Worcester newspaper with the editors of newspapers in Flint, Mich., and Waco, Texas, which had also been victims of nearly simultaneous, if not so devastating tornadoes.

The success of the local relief effort also led to a thorough examination of the administration and financial records of philanthropic organizations, particularly the American Red Cross and the United Fund, or United Way.

The ratio of fund-raising and relief disbursement revealed by a series of articles on the subject struck a blow at the fund-raising efforts of those organizations in the city for years.

The Salvation Army, whose teams were dispatched to the disaster scene immediately and worked tirelessly throughout the rescue effort, was the only organization that came through this examination unscathed.

The series taught me a valuable lesson: To ask for a financial report from any solicitor of a charity.

I have yet to receive one.

It was an honor to have worked for Frank Murphy, if only during those three tornado-driven months of 1953 and the six months after my graduation from school and enlistment in the Army a year later.

I had worked as an office boy for the afternoon Gazette during the summer of 1952, and had decided to apply for a reporter's job at The Telegram. Frank Murphy's reputation was an inducement.

I wrote several feature stories during that first summer of the tornado, and on my return, decided to do a couple of follow-ups.

One of them went straight to Frank Murphy's desk for editing, perhaps because it was going in the Sunday feature section.

He called me into his glassed-in office.

He commended me in general, but gruffly pointed out a gaffe.

I, in my virginal innocence, had misused the adjective consummate.

"Marriages are never consummated in a newspaper," he warned, "only in bed."

Frank Murphy was also a consummate editor.

I went off to the Army, Fort Dix, N.J., Fort Holabird, Md., the Army

Language School at the Presidio of Monterey, Calif., and service with the Army in Germany and studies at the University of Munich.

On my return, I went to Frank Murphy for a recommendation as I applied to news organizations that were most likely to give me an opportunity to be assigned overseas as a foreign correspondent.

He was kind enough to put me in contact with Dick Steele, a former Telegram executive who spent a short stint in the effort to rescue the ill-fated New York Herald Tribune.

Mr. Steele gave me time and every courtesy in New York, but I was not hired, the Herald-Tribune could not be saved, and Dick Steele eventually ended up back in Worcester.

In retrospect, I feel more now than then, that it was a gross presumption on my part to ask Frank Murphy for a recommendation to work for another news organization. But there was no evidence, in his facial expressions, his words, or his actions, that it was. Apparently he perceived, understood and accepted what I really wanted.

R. H. DAVIS;
EX-TELEGRAM CITY EDITOR
1907-1962

Richard (Dick) Harris Davis of 41 North Main Street, Oakdale, a former reporter, aviation writer, and night city editor of The Worcester Telegram, died yesterday in Holden District Hospital after a long illness. He was 55.

Except for service with the U.S. Army Air Corps between 1942 and 1945, Mr. Davis worked for The Telegram from 1931 to 1946, when he entered the auditing business with his father. He joined The Telegram after attending Amherst College.

He resided his entire life at the same address in Oakdale. He was the son of Hazel W. (Harris) Davis and the late Archibald Davis. His father was West Boylston town clerk for many years.

Mr. Davis was graduated from West Boylston Elementary School and North High School, Worcester, before attending college. He was a police and general assignment reporter before his assignment as night city editor in the late 1930s. He was reputed at that time to be one of the youngest city editors in the United States.

Mr. Davis, a private pilot, flew over most of the Atlantic seaboard. He was associated in flying activities with Mason Jennings of North Grafton and the late Laurence O. Hanscom, state house reporter for The Telegram and The Evening Gazette in the 1930s. L. G. Hanscom Field, Bedford, is named for Hanscom, who was killed in a plane crash at Saugus.

Hanscom, Mr. Davis and William C. Chaplis, former Telegram photographer, narrowly escaped injury on the afternoon of the 1938 hurricane while on an air survey of flood damage in the Ware River Valley. They were caught in the hurricane's outer spiral and barely made it back to Grafton Airport before trees began falling throughout the area.

Before his Army Air Corps service, Mr. Davis was a prime organizer of the Massachusetts Civil Air Patrol. He rejoined The Telegram in the late 1940s but left again to become editor of The West Boylston Times, a weekly newspaper.

He had been in ill health in recent years.

A memorial service will be held at 7 p.m. May 17 in Oakdale Methodist Church. Rev. Horatio Robbins will officiate. The family requests that flowers be omitted, and suggests contributions may be made to the American Cancer Fund.

The Gould Funeral Home, 1 West Boylston St., West Boylston, is in charge of arrangements.

Died May 8, 1962   ***The Worcester*** (Mass.) ***Telegram*** *May 9, 1962*

"STALAG 17"

Dick Davis was involved in my first byline.

I'm not sure whether Bill DeBourke on the city desk or Dick on the copy desk actually wrote my name on the copy, but both of them edited the story.

It was based on an interview with an airman from Worcester, Mass. who had been imprisoned in the German POW camp made infamous by the hit film with William Holden.

The Worcester airman lent me a book that the POWs published after the war to record their experiences and their ordeal.

Thanks to the interview and the book, the story wrote itself.

Dick was enthused by the story, and offered a commendation as to how it was handled. For a rookie general assignment reporter, that is enough of a Cloud 9 to float you out of the city room and into the nearest bar.

In the Worcester of that era, that was the Eden, just downstairs.

I came to understand why Dick was so interested in the story nearly 50 years later, when I read his obituary for the first time.

He was a flier himself. His obituary catalogues his interests.

He would have been even more interested in how "Stalag 17" came to be published.

That story was recalled years later by Andy Rooney in his book, "My War."

Two prisoners of Stalag 17, Ron Bevan and Ed Trzynski, had written a play about their experiences and were seeking advice how to get it published.

Bevan had collaborated with Rooney by providing combat sketches for the European edition of The Stars and Stripes, the Army newspaper, before his B-17 was shot down.

Bevan approached Rooney because the latter already had achieved a small measure of what was to be greater success in future with the publication of "Air Gunner" with Bud Hutton.

Rooney candidly acknowledges in his book his lack of literary perceptiveness.

He gave them little encouragement, attributing their enthusiasm to the euphoria resulting from having been released from Stalag 17.

But he did pass on the name of an agent, and then forgot about it.

"You can imagine my amazement," Rooney wrote in "My War," "when shortly after the war, Don Bevan and Ed Trzynski's 'Stalag 17' was made into a wonderfully successful and Academy Award-winning movie."

Rooney added an aside that probably made a few attorneys at CBS blanch.

He mentioned that Bevan and Trzynski eventually were forced to sue the television network—successfully it turned out—for having pirated too much of Stalag 17 and morphed it into the dumbed-down series "Hogan's Heroes."

Dick Davis would have loved Andy Rooney's take on all this.

Dick was articulate, meticulous, kind, flamboyant and alcoholic.

Every occupation has its occupational hazards.

The No. 1 hazard in the news and wire service field is alcohol.

And each one is an individual case.

Dick would arrive at work in late afternoon for the evening run to produce the morning paper.

A very thin graying man with hollow cheeks and deeply set dark eyes, he would arrive spiffily dressed and soberly serious or witty, as the case might be.

Horrible reporting or writing would produce an eruption of creative and imaginative epithets from the rim which were a joy to the literate ear.

The outbursts were not too often to be disruptive. In fact, they were a welcome safety valve on a copy desk whose members were only too willing to share their observations of folly.

After the first rush to deadline, members of the various desks would take their staggered dinner breaks.

For many, this would be the Eden, a journalistic paradise with a long bar and comfortable booths.

It was also within immediate reach by telephone for any newsroom emergency.

Dick frequently returned from dinner with that alcoholic spark that made him even more perceptive than while sober.

Occasionally, he would return unable to function well at all, but still joined in putting the last editions to bed.

And rarely, he would not return at all.

Protective staff members and editors would then come to the rescue.

I was enlisted to that team.

There were two solutions.

One, whenever I was on night police, was to bundle Dick into the 1950

Ford that The Worcester Telegram provided the night police reporter to occasionally beat the cruisers and/or ambulances to the accident or crime scene.

I then drove him dutifully to his home in the Oakdale section of West Boylston.

Occasionally, a second solution was deemed prudent. Several colleagues would repair to one of the all-night diners in downtown Worcester to share in a huge breakfast that would serve as a solid foundation to absorb the sea of alcohol.

This served as excellent training for later confrontations with the alcoholic colleague as friend, although these were more productive because they more often led to moderation, abstention and even sobriety.

One looks forward to applying that experience with Richard (Dick) Davis.

DOUGLAS E. KNEELAND

1929 – 2007

LINCOLN, Me.—Douglas E. Kneeland, 78, a reporter and bureau chief for The New York Times and later national and foreign editor of the Chicago Tribune, died Dec. 15, 2007 in hospital. The cause was lung cancer.

Kneeland returned to Lincoln, his hometown, after his retirement from The Tribune in 1993.

Kneeland was born July 27, 1929, the son of Vernis Bruce and Sadie Kneeland. After his graduation from Mattanawcook Academy in Lincoln in 1947, he entered the U.S. Army and served in Korea before the outbreak of the Korean War.

He began his studies at the University of Maine in 1949, majoring in history and journalism.

Upon graduation in 1953, he joined The Worcester (Mass.) Telegram and immediately participated in the coverage of the June 9 tornado which killed 94, left 1,288 injured, leveled or damaged 4,000 buildings, leaving more than 10,000 homeless and caused damage estimated by insurers at 53 million in 1953 dollars, or more than $1.5 billion today.

Kneeland soon was the top reporter on The Telegram's general assignment staff and remained there until 1956, when his former professor and mentor at the University of Maine, Wayne Jordan, recruited him to work at the Lorain Journal in Ohio.

He remained at the Lorain paper until 1959, when he was hired by The New York Times, with which he would be associated for 22 years. He was assigned to both the foreign and metropolitan desks

In 1967, he became a roving national correspondent for The Times, based in Kansas City. Two years later, he was persuaded to return to New York by national editor Gene Roberts to assist in the transformation of The Times into a national newspaper.

He was rewarded with subsequent national assignments working out of bureaus in Los Angeles and Chicago.

During this period, he covered a wide range of stories including the trials of the assassin of presidential candidate Robert F. Kennedy, Sirhan Sirhan, the trial of mass killer Charles Manson, the arrest of the kidnappers of Patricia Hearst and the killing of Kent State University students by members of the Ohio National Guard during anti-Vietnam war protests.

He also covered race riots, several presidential campaigns and the Watergate burglary, the investigation of which led to the resignation of President Richard M. Nixon.

He always regarded the highlight of the latter story was the breaking of the news of the Saturday night massacre, the resignation of Attorney General Elliot Richardson and other members of the administration over the refusal to fire Watergate special prosecutor Archibald Cox.

Kneeland left The Times in 1981 and joined the Chicago Tribune, where he served as foreign and national editor, and later as associate managing editor.

Tribune Editor Jim Squires indicated he hired Kneeland for his genial personality as well as his writing and editing skills.

"He never acted like he was from The New York Times," Squires said. "He acted like he was from the Maine Times, and that made all the difference in the world."

During the latter part of his career at The Tribune, Kneeland became a writer and editor for The Tribune's editorial pages. In 1990, he was named the paper's public editor responsible for seeing "that legitimate complaints about the newspaper's behavior" were heard and redressed and that "errors of fact and taste were aggressively corrected."

Kneeland was predeceased by his first wife, Anne Libby Kneeland, who died of cancer in 1989. After surgery during his own bout with the disease, he took early retirement and returned in 1993 to his hometown in Maine.

Back home, he was recruited to write a column for the local newspaper, the Lincoln News, and subsequently also taught journalism courses at the University of Maine, his alma mater. He was later inducted into the Maine Press Association Hall of Fame and honored by the university with an honorary doctorate.

In the mid-90s, be became reacquainted with an old friend from high school, Barbara Jordan Lees, and they were married in May of 1997.

Besides his second wife, he is survived by two sons, Bruce and Wayne Kneeland of Bristol, R.I.; two daughters, Debra Wentz of Sioux City, Iowa and Libby Williams of San Jose, Calif.; and a sister, Pamela Greene of Chatham, N.J.

A memorial service is planned for the spring.

Died Dec. 15, 2007   *Compiled by the author from obituaries published in the* **Bangor** (ME.) ***Daily News,*** *The* **New York Times** *and* ***The Chicago Tribune***

⌒

THE ATYPICAL MAINIAC

Maine native Larry Perkins (See Well-Schooled, Chapter 44) told me this one.

He asked me whether I knew what a Mainiac was.

I professed ignorance.

Well, it isn't a native of Maine, Larry explained, being one himself.

It is a native of Maine who leaves, and then returns to stay.

Doug Kneeland was a Mainiac, but highly atypical.

He had left the first time for Somerville, Mass., had worked a short time for a newspaper there, and then like any aspiring young man, had taken Horace Greeley's advice and gone west, joining the staff of The Worcester (Mass.) Telegram, about 25 miles to the west, in Central Massachusetts.

He picked the newsiest summer of that newspaper's life.

A tornado had whipped through the northeast quadrant of the city on June 9, 1953, and Doug Kneeland, the new reporter, quickly distinguished himself as one of the paper's savviest hires.

The eventual 94 deaths, injuries and millions of dollars of destruction provided grist for the newspaper's mill for the entire summer.

This writer was scheduled to join the staff the following week, but our boss, Frank Murphy, showed his flair for mobilization by calling my mother 14 miles to the south in Whitinsville and asking her if I could start immediately.

I hopped a flight in Youngstown, Ohio, 18 miles west of where I was finishing my junior year at Westminster College in New Wilmington, Pa.. My first flight ever got me back to New England via Newark and I was quickly thrown into the cauldron that was the tornado coverage of June, 1953.

Doug was also a rookie, but one who was a little older than the rest of us, having served in the U.S. Army in Korea. And unlike the rest of us, he turned out to be married.

He quickly earned the top assignments emanating from the day desk of A. Alfred Marcello, and the frequent bylines that come, both on Page 1 and inside, to that gifted combination of both writer and reporter.

One of the major public services performed by The Telegram that summer was the reuniting of householders with their possessions that the twister had lifted from their homes or the remains of them and deposited eastward across the state and as far as the Atlantic Ocean or Cape Cod Bay.

I could identify with those losses in that a parallel twister had hopped and skipped across the state just south of Worcester, had destroyed my uncle's chicken farm on a hilltop in Northbridge, Mass., and taken off the roof and attic of the old farmhouse. The winds deposited the family Bible, histories, letters, passports, citizenship papers and other heirlooms to what the family still presumes a watery grave.

But fishermen collected items and memorabilia from the waters off the Massachusetts coast for weeks and sent them back to The Telegram, which catalogued them and formed a depository for claims by grateful residents.

It wasn't until 54 years later that I was able to go to Northern Ireland and obtain the historical family background from a Presbyterian Church in County Down that had been lost.

Doug's abilities were recognized so quickly and utilized that he did not have to go through the regular apprenticeship of the rookie reporter on the obit desk that summer.

But even that graveyard of some reporters became an important backstop because of the tornado. An important task was to track the condition of the injured from the tornado and to determine whether those who died may have done so as a result of injuries from the disaster.

I can recall writing the obituary of victim No. 93 in September before my return to school for my senior year.

By the time of my return to the staff the following June, Doug was the star reporter there, and a self-effacing friend who invited me over for dinner with his wife Anne. He was also an occasional companion at the Eden, the restaurant and bar downstairs from the newsroom which served as the watering hole for the staffs of both the afternoon Gazette and the morning Telegram.

We kept in touch after I entered the U.S. Army in January of 1955 to do my stretch. When I learned that the lieutenant in the chain of command of our training battalion at Fort Dix was a graduate of the University of Maine, Doug was able to provide me with a wealth of background material on him in case I needed it.

That didn't prove to be necessary, but I was called before the captain once to ascertain why I was the only member of my platoon not to have contributed to the Red Cross drive. The goal of every unit was to have 100 % participation.

My explanation, denoted more fully in Frank Murphy Chapter 9, revolved around the investigative series on the Red Cross response to the Worcester tornado disaster and its implications for the community.

I am not sure how large a role Doug played in pulling together that series, but I am certain it was a significant one. The series itself influenced my decisions on charitable giving and philanthropies for a lifetime.

The captain, upon hearing my explanation, gave me a reprieve.

By the time I returned to Worcester for occasional visits during my period in the service, Doug had moved on to the Lorain Journal in Ohio.

And when I returned from four years in Germany, he was at The New York Times.

I was unemployed.

I had returned from four years in Germany with varying degrees of fluency in German, Russian and Ukrainian, experience with the Counter Intelligence Corps during the Hungarian crisis, and the study of history and foreign languages at the University of Munich.

I was also full of myself, and certain I would be immediately snapped up by the first eligible employer.

So why not try the Big Apple.

Doug agreed and invited me to stay at their place in Jackson Heights while I underwent a series of interviews at newspapers and magazines in Manhattan. I came away with a heightened appreciation of the generosity of both Doug and Anne.

But no job.

I also came away with a couple of vignettes from that visit, "Jackson Heights" and "Taxi", which are collected in a separate published volume, "Foibles."

For those too, I can thank Doug Kneeland.

THOMAS HAL BOYD

1896 – 1990

Thomas Hal Boyd, 93, of Carmel Highlands, an artist, builder and sportsman, died Saturday at Carmel Convalescent Center.

Born on Dec. 6, 1896, in Portland, Ore., Mr. Boyd was a graduate of the California School of Fine Arts. He had his first major art show in oils and watercolors at the Palace of Fine Arts in San Francisco in 1915.

He was an Army Air Corps veteran of World War I, flying the Curtis Jenny biplane.

Mr. Boyd homesteaded in the Shasta Valley after the war, then moved to Oakland, where he was manager of Joaquin Miller Park. He was active in producing operas performed by the Pacific Opera Company at Woodminster Amphitheater, as well as performances by the Oakland Symphony. He also sang with the Orpheus Club Chorus in Oakland.

In 1946, Mr. Boyd moved to Carmel Highlands. In 1949 he was involved in producing the first opera to be performed at the Forest Theater in Carmel by the Pacific Opera Company.

In the early 1960s, he developed Boyd Acres in Carmel Highlands. He also served as president of the Carmel Highlands Association, Carmel Pistol Club, Carmel Associated Sportsmen and the Monterey Peninsula Barbershop Cypressaires Chorus, and was an illustrator for the Department of the Army.

Mr. Boyd is survived by his wife, Ruth, and two daughters, Charlotte Hallam of Edgewater, Md., and Carol Hallett of Alexandria, Va.

No services will be held. Private cremation will take place at the Little Chapel by-the-Sea under direction of the Paul Mortuary. Private inurnment will follow.

The family requests that any memorial contributions go to the Harmony Foundation, care of Monterey Peninsula Cypressaires, P.O. Box 1301, Monterey 93942.

Died Feb. 10, 1990   *The* (Monterey, Ca.) ***Sunday Herald,*** *Feb. 11, 1990*

⮑

THE BOYDS

The Boyds were a wonderful couple.

I would never have met them if it hadn't been for Tom Barthelemy and Bill Reedy.

Tom and Bill were students of Russian at the Army Language School (later Defense Language Institute) in Monterey, Calif.

They were vetting fellow students to fill a vacancy at a house in Carmel Highlands. Five of the students rented the place for a weekend getaway from school and the military style barracks that climbed the hill above Monterey Bay in the mid-1950s.

They picked me.

It was an offer I would have been a fool to refuse.

The Boyds owned two homes overlooking the Pacific Ocean.

A tradition had developed of renting one of them to students at the language school. It was mutually advantageous.

The tenants also served as rental agents.

As soon as one got set to graduate, the others looked for a replacement.

I was chosen, given a preview of the site, and agreed to the terms.

The Boyds charged a rent of $70 a month. That divided by five amounted to $14 each. And at least one of the five had to own a car for the 15-minute drive up the hill and across the peninsula.

I didn't qualify on that last score.

I was a late bloomer in car ownership, just like in a number of other things.

I was 22 years old (turned 23 during the 48 weeks of language training) and had never owned a car, although I was having one $25 bond taken out of my Army pay each month toward the purchase of a Volkswagen Beetle on my posting to Austria or Germany.

Tom and Bill first introduced me to Jim Terrell and Bob Benton, the other two students with whom I would be sharing a roof and the rent.

It was an interesting group.

Jim was the oldest and most experienced. He was the furthest along in the demanding course, was therefore the most fluent and soon would be eager to leave.

He was adding Russian to the German he had learned at Marburg University.

Before graduating at Monterey, however, he kindly offered to get me started on German too, before my eventual posting there.

I had originally applied to take Russian as well, but the quota had been filled.

I had listed two alternate languages in my application, Turkish and Ukrainian.

The latter was one of two new languages added to the curriculum at the school in the autumn of 1955.

The foreign policy during that first term of the presidency of Dwight D. Eisenhower was one espousing the rollback of Communism, not its containment.

The name of the CIA-supported organization which beamed broadcasts in a number of languages behind the Iron and Bamboo curtains had still not been changed from Radio Liberation to Radio Liberty, a less aggressive title reflecting a softer policy.

The two new languages, Ukrainian and Vietnamese, reflected the policy of liberation.

I was assigned to the first Ukrainian class, a group of three officers and six enlisted men, all non-commissioned officers except myself, a lowly private.

I immediately became immersed in the six hours of class work and three hours of homework a day which constituted the course, which was conducted almost exclusively in the new language.

In addition, I was subjected to a sort of Western Hemispheric Russification. During the week, I lived in a barracks of Russian students and speakers, and on the weekend I escaped to an idyllic retreat, again dominated by Russian speakers.

It turned out to be a boon, learning one language and constantly exposed to another.

The Boyds turned out to be a friendly couple in their 50s with two daughters who were on the East Coast.

We paid our rent, and strangely, were almost monastic in behavior. It seemed that most of my housemates had girl friends at home.

Tom Barthelemy was a graduate of Miami University of Ohio, and a native of Massillon.

Bill Reedy was a graduate of Yale, and a native of Reading, Pa.

Jim Terrell had graduated from the University of Kansas at Lawrence before going to graduate school in Germany.

Bob Benton had lived abroad with his parents. His father had at one time been posted with the U.S. Foreign Service in Copenhagen, and Bob spoke Danish.

His folks lived in Southern California, so he made the most frequent trips home.

Monterey had a much more academic than military atmosphere, and thus was very conducive to learning and the broadening of one's horizons.

The 48 weeks of training (students of Chinese took 72 weeks, Romanian

36 and the Germanic and Romance languages 24) passed more swiftly than any other 48 weeks in my lifetime, with the exception of one when we didn't even go to class.

The school closed for one week in late December for Christmas vacation.

The school's mess hall closed down.

The other four guys went home on leave.

I, frugal as ever and looking forward to buying that Beetle, holed up at my idyllic Carmel Highlands retreat, and awaited the return of my housemates, their wheels, and the opening of the mess hall.

I didn't prepare very well for that very first period of total self-dependence.

I had always been fed very well, at two separate homes in Whitinsville, Mass., at three college dormitories and one fraternity house, and in the Army.

I had been caught unawares by this sudden abandonment, and hadn't even shopped.

My housemates, looking forward to home, hadn't bothered either.

The cupboard was nearly bare.

It was my first Christmas away from home, and the loneliest I ever spent.

There was a little relief, and social contact, just below us.

Language students had over the years cultivated ties with the management of the Highlands Inn, an exclusive escape and honeymoon retreat.

We were welcome at their bar and restaurant, and had ready access to their outdoor pool.

We were grateful for our privileges and behaved accordingly.

Unfortunately, what little substance I had that week was squandered on what was hardly riotous, but for me extravagant living at the Highlands Inn.

By the time school reopened, and pay day, I had eaten everything that was in the pantry.

My last meal consisted of bread and peanut butter and crème de menthe (green).

What a contrast to one of the last meals I enjoyed before leaving California for Germany.

The Boyds invited us all down to their house for dinner before our respective graduations.

We used to joke that they were trying to marry off their daughters to us, but we should have been so lucky.

After dinner and a performance of piano duets (I believe it was Bach) by Jim and Bill, Mr. Boyd made an announcement.

He thanked us for the respect we had shown for his property, and commended us for having been one of the finest groups of tenants from the language school that they had experienced. He added, somewhat sadly, that their daughters appeared to be planning their futures for the East Coast, and were not interested, at least for the foreseeable future, in the house we were inhabiting.

He asked us if we were interested in an option on the property.

Mr. Boyd acknowledged that we were all probably going to be assigned overseas, and that picking up that option might not occasion itself for some time. But he wished to make the offer anyway.

His price was $800.

None of the others envisioned returning to California.

I did. And I had $1,000 in savings bonds.

But I had my eyes on another prize, my new Volkswagen as soon as I arrived in Germany.

We all sadly passed.

Jim, Tom, Bill and Bob graduated from the school in turn and were reassigned, and I went about recruiting replacements.

The first was Tom DeBettencourt, a native of Martha's Vineyard who had decided not to enter the priesthood shortly before the decision to take his last vows.

He did the rest of the work for me, enlisting three other former fellow students from St. Mary's Seminary near Baltimore.

The monastic-style regime became suddenly festive.

The ex-seminarians, otherwise model citizens, evidenced an enthusiasm for female companionship and partying to which I was not used to. I was forced to indulge.

Fortunately, my fluency and proficiency in Ukrainian allowed me to absorb the new lessons in much less time than the three hours of homework recommended at the beginning of the course, so this allowed for some social license.

But I must concede that near the end of the course – and a hectic new social life – I was ready to yield my spot at Carmel Highlands and move on.

For years afterward, I wondered if any one of my former housemates had ever returned to the idyllic house on the hill.

Tom Barthelemy and Bill Reedy had maintained contact, and we had a reunion in Washington, D.C. in the mid-60s. None of us had gone back.

In 1979, I want job hunting to California, and put a stop on the Monterey Peninsula on my itinerary.

As I drove past the Carmel Highlands Inn in my rented Nova, I wondered if Mr. and Boyd were still alive.

They were, now in their 80s.

We reminisced, and one of my first questions was whether any of my contemporaries had ever returned to say hello, and thank you.

Only one, they answered.

It was Tom DeBettencourt.

I asked if they had his address.

They fetched the address book.

He was now a resident of Lafayette, Calif., just over the Berkeley Hills east of San Francisco. I jotted down the address and telephone number.

I was booked to fly back east out of San Francisco.

When I called Tom from Berkeley, he was ecstatic.

When I knocked on the door, his wife was more so.

I got a wonderful hug. It turned out that I was with her and Tom on their first date. I had been with a cute blonde whom I'd almost forgotten.

Tom had been with a pretty brunette that he hadn't.

He had returned to California, gotten married and the couple had five children. He, his wife, and the children were all active in the local parish.

We had a heart-warming meal together, and I thanked Tom for having returned to Carmel.

We talked about the Boyds.

I had asked Mr. Boyd what had become of the second house. He had advised me it had just been sold.

I didn't have the nerve, the effrontery or the courage to ask him for how much.

I still don't know, and don't dare inquire of the Carmel board of assessors, or its counterpart.

BORIS ALEXANDER

1910 – 2007

MONTEREY – Boris Alexander was born near Kiev, Ukraine and he left there during WWII. He died at the Westland House of Monterey at the age of 97.

He lived with his wife, Halyna, in Monterey since 1953. At that time he started to work at DLA (Defense Language Institute) as a teacher of Russian. Subsequently he served as head of the Ukrainian Department. His numerous students admired his talent, sense of humor, profound intellect, and great knowledge in various fields of science and culture, and authentic professionalism. They greatly appreciated him and loved him dearly. Many kept in touch with him until his very old age. Boris is survived by Halyna, his wife of 67 years. He is also survived by a niece, Tetyana and a nephew, Valeriy and their children and grandchildren.

He will be remembered and will be missed for his charm, wit, kindness and great strength of spirit, which impressed and touched all who knew and loved him.

Memorial services will be held at Saint Seraphim's Russian Orthodox Church in Seaside (Canyon Del Rey) on Saturday, July 21, 2007 at 5:30 p.m. and on Sunday, July 22, 2007 at 6:00 p.m. Funeral services will be held at the same location at 10:00 a.m. on Monday, July 23, 2007. Interment will follow in the Monterey City Cemetery. A reception at

Chef Lee's Chinese Restaurant in Monterey will follow the interment. All friends are invited.

Died July 18, 2007   ***The Monterey*** (CA) ***Peninsula Herald,*** *July 20, 2007*

⌒

FRUSTRATION

It was very difficult finding an obituary of Boris Alexandrovsky, the former chairman of the Ukrainian Department at the old Army Language School, now Defense Language Institute, at Monterey, Calif.

The (Monterey) Peninsula Herald responded to my request, but insisted it had none in its files.

Later, I made direct contact with the institute, and learned that Boris was still alive, and still living at the address on Via del Rey in Monterey where I had visited him a quarter century earlier.

He responded, at the age of 95, to my letter, complaining about the loss of his driver's license, the failing eyesight and the loss of friends.

He complained that his Christmas card list had dwindled to two.

I asked him whether it would be an imposition to read, or have read, for historical accuracy, a piece about him that I had written.

He not only did so, but filled in the geographical gaps in my story.

I was only too happy to notify two of my Witness friends on the Monterey Peninsula to look in on my old mentor and friend.

GEORG GRAF VON EINSIEDEL
1910 – 1983

WILHELMSHAVEN, Germany – Georg Graf von Einsiedel died on October 26 in Wilhelmshaven. He was 73.

He was born in Dresden-Blasewitz and after World War II settled in Straubing, Germany, where he worked as a typesetter for the daily Straubinger Tagblatt.

No death notice appeared in the Wilhelmshavener Zeitung after his passing and the city archives were unable to provide any further information.

GEORG GRAF VON EINSIEDEL

Graf von Einsiedel reminds me of the story of the Bavarian mother confronted by her little son. He had noticed that the neighbor girl didn't display the same genitalia as he when they showered naked under the garden hose on a hot summer day.

Oh, she is a refugee from the East, his mother explained.

They lost everything.

Graf von Einsiedel hadn't lost everything in the war, but he had lost a great deal.

A leg, for example, on the Russian front.

And his home, in Dresden, Saxony, now part of the German Democratic Republic.

And his wealth.

During my very first weeks in Germany, I tried learning the language by going into town, Straubing on the Danube in Lower Bavaria (Niederbayern,) as often as possible. I was attached to the 6th Armored Cavalry Regiment which was assigned to patrol the Czech border during the earlier years of the Cold War. It was easy for me to travel freely because I was in a Counter Intelligence Corps unit and wore civilian clothes. I had purchased my own car immediately on arriving in September of 1956, so had almost absolute freedom of movement.

I started dining in various hotels and restaurants in town, attending movies and doing everything possible to immerse myself in the language pool.

One of the spots was a popular café, possibly more popular among the German elite of the small city because Americans, particularly those in uniform, rarely frequented it.

On one weekend afternoon, I was interrupted while reading my German newspaper over my Kafe and Kuchen.

An older gentleman at the next table asked me whether I was trying to learn the language.

It was obvious that was the case. I was holding a copy of the Straubinger Tagblatt, the local daily, in front of me.

My captain already was impressed with the progress I had made with German in the few weeks I had been in the country. Jim Terrell, a fellow student at the Army Language School (now Defense Language Institute) in Monterey, Calif., had started teaching me German even before I knew that I had been assigned there.

Jim, a student of Russian at Monterey, already had studied abroad, at Marburg University in Germany, and was fluent and very generous with his assistance and encouragement.

At Straubing, I started reading the Tagblatt every day to find out what the German press was saying about the Americans and in particular the U.S. Army units that were stationed just outside town at a small former Luftwaffe base.

It turned out that Graf von Einsiedel was a typesetter at the Tagblatt.

He suggested that I return to the café the following week at the same time, and he would introduce me to some younger German residents of the city.

The first was the owner-operator of a radio shop, which was just what I needed.

I had considered buying a Telefunken radio ever since I had first heard of the brand several years earlier, but was dissuaded by the store owner.

Gründig up in Fürth , Henry Kissinger's hometown, had made a quantum entrepreneurial leap in the postwar radio industry.

Stymied by the Allied occupation forces from getting back into the radio and communications industry because of the military implications, Gründig had received permission to build toy radios.

When permission was finally given to produce radios in Germany, Gründig was far ahead of its German competitors, having set up a production and assembly line for its toy radios. All that was needed was to insert the works.

My radio store owner was ahead of them all.

He was importing Phillips radios from The Netherlands, and that was the first one I bought, from him.

That enabled me to listen to the Bayrischer Rundfunk for news and weather reports, and the classical music programs which were then being directed by the internationally acclaimed conductor Eugen Jochum.

It also got me acquainted with the jazz programs broadcast by the Voice of America with Willis Conover, one of the best ambassadors the United States had overseas.

In subsequent weeks, I met Frau von Einsiedel, and she introduced me to her youthful companion, a University of Munich student who also happened to be the mayor's daughter. This led to several other university acquaintances, including the son of a local dentist.

These young Germans were instrumental in my receiving an invitation to a major social event in the city attended by only two Americans. One of the colonel in charge of the base, there as a courtesy. I was invited for ostensibly other reasons, and I was subsequently told that the colonel was not entirely pleased that I was there.

In any event, it was Graf von Einsiedel who had opened the gate to the immersion pool. I am still swimming in it and am grateful for it.

CHAPTER 16

HANS HUDERT

An obituary for Hans Hudert could not be obtained for this printing.

⁓

THE HUDERTS

It had been my intention all along to wed Maria as soon as it was possible.

That did not change when the military transferred me from Straubing, Germany to Nuremberg.

There were multiple reasons for the transfer, one of which may have been to get me away from that German girl and all the complications that fraternization, as it was still called in the mid-1950s, might entail.

If that was one of the reasons, it didn't work.

I took Maria with me.

This was before the time that shacking up was morally or sociologically defensible, so we didn't.

The goal was to find a nice room where she could stay until the few months passed that we could marry and set up a household — probably in Munich.

I can't remember how we found the room, but it was at the Huderts.

Herr and Frau Hudert operated a haberdashery in the northern part of the city, and lived in a nice home in the suburban outskirts, not far from their shop. They had one son, and he was either away at school or at the start of his professional career, and out of the house.

It was perfect, at least for me.

I was at work all day, either at the office near the parade ground where Hitler mesmerized thousands before the war. If I wasn't visiting units in the city, I was traveling all over Franconia to line units, some of which stored nuclear weapons which had to be kept secret and protected. Nuremberg was the headquarters for armored cavalry units that guarded the northern border of Bavaria with Czechoslovakia at the height of the Cold War.

What Maria did with her days, I'd have to ask.

Evenings, we spent in a very petit bourgeois fashion, dining out, a movie, getting acquainted with my American colleagues and their spouses and the Huderts.

We became so comfortable with the Huderts that they eventually inquired whether we played bridge.

We did, and we began to play cards in their sitting room.

I had intended our stay in Nuremberg to last only three months until my tour of duty was up, and I could be discharged.

The original intention had been to be mustered out on the 3rd of January and start school immediately.

Two facts mitigated against that.

The German university system was in the middle of semesters.

The earliest that I could start was in the spring.

I had been planning over the last few months of my Army tour to attend the universities at Marburg, Heidelberg or Munich.

Several factors, including the relative strengths of the faculties in Slavic studies and the location of the Oktoberfest, affected the decision. I had gone to Munich, taken entry tests, and passed them already.

When I learned that the earliest that I could enroll was the first of May, and that there would be no G.I. bill payments until then, the decision was made to extend my enlistment three months.

Thus, we spent the rest of the winter in Nuremberg, celebrated the beginning of the new year, 1958, with the Huderts, and experienced the warmth of Muehlwein, a particular delight of the city.

After several months of warming relations with the Huderts, Herr Hudert interrupted one of our bridge games.

He directed our attention to one of the living room walls.

"Do you recognize that work of art?" he asked.

I confessed ignorance.

It's a Rembrandt, he said.

He then proceeded to explain its background, including its loss immediately after World War II.

It, along with many art works after the war, had been confiscated by the occupying American military.

Spoils of war, Herr Hudert figured, never expecting to see the valuable piece again.

Many months later, there was a knock on the door.

It was an American Army captain, and he was carrying a package under his arm.

He was received into the Hudert home, and proceeded to inform them that a thorough vetting of the Rembrandt had proved that it was a rightful possession of the Hudert family.

The Army, Herr Hudert said, was seeking to determine whether such artworks had been extorted or stolen from their rightful owners, including many of the German Jews who had either been forced out of the country or into concentration camps before and during the war.

The return of the Rembrandt was at least one reason we were so welcome in the Hudert home.

DR. FRANZ SCHNABEL

1887-1966

The historian Franz Schnabel was born in Mannheim on December 18, 1887, the son of merchant Carl Schnabel and his wife Maria.

He passed his examination at the gymnasium in the humanities there and studied history and philology for the next four years in Berlin and Heidelberg under Erich Marcks and Hermann Oncken One year after completing his dissertation on "The Alliance of Political Catholicism in Germany in the year 1848" he passed his state examination. He maintained during this period of study a programmatic preparation for the teaching profession.

Franz Schnabel taught, with the exception of the war years of 1914 to 1918, first in Mannheim and then at the Lessing Gymnasium and the Goethe School in Karlsruhe, and then was named Gymnasium professor on April 1, 1920. It was at this time that the Technical Institute of Karlsruhe (Technische Hochschule Karlsruhe) called him to the newly established chair for history there. He delivered his formal hypotheses with his introductory lecture there in 1922. a "History of Ministerial Responsibility in Baden." On March 1, 1924, he assumed directorship of the General State Archives of Baden.

Schnabel was an untypical representative of his profession in several ways: First he taught at a technical institute, not a university, and he followed a very different research path than his colleagues in the study of history. His students were also unusual; young engineers and technicians, interested members of the Karlsruhe public, but hardly the classic history student circle.

His methodology was also extraordinary, whereby history was studied as it applied to the general culture of the time instead of the political culture, thus reducing the focus on the history of states and their interrelationships. His principal work was the four volume German History in the 19th Century (Deutsche Geschichte im 19. Jahrhundert) which he began in 1922.

Although Franz Schnabel was close to the Catholic Central Party, he was not a party member, so could not be dismissed from his post in 1933 based on the newly enacted "Berufsbeamtengesetzes" which affected professionals in state employ who had party affiliations. Instead he was pensioned off on Oct. 1, 1936 when the Baden Cultural Ministry transferred his chair in history to the chemistry department and declared it superfluous.

He was thus unable to return to his profession (Fridericiana, or the unimpeded teaching of history reminiscent of the former times of Frederick II (of Prussia) until 1945. Until his departure for the University of Munich in 1947, he conducted guest lectures but was unable to undertake any formal instruction because on September 5, 1945, the American military government named him State Director of Culture and Instruction in order to reorganize public school and university education in North Baden.

He took his Munich post with the stipulation that he could make his own decision on retirement. He did so in 1962. He died Feb. 25, 1966

Died Feb. 25, 1966   **Universität Karlsruhe, Fakultäet fuer Geistes**
                            u. Sozialwissenschaften

DR. FRANZ SCHNABEL

It was nearly impossible to get into one of Dr. Schnabel's seminars.

The next best thing was not to miss one of his weekly lectures in an auditorium of the Maximilian Universität (University of Munich).

It was standing room only, and there were more than 800 seats.

The topic was the 20th Century.

He had been born in the 19th, in Mannheim, Germany, but was only 13 at the new millennium.

After completing his secondary education in Mannheim, he studied history at the universities of Berlin and Heidelberg.

He passed the state examination to qualify to teach at the gymnasium (secondary school) level in 1910, and also completed his thesis on "The Alliance of Political Catholicism in Germany in 1848."

Except for three years served in the German military during World War I, he served as a teacher at the gymnasium level from 1910 to 1922.

After further academic study in history, he was named as a professor at the Karlsruhe Technical Institute. (Technische Hochschule Karlsruhe).

The work resulting from his study and research in those years was

"Deutsche Geschichte im neunzehnten Jahrhundert" (German History in the 19th Century), which appeared in 1929.

He was dismissed from his post in 1936 because of his opposition to the Nazi regime, and wrote magazine and newspaper articles for such publications as the Frankfurter Zeitung' and Hochland until they also were forced to cease publication.

From then until the end of the war, he lived in virtual house arrest in Heidelberg as part of what the Hitler opposition called the internal emigration.

In 1945 he was named director of instruction and culture for North Baden, a section of southwestern Germany which was incorporated into the state of Baden-Wuertemberg in 1951.

In 1947, he accepted a call to the University of Munich., and remained at that post until he reached the age of 75 in 1962.

Author Konrad Fuchs, in his biographical synopsis published in the "Biographisch-Bibliographisches KIRCHENLEXIKON, Volume IX" in 1995, wrote that Dr. Schnabel had a major and lasting influence on the student generations immediately after World War II.

This, Fuchs wrote, was based not only on his academic qualifications, but his Catholic faith and steadfastness of character.

This effect was particularly evident at one lecture during which he addressed the implications of the attempt to kill Adolf Hitler on July 20, 1944.

Without addressing the moral questions of assassination, he recounted a stunning fact of life and death.

More German citizens died, he told the silent lecture hall, between July 20, 1944, and May 8, the end of the war, than had died from the first attack on Poland in September of 1939 to July 20, 1944.

The memory of that lecture, 60 years later, led me to read through the servicemen's album of my small hometown in the Blackstone Valley of Massachusetts.

The album compiled by Augusta H. Lorenz and Lawrence M. Keeler in Whitinsville, Mass. for the town of Northbridge, listed 17 residents of that milltown of 10,000 souls who had died, in Europe alone, between July 20, 1944 and the end of the war.

Compound that by thousands of cities and towns around the country and the globe.

Rudolf Goldschmit paid final tribute to Dr. Schnabel in the Munich daily Süddeutsche Zeitung three days after his death on Feb. 25, 1966.

He expressed regret for the loss of his teaching and guidance during the 11-year period of the Nazi regime.

He cited the fact that his great history of the 19th century had been banned during that period.

The writer blamed politics that this professor gained academic distinction so late in his career.

It was a late, but a rich harvest, Goldschmit wrote.

"There is hardly an institution of higher education in Bavaria," he wrote, "that does not have faculty members who were not Schnabel's students, and countless others audited and eavesdropped on his lectures, and thereby learned a little history and how to think historically as well. They all understand what we have lost with the death of this historian."

IN REMEMBRANCE OF GEORG STADTMÜLLER

By Helmut W. Schaller

Dr. Georg Stadtmueller, former professor of East and Southeast European history at the University of Munich and seminar chairman, died on Nov. 1 in Passau. He was 76.

He was born on March 10, 1909 in Bürstadt/Hesse and after completion of his studies in the Humanities Gymnasium there, enrolled at the Universities of Freiburg and Munich to study history, law and Slavic and Semitic philology.

He majored in Byzantine studies under Franz Dölger in Munich.

He passed his state examination in 1931 and attained his doctorate two years later under Dr. Dölger with the publication of his dissertation entitled "Michael Choniates, Metropolit von Athen" (ca.1138-1222).

While including work on his doctorate, he took on the question of early Albanian history. He was at the same time associated professionally in a library post.

The results of this research led to his early appointment to the faculty of the University of Breslau as a lecturer in 1936.

His work there, entitled "Research into Early Albanian History", was published in Budapest in 1942.

It appeared in two volumes in 1966 in Wiesbaden as part of the Albanian Series founded by Dr. Stadtmüller.

This work and his dissertation clearly signaled the future direction of his academic interest in Southeast Europe; but despite this, there was also interest in the questions of the history of Eastern Europe.

After a short period as docent at the University of Breslau, Stadtmüller was named as lecturer at the University of Leipzig. He began his academic career at Leipzig on June 14, 1939 with a lecture series entitled "Ottoman Empire Law and the History of the Balkan Peoples." In this he sought to achieve a synthesis of understanding of the two spheres.

He was called to military service in 1943, and served as a translator on the Southeast General Staff in Greece.

After resuming his academic pursuits at the end of the war, he was named a professor of comparative history at the University of Munich in 1950. In 1959, he was named full professor of history for East and Southeast Europe and chairman of that seminar.

He later served as director of the East European Institute (Osteuropa Institut) in Munich from 1960-63 and also directed the Hungarian Institute (Ungarische Institute) when it was founded in 1968 and the Albanian Research Institute (Albanische Forschungs-Institut).

He led both latter institutes until his retirement in 1975, and both are now led by his students Horst Glassl and Peter Bartl.

Only a few works in his many-faceted academic career can be mentioned here, but the first among them must be his "History of Southeast Europe" (Geschichte Südosteuropas), which was published in 1950, and remains to this day the single work with a comprehensive grasp of this theme.

This is not surprising considering the knowledge of languages that is required to do the research in this varied ethnic sphere.

This entailed study of Roman rule and its effects, the migrations of the German peoples and the influx of Slavic peoples around 600 (A.D.) and the subsequent colonization of the region by the German peoples in the Middle Ages.

Several of the themes represented in this work include Hussitism and the national Bohemian religious revolution of the Czechs, the reformation and the counter-reformation, the Habsburg state and the national movements under the Habsburg Empire

Stadtmüller concluded from his studies that the history of East and Southeast Europe could not be split up into special regions for research, study and teaching, but had to be regarded as a special sphere of world history.

He spent 10 years researching this subject from his first lecture in 1937 under the title "A View of the History of Southeast Europe." (Geschichte Südosteuropas im Überblick)

Another work, which embraced both central and Eastern Europe, was titled "The History of Habsburg Power" (Geschichte der habsburgischen Macht), which was based on a series of lectures which he delivered at the University of Leipzig from 1939 to 1942 and the University of Munich from 1964 to 1968.

This latter work, which was published as an "Urban-Buch" in 1966, seeks, based on Stadtmüller's assertions, to provide the general reader of history a universal overview of the entire Germanic and entire European experience, in as much as this has been determined by the Habsburg Empire or is related to it.

Other works deserving of regard on east-central Europe are Stadtmüller's "The Historical East" (Geschichtliche Ostkunde), which appeared in Munich in 1959, and was published with an expanded second volume in 1963 and the subtitle "The 20th Century"; "The Principles of European History as Problem," (Grundfragen der europäischen Geschichte als Problem) published in 1965, as was "Poland in European History" (Polen in der europäischen Geschichte).

Several other Stadtmüller works published in Leipzig and Munich should not remain unremarked.

He was editor of the "Leipzig Quarterly for Southeast Europe" as early as 1939. From that period on, he was associated with Franz Dölger, Carl Patsch, Paul Kretschmer and Gerhard Gesemann in association with the Deutsche Akademie and its Southeast Institute, as well as with the Balkan Commission of the Wiener (Vienna) Akademie der Wissenschaften.

During his Munich period, Stadtmüller founded several periodicals and series, such as the "Hungary Yearbooks" (Ungarn-Jahrbücher), the "Studia Hungarica",. and the "Albanian Studies" (Albanischen Forschungen).

He founded the general history quarterly "Saeculum" in 1950, and published the "Jahrbücher für Geschichte Osteuropas" (The Yearbooks for East European History) from 1960 to 1965.

In 1962, he became a co-founder of the "Arbeits- and Förderungsge-meinschaft der ukrainischen Wissenschaften" (The Association for the Advancement of Ukrainian Science). The Law and Economics Faculties of the Free Ukrainian University awarded Stadtmüller an honorary doctor's degree on June 8, 1979.

Whoever participated in Dr. Stadtmüller's seminars on East and

Southeast European history swiftly learned that German and English language source materials would not be the only ones utilized in their research. On the contrary, research would have to be undertaken in a number of varied languages. Latin and Greek were taken for granted by him as foundation stones. For historians, the knowledge of English, French and Italian were essential. It was his view that the knowledge of Slavic languages was an obligatory tool of the historian of East- and Southeast Europe. The student who has followed in his path is grateful today to have had a relationship with this exceptionally multi-dimensional and stimulating teacher. Many of his writings will be irreplaceable for many years to come and the memory of this great historian will remain alive.

Died Nov. 1, 1985   **Zeitschrift für Ostforschung** (ZfO) **35,** *1986, Pages 403-405*

DR. GEORGE STADTMÜLLER

Georg Stadtmüller was a member of the faculty in the history department at the University of Munich, formally known as the Maximilian Universitaet.

His was the fourth seminar I had managed to squeeze into during six semesters at the university, which I considered quite an achievement.

The first three had to do with Pan-Slavism, the Bolshevik revolution with specific emphasis on the links between the Russian Bolsheviks and their allies in other European countries and Sören Kierkegaard's "Furcht und Zittern," a dabbling in Christian existentialism.

The fourth was Georg Stadtmüller's.

The professor was focusing on the potential clash of Russian and Spanish imperialism on the West Coast of North America at the time of the discovery of gold in California.

He assigned me the task of distilling the American historian George Bancroft's analyses of that confrontation, and then double-distill it into German.

I had already written a monograph in German on the Polish revolutionary Julian Machlevski and knew enough Spanish and Russian to do some rudimentary research into the subject.

But my infant son's serious illness interrupted these studies, and medical costs forced me back to the United States, and gainful employment.

But the seminar piqued my curiosity on the subject and I returned to it in my later professional life.

One other incident during Professor Stadtmüller's classes remains a constant in historical memory.

The groves of academe in the Federal Republic of Germany in the late 1950s had much tinder.

It consisted of the biographies of the faculty members.

Many of them had embarrassingly long blanks regarding their careers before and during World War II.

The bigger the blanks, the greater the suspicion that the professors had been deeply involved in the German military, or worse, Nazi Party activities.

Young German student activists were engaged in outing such faculty members.

Many members of the faculties were revered for having been persecuted before and during the war, forbidden to teach or worse. Many others were non-Germans who had remained in Germany after the war, fearing the results of returning to the Sovietized east.

There were many who had prominent roles in the German military whose expertise was highly valued in the new battle against the Soviets, such as German rocket scientist Wernher von Braun and his colleagues.

Gen. George Patton was much maligned for his utilization of Nazis or ex-Nazis during the early months of the occupation of Germany, but his rationalization was that to keep the trains running, you had to employ those who already knew how to do it.

In retrospect, that policy might have been more advisable for the American and British occupiers of Iraq a half century later.

Dr. Stadtmüller, during the outing process that was unfolding at the university, gave his closest students an intimate account of his own activities during the war.

Stadtmüller, an officer in the German Wehrmacht, had been assigned to a Greek island as part of a detachment of civil military administrators.

This detachment had a specific mission.

It was to establish ties with Arab and other dissidents in Mesopotamia to prepare for the overthrow of the Iraqi regime put in power by the British after World War I. The result would be a new independent regime in Baghdad allied with Germany, Italy and Turkey which would open the fuel lines of Kurdish and Arab oil to central Europe.

Unfortunately, the Baghdad putsch never came, and the detachment remained quite inactive on the island until near the end of the war.

Eventually, many of the German soldiers had to fight for their lives through the Balkans to get back home.

That is one of the battles recounted by Yugoslav Partisan leader Milovan Djilas in his memoir "Wartime."

He acknowledged to me personally in Belgrade in 1989 that some of the most bloody battles he experienced was near the end of World War II between the Yugoslav Partisans and retreating German units.

It would have been interesting to learn how Dr. Stadtmüller had survived his own repatriation.

SADIK T. DUDA

1925-2007

DURHAM, N.C. – Sadik T. Duda passed away May 30, 2007, in his home at 3115 Kenan Road, Durham. He was 81.

As an educator, friend and family man, he enriched the lives of many people

Dr. Duda led a full and eventful life that ended peacefully.

He is survived by his wife, Sophia; a son and daughter, Turan and Tulin; his daughter-in–law, Linda; and his beloved grandchildren, Aisander and Sophia Ellen.

He was laid to rest in a private family ceremony at Wake Memorial Park in Cary.

Arrangements are by Walker's Funeral Home

Died May 30, 2007　　　　　*The* (Durham, N.C.) ***Herald-Sun,*** *June 7, 2007*

≈

SADIK DUDA

Sadik Duda was a Karachai.

I met him in Munich in 1958 when I was trying to pick up a few bucks during the months when the University of Munich was not in session, and GI Bill checks were not forthcoming from the U.S. government for my studies there.

I started out translating radio broadcasts from Radio Liberty, an organization broadcasting news to the peoples of the Soviet Union in Russian and a number of the other languages in that huge and multifaceted country.

Both Radio Free Europe and Radio Liberty, funded by the U.S. government under the aegis of the Central Intelligence Agency, had begun to monitor the broadcasts more closely after the Hungarian uprising of the autumn of 1956.

There had been accusations that some of the broadcasts had fomented and encouraged the uprising, and the monitoring was meant to curb or respond to that criticism.

My translation efforts led to another adjunct of Radio Liberty, an office that coordinated the efforts of émigrés from other non-Russian nationalities in the Soviet Union to publish news and information for their peoples behind the Iron Curtain.

I was introduced to Sadik Duda, an émigré from the north Caucasus who had landed in central Europe after World War II with hundreds of thousands of other DPs, the acronym for displaced persons.

I worked with the group for only a brief time, learning how to type on a Cyrillic alphabet typewriter, polishing my Russian and communicating primarily in German.

Another commission was to compile and edit the reports of a group of Soviet exiles who were dispatched to Vienna to attend sessions of the Communist Youth Festival in 1959 and contact young Soviet citizens who were delegates to the festivities.

Eventually, I decided to curtail my studies at the university when my family situation dictated that I return to the United States after four years in Germany and obtain gainful employment at the age of 28.

But Sadik Duda and his colleagues had opened my eyes to the impossible task the Russians had set for themselves of Russifying and Sovietizing a mammoth swath of the globe peopled by hundreds of varied ethnic groups speaking that many languages and dialects.

Sadik never provided me with the details of his fate during World War II, and the circumstances leading to his landing in Germany. But there were two principal options for the Karachais during that period, either fight with the Russians against the invading Germans or join what were regarded as the liberating Germans and fight the oppressive Soviet Russian regime.

Most chose the latter, leading the Soviet Union to expel the remaining Karachais to Kazakhstan and Uzbekistan in 1943.

One census listed the number of Karachais who lived in the district in the north Caucasus now known as the Autonomous Soviet Socialist

Republic of Karachay-Cherkessia as 70,932 in 1939, 29.2 % of the republic's population..

As the result of war and expulsion, it had shrunk more than 3000 to 67,830 by 1959, two years after the Karachais had been rehabilitated by the Soviet government. The percentage of Karachais had dropped to 24.4 %.

Today, the Karachais have recovered to form 38.5 % of the population of the republic, a much smaller ratio than in 1926, before Soviet national gerrymandering began.

In the volatile mix of this one small region in the Caucasus are Abazins, Russians, Nogais, Ossetians, Ukrainians, Armenians and Tatars. It is bordered by the Abkhazians to the south, constantly seeking independence from the Georgians, and Kabardino-Balkaria, North Ossetia, Ingushetiya and Chechnya to the east, all incendiary centers of national and tribal dispute.

Forty-five years after my association with Sadik Duda, a piece by Ian Johnson, then of The Wall Street Journal, on the Islamic Center of Munich brought it all back to mind. I realized that several sources cited by Johnson in his excellent historical analysis might enable me to reestablish contact with one of the men who had contributed to my understanding of that obscure part of the world.

Ian Johnson responded immediately to my letter commending him for his piece, provided several contacts and questioned me further about that period in postwar history.

One of the contacts advised me that Sadik had emigrated to the United States, and further queries established that he was a resident of Durham, N.C., and had written a doctoral dissertation on "The Theme of Caucasus in Russian Literature of the XVII-XIX Centuries."

Chapter 19

Unfortunately, Sadik was terminally ill by the time I contacted his wife Sophia, and I was unable to see him again. But I will get to know him still better as I read the result of his labors.

He opened the door on a once obscure part of the world where people had lived, suffered and died for centuries without much being known about them.

Now these people and their agonies, the Karachais, Chechens, Ingush, Daghestanis, Cherkassians, Georgians, Azeris, Armenians , Abkhazians and Ossetians are on the front pages.

CHAPTER 20

MISBAK MIFTAFOGLU

One of Misbak Miftafoglu's superiors advised me years after the fact that Misbak, a displaced person due to World War II, had defected and returned to the Soviet Union. This author made no effort to trace him.

.

MISBAK MIFTAFOGLU THE TARTAR

Misbak was in a sanatorium when I last saw him.

At this writing, I don't know his fate.

Misbak (and it was pronounced softer than so could also be spelled Mizbach) was a Tatar.

And looked the stereotypical part.

He had the wide moustache.

And the black hair.

And the slanted eyes.

But after that, he defied the stereotype,

He was a smiling, jovial man, and devoted to helping achieve a greater measure of freedom and autonomy for his fellow Tatars, deep inside the Soviet Union.

World War II had deposited him and hundreds of thousands of other displaced persons into the bowels of Central Europe, and by the middle of the 1950s, many had already found new lives through emigration.

And others had opted to join organizations seeking to inform the world of the plight of non-Russian peoples behind the Iron Curtain or to broadcast news to them of what was happening in the Free World.

Misbak was engaged in that work under American auspices when I met him.

Until he was diagnosed with tuberculosis. I felt uneasy visiting him in the sanatarium, myself having two young children, one of whom had been hospitalized in infancy for respiratory disease. But I did so, with staff counseling, and never had to regret it.

I shortly thereafter left Europe, and thought about Misbak frequently, primarily when I read about the Tatars. Miftafoglu was a hard name to forget once one had memorized it.

Years later, Ian Johnson, then with The Wall Street Journal in Berlin, provided me a possible contact with Misbak, a countryman and former colleague. The former colleague advised me that Misbak had chosen to return to the Soviet Union. It left unanswered the question whether he had been a double agent.

CHAPTER 21

HENRY MINOTT, 71
WAS TOP UPI NEWSMAN

WOBURN — Henry (Hank) Minott of 137 Winn Street in
Woburn, died suddenly yesterday at his Winn Street home of a heart
seizure. Minott had been a well-known and well-respected newsman
for a quarter of a century. He was the New England news manager of
the United Press International for twenty-four years at Boston. He held
this position from 1941 until he retired in 1965. Since 1965, he had
been a familiar figure in Woburn, around his Winn Street home, and in
the affairs of his church. And he was an often-times visitor to The Daily
Times, where many of the staffers talked frequently with him.

Minott, who had a penchant for detail, wrote his own obituary on
October 24th, 1963, and simply noted: "If you ever need it, it's filed."

The obituary follows:

"Henry Minott was born in Gardner, Mass., on Sept. 26, 1900, son
of Postmaster George L. and Jessie Gourley Minott. After attending
Clark College and Boston University, he began his newspaper career as
a reporter for The Gardner Daily News in his native city.

Subsequently, he was a member of the staff of the Boston Bureau of
The Associated Press, a reporter for the Greenfield, (Mass.), Recorder,
a deskman for The Springfield Republican, a reporter and deskman for
The Worcester Telegram, a reporter for The Boston Post, and a member
of the New York staff of United Press.

In 1925, Minott became manager of the Boston bureau of United Press, and in 1941 was named New England news manager of that organization.

One of Minott's first acts after becoming Boston manager of UP was to add to his staff a young man freshly graduated from Boston University. This was Boyd Lewis, now president of the Newspaper Enterprise Association (NEA), who became the first of scores of trainees that have gone from Minott's "school of journalism" to jobs in the newspaper and kindred fields in various parts of the world.

In developing talent among young college graduates, Minott always placed great stress on spelling. A year ago, he compiled a list of "One Hundred Commonly Misspelled Words." This list (appeared) in whole or in part in Time, Newsweek, The New Yorker, Editor & Publisher, The New York Herald Tribune and a paperback book on how to learn to spell.

In 1963, Minott was elected to the Academy of New England Journalists, sponsored by the New England Professional chapter of Sigma Delta Chi.

During his years with United Press and since the 1957 merger when it became United Press International, Minott worked on a host of major news stories. Among these were:

The Sacco-Vanzetti case, a cause celebre that still makes news. A letter written by Vanzetti in his death cell, which was obtained by Minott, is now in the Boston Athenaeum.

The Charles Ponzi "get-rich-quick" swindle, a multi-million-dollar bubble that burst in the faces of gullible Boston investors soon after World War I.

New York's Daddy Browning case.

The surprise hurricane that devastated New England in 1938.

COMMENT

While Minott considered his obituary sufficient, those who worked with him over the years felt that he left out too much that made him such a colorful and dominant figure in the business.

His successor, Stanton Berens, recalled the short, slim newsman as a contradictory figure.

"Mild-mannered, of Yankee restraint and shrewdness," Berens wrote on Minott's retirement, "he was a tyrannical giant on the news desk. His nasal twang could erupt in high-pitched rage or joy at the foibles and feats of newspapering."

One of Minott's many protégés, Berens wrote in awe of the man's "explosive enthusiasm, his fierce competitiveness and an inbred talent to write with accuracy, crispness and speed." And it was noted that Minott "hammered and hounded and injected and inspired generations of newsmen" to emulate him.

Minott mentioned his pre-occupation with correct spelling but Berens added to that picture by recalling that when the demanding editor spotted a misspelled word in a news story, "he would jump from his chair and verbally devastate the offending newsman."

It was recalled also that the colorful editor seemed to be a magnet for "characters." Perhaps best remembered in the UPI's office was the office boy who trapped pigeons for food on the 10th floor ledge overlooking downtown Washington Street. Minott, those who knew him then relate, protested only when the boy would curl up on the ledge for an unauthorized nap.

When not striving for excellence in the news field, Minott relaxed by touring and studying the historic and ancient sites of Boston. On his retirement, he announced his plans were "to go boating on the Concord River with my copy of Thoreau and tend to my 100-year-old house in Woburn."

He leaves his wife, Mrs. Wilma (Horwood) Minott; a son, Edward; and two daughters, Susan Minott and Mrs. John Zink.

Died June 6, 1972   **Daily Times,** Woburn, Mass. *June 7, 1972*

HENRY (HANK) MINOTT
1900 – 1972

I only got to work closely with Hank Minott for six weeks.

Then he farmed me out for seasoning.

But it was the way he did it.

The Boston bureau of United Press International was an exhilarating place to work in the early 1960s.

I had returned to New England from four years in Europe on the first of August, 1960, and was full of myself regarding my experience and worldly knowledge.

Unfortunately, none of that was of much use during a recession.

So after trips to Boston and New York during which I had failed to impress United Press International, The Associated Press, The New York Times, Time and Newsweek magazines and even the Central Intelligence Agency, I took a job as a substitute teacher of English at Shrewsbury Junior High School, a short jaunt now that my Volkswagen Standard had arrived at Boston from Amsterdam.

I had resigned myself to become as good a teacher as I could be when the call came from UPI in Boston that a slot would be open in the Boston bureau the last week of December, 1960.

John F. Kennedy had just been elected to the presidency, and I had watched the election excitedly from the Hotel Taft in New Haven, where I was being interviewed for a p.r. (public relations) job with United Illuminating Co.

One of the first assignments I was given in Boston was to take dictation from Merriman Smith, the UPI's White House correspondent, who was covering Kennedy's visit to Harvard Yard in Cambridge shortly before his inauguration.

Smith and Minott were both institutions, and there was I in the middle.

Hank was handling the editing of the copy directly on the A wire, the principal quality and speed wire that carried news instantly to New York and from there all over the world via wire and radio in seconds.

Smith kept me busy and I kept Hank busy.

First Lead Kennedy

Rapid fire dictation.

First Add, first lead Kennedy

Rapid fire dictation.

Second add, first lead Kennedy.

Rapid fire dictation.

Third add, first lead Kennedy.

Rapid fire dictation.

Sidebar Appointment, Kennedy.

Rapid fire dictation.

Sidebar, first add appointment, Kennedy.

Rapid fire dictation.

Fourth add, first lead Kennedy.

Rapid fire dictation.

Fifth add, first lead Kennedy

Rapid fire dictation.

Sidebar, Harvard yard, Kennedy.

Rapid fire dictation.

Sidebar, first add, Harvard Yard, Kennedy

Rapid fire dictation.

Sixth add, first lead, Kennedy.

Sidebar, second add, Harvard Yard, Kennedy.

Rapid fire dictation.

Seventh add, first lead, Kennedy.

Rapid fire dictation.

Sidebar, third add, Harvard Yard, Kennedy.

Rapid fire dictation.

Eighth add, first lead, Kennedy

Rapid fire dictation.

Second lead, Kennedy

Rapid fire dictation.

1st add, Second lead, Kennedy

Rapid fire dictation

2nd add, Second lead, Kennedy

Rapid fire dictation

Pickup 3rd add, first lead, Kennedy xxxx at

You get the idea.

This was in the era of copy paper and carbon paper.

And even though the books were devised for swift and easy handling, dictation and composition, one could stumble, especially when finishing a take and reinserting another book into the typewriter.

Once or twice, Merriman Smith grumbled at the slow pace of the dictation or the request for a repeated word or phrase.

And I regarded myself as a speed typist.

At the end of the dictation of the stories from Harvard Yard, Hank looked across the desk and nodded, what I took as approval.

During those six weeks, I got several baptisms of wire service fire.

Eliot Richardson, the then U.S. Attorney in Boston and future secretary in four cabinet posts in Washington, was chasing down Bernard Goldfine with a subpoena in the Sherman Adams vicuña coat caper.

The Federal Aeronautics Administration was conducting an inquest into the cause of the fatal crash at Logan International Airport of a Lockheed Electra airliner that killed 62 persons, including Evan Bedigian, a Whitin Machine Works salesman from my hometown (It eventually was determined that the plane struck a flock of birds, the parts of which were found in the plane's engines.).

Kennedy had appointed McGeorge Bundy to his White House staff, and I was sent over to Harvard to interview staff and faculty members for a profile of the appointee. The hardest nut to crack proved to be John Munro, the university provost who subsequently abandoned his Ivy League career to take over the administration of a southern Black college to improve its academic standing. Munro argued that Bundy was a friend of his and that he was disinclined to provide any information to a rookie wire service reporter who might embarrass him and his friend in the report. He relented during a second interview in which I advised him that Bundy had enemies as well as friends at Harvard and that it was my goal to get as balanced a view as possible.

Dick Dew, a veteran wire service staffer who later covered sports at UPI and elsewhere, was running the desk on a quiet Sunday morning when there was a fatal crash in Maine and we were able to make telephonic contact with a surviving victim of the crash. He was more unimpressed by the questions I had failed to ask than the information I did come up with. He and his colleague Al Wade, who ran the radio wire at UPI in Boston at the time, taught me how to work the phones.

After five weeks of this hectic activity, Hank called me over.

"How much are you making?" he asked.

"$85 a week," I responded, although I thought he already knew.

"Where are you going to live?" he continued.

I, my wife, and two children (the youngest born four months before, in September) had been living with my parents 37 miles away in Whitinsville, but I had been looking for a place closer to Boston.

"We've found an apartment in Ashland," I replied.

"How much will your rent be?" Hank asked.

"$135 a month," I answered.

"That's going to be rough, with two kids," Hank reflected. He then floated an alternative. "How about this?" he proposed. "Phil Keohane is the bureau manager in Springfield," he said . "We are promoting him to take over the Albany bureau. How would you like to go to Springfield?"

He added that living in Springfield would be a lot less expensive than Greater Boston. I accepted the job and he turned out to be right. The four years in Springfield were just what was needed to allow members of a young family to get their feet, some of which were not even walking, on the ground, establish a home and a career.

Hank Minott was in addition to being a topnotch newsman, something both German and Yiddish speakers can agree on, a "Mensch."

ALAN WADE

1921 – 1995

(The following obituary is compiled from accounts in the Washington Post, the Boston Globe and a publication of Worcester (Mass.) *Academy.)*

Alan B. Wade of Lexington, 74, a former editor at United Press International in Boston and public affairs officer for the U.S. Treasury Department in Washington, died Saturday of prostate cancer at Massachusetts General Hospital in Boston.

He was born in Boston and was a graduate of Worcester Academy and Clark University in Worcester.

During World War II, he served in the U.S. Army with the 65th Infantry Division that fought in France and Germany.

After the war he worked as a reporter for The (Worcester) Evening Gazette and in public relations for the former Northeast Airlines in Boston before joining the United Press in Boston in the 1950s.

He served with that news agency, which became United Press International after the merger with International News Service, for 20 years, as reporter, New England radio news editor and as an executive sales representative.

He joined the U.S. Department of the Treasury in the 1970s, and served as a public affairs officer under secretaries David Kennedy, John B. Connally, George P. Shultz and William P. Simon..

He also served as a special assistant for public affairs in the White House Office of Management and Budget.

He retired in 1983, after five years as a public affairs officer for the U.S. League of Savings Institutions.

He leaves his wife, Helen (Weymouth); two sons, Stephen of Lexington and Eric of Halfmoon, N.Y.; a daughter, Alison of Raynham; three sisters, Virginia Sampson and Miriam Butts, both of Lexington, and Anne Wade of Boston; two brothers, Harold of Salisbury, N.H., and Paul of Brunswick, Me; and three grandchildren.

A memorial service will be held at 2 p.m. Sept. 16 in First Parish Unitarian Church in Lexington.

Died Sept. 2, 1995

LITTLE AL

Al Wade was a small man with great energy.

The last time I saw him was in Washington, D.C. in 1979, where he was winding down his career as a public affairs officer with the U.S. League of Savings Institutions.

We reminisced about the Boston office of UPI in the early 1960s.

I was considering a career change, going into the 1980s, and was visiting Washington and Baltimore, among other cities, to gauge the prospects.

"Anybody who worked in Boston for UPI in the early 1960s can make it in Washington," he said.

Could make it anywhere, when one reflected on it.

Frank Jackman, who went on to the N.Y. Daily News, China Altman and Dick Growald, who went to Europe, Bill Ketter, Bernie Caughey and Dick Dew, who went on to newspaper editorships. And the war horses who remained in Boston, Hank Minott and Stan Berens.

Al had become my immediate superior after I accepted Hank Minott's offer to go to Springfield and take over that bureau.

As such, I wrote radio copy every morning for the New England radio wire that Al supervised out of Boston.

Al was not only the fastest and best radio news writer I ever met. He was also easy to get along with. Which didn't mean he wasn't competitive.

One of his favorite tricks, as if he didn't have enough to do, was to get wind of a story in each or any of his precincts, Maine, New Hampshire, Vermont, Rhode Island and Connecticut as well as Massachusetts, and beat you to the story.

He was one of the best newsmen with a phone as well.

Al invited us out to his house in Lexington before we left for Springfield.

It was a Walter Gropius house, and this was before I had learned much about architecture, never mind the Bauhaus culture.

But if I only got to appreciate his enthusiasm about his environs much later, I appreciated his enthusiasm about his work instantly.

And when we got an accelerated approval to obtain citizenship for my German-born wife by going to Boston, he agreed to be a witness.

That he was a great friend can be attested to also by the family and friends of Frederick C. Murphy, a Medal of Honor winner who was killed by land mines while trying to assist fellow soldiers wounded on the battlefield near Saarlautern (Saarlouis) in Germany during World War II.

After the war, a veterans hospital in Waltham, Mass. was named after the fallen hero.

But 30 years later, the hospital closed, and the name slipped toward obscurity with its closing.

Al, and a fellow veteran, former Waltham Fire Chief Edward A. Cloonan, conducted a drive to rename the recently opened Waltham Federal Center after Murphy.

Division veterans also arranged to fly his daughter out for their 50th reunion.

Frank Callahan, a Worcester Academy archivist and chronicler, also notes Al Wade's consideration of others.

Callahan, in one of the academy's publications, records that Al, a member of the prep school's Class of 1940, compiled with his brother and fellow alumnus Harold, a 236-page report on the accomplishments of the members of that class.

Each member of that class must read each account with pride – that they had a classmate like Al.

K. F. LEMERE
NEWSCASTER
DEAD AT 53

Kenneth F. LeMere, 53, of 160 Alden St., radio-television news commentator, died Sunday night in Springfield Hospital. Mr. LeMere had been employed by several radio and television stations in this city and had covered the Western Massachusetts area for a Boston newspaper.

Mr. LeMere underwent serious surgery last December, and had only briefly been able to resume his activities since that time.

The well-known local newsman began his career in 1957 when he joined the news force of WWLP-TV, Channel 22. In 1959 Mr. LeMere became news director at radio station WMAS. He joined the staff of WHYN Radio and Television in 1962. For WHYN Mr. LeMere had charge of the field work, writing and editing for the station's "News at 7".

In 1963 Mr. LeMere returned to WMAS as news director to supervise all news activities at WMAS and to resume his "Editor's Corner" feature at 7.40 a.m. and 6.15 p.m. His provocative, unorthodox approach to many local issues gave him wide popularity.

He was the winner of three Tom Phillips Awards by United Press International Broadcasters of Massachusetts, and had won the top award for a radio station editorial on WMAS in 1961 and for a TV documentary for WHYN-TV in 1962.

Globe Correspondent

Mr. LeMere had been news correspondent for the Boston Globe for more than six years, and had contributed articles and fiction to many industrial and commercial magazines.

Prior to entering the news field in 1957, Mr. LeMere was a letter carrier for the Springfield Post Office for 21 years. He served as president and vice-president of Branch 46, National Association of Letter Carriers.

For three years he was secretary of the Central Labor Union and had served on the board of trustees of Wesson Maternity Hospital, United Fund and the United Cerebral Palsy Associations. Mr. LeMere was chairman of the executive budget committee of the United Fund and was a member of the city Public Utilities and Human Relations Commissions.

He was born in Thompsonville, Conn., Sept. 30, 1911, son of Mrs. Ann (McCarthy) LeMere and the late Frederick LeMere, and lived in this city for the past 46 years. He graduated from Classical High School, attended Brown University, Springfield College and American International College where he majored in history and political science.

He was a member of Holy Family Church, the Holy Name Society of that church and was a director and former secretary of the Valley Press Club.

Besides his mother, he leaves his wife, Mrs. Eleanor M. (Paro) LeMere, a daughter, Ann Marie at home, and two brothers, Elmer J. of East Longmeadow and Armon L. of this city.

The funeral will be held Wednesday at 9 a.m. at Hafey's funeral home, with a requiem high mass in Holy Family Church at 10. Burial will be in St. Thomas Cemetery, West Springfield. Visiting hours are tonight, 7.30 to 9.30, and Tuesday, 2 to 4 and 7.30 to 9.30 p.m.

Died June 27, 1965   ***Springfield*** (Mass.) ***Daily News,*** *June 28, 1965*

⇀

KENNETH F. LEMERE
1911 – 1965

Ken LeMere was the first newsman I met on my arrival in Springfield, Mass. in February of 1961.

My two predecessors as bureau managers of United Press International there had groomed Ken as one of their principal stringers for what was primarily a radio wire in Western Massachusetts.

Although UPI, recently formed by the merger of Scripps-Howard's United Press and Hearst's International News Service, had contracts with The Springfield Newspapers, then consisting of The Morning Union, the evening Springfield Daily News and the combined Sunday Republican, and The Berkshire Eagle in Pittsfield, the bureau was established primarily to serve the numerous radio stations in the four-county region.

The cumulative revenues from contracts with stations in Springfield, Holyoke, Northampton, Westfield, Pittsfield, Great Barrington and North Adams possibly equaled or surpassed those received from the two newspaper companies, so they were a valuable asset to the wire service.

There was another consideration.

Springfield was next door to Chicopee Falls, home of Westover Air Force Base and the Eighth Air Force of the Strategic Air Command. The Eighth Air Force headquarters was at Westover, and thus was the source of any news about the base and its B-52 bombers and KC-135 tankers, which flew out of Westover and three other air force bases in Maine and New Hampshire. The SAC base had a range of responsibility from Puerto Rico to Thule in Greenland.

That was the biggest beat I ever had to cover as a newsman.

UPI was there in case the balloon went up with the Soviets, the balloon being a euphemism for the outbreak of World War III. My contemporaries and readers of history will recall that a year later, it almost did.

More about that later in another segment.

Ken became more than just a stringer that winter. He became a friend and a benefactor.

We came into Springfield with furniture cobbled together from several families.

But something was missing for a young family with two children three years old and under. There was no washing machine. And no money to buy one. And no credit to borrow any money. And a stubborn insistence not to impose on parents who had just suffered the inconvenience of having a family of three, soon to become four, descend suddenly on their domestic peace, and then linger for six months.

I broached the problem to Ken, and he immediately agreed to introduce me to his brother Armon, who was associated with Gray Supply, an appliance wholesaler and retailer in the North End. Ken, who was of modest means himself, agreed to countersign the loan, and the first significant problem of settled domestic life had been solved.

Ken handled the radio news for station WMAS in Springfield at the time. He was responsible for the noon and evening newscasts, the latter of which was the most important for the commuting public.

He would then also string during the evening for both the Boston Globe and United Press International, alerting the Boston bureau to anything that might be transpiring while I was off duty.

My shift began around 5 a.m., with significant news splits on the radio wire every hour on the 10s, similar to the on the eights segment instituted by television's Weather Channel a generation later.

The job consisted of combing several editions of all the newspapers published in Western Massachusetts and then following up on all the tips provided from the several stringers at radio stations and newspapers in the region.

Sam Kuczun and Phil Keohane had built up a reliable stable of stringers, and the news flowed in at a steady pace.

The UPI bureau had been located in a rear room of the Bowles Building on Main Street.

This office was close to the main office of The Springfield Newspapers, then on Cypress Street, and the rent was low, and payable to a principal customer, The Republican Co. But it was several blocks away from some of the biggest news sources in town, the Springfield City Hall and Symphony Hall, the Hampden County Superior Court, the Springfield District Court, and the police and fire stations, all bunched around Court Square.

The mayor at the time, Thomas (Tommy) O'Connor, was amenable to our idea to turn the underused Press Room at City Hall into an active news center by allowing UPI to use it as an office with a wire machine and constant flow of city reporters --newspaper, radio and television.

Not lost on those cognizant of UPI's propensity to downhold expenses was the fact that the office was rent-free. I offered a sop to passersby by posting the news of the day in compartmentalized form on a news bulletin board outside the office.

This largesse from the Springfield taxpayers continued into the next administration of Mayor Charles V. Ryan, Jr., who permitted it until shortly after my posting to London in 1964.

Transferring the office from the curious complex of Bowles buildings that dotted downtown Springfield over to City Hall greatly enhanced the news gathering effort.

Ken, and his colleagues and competitors in the busy Connecticut Valley news field, would meander in and through the offices every day, sharing tips and tidbits.

It was the quickest way to get to know Durham Caldwell and Keith Silver of WSPR, Ed Kennedy of WWLP-TV, Bob McClellan of the Daily News and a stream of other regular beat men on the papers.

And eventually, contacts were made with the editors and executives of both major newspaper organizations in Springfield and Pittsfield, Springfield newspapers publisher Sid Cook and ad exec John Mannix, Dick Garvey and Carroll Robbins of the Daily News, Paul Craig of The Union, and Rex Fall and Tom Morton of The Berkshire Eagle.

There was a lot to learn.

The immediate goal was to keep up with any breaking story to provide all the local radio stations with updates for their broadcasts.

Another goal was to jump on any story that had any implication outside Western Massachusetts. This was still the era of the afternoon newspaper (afternoon papers outnumbered morning papers in Massachusetts by a ratio of 20 to 1). That meant that radio stations gave a wire service the jump on any story that might be sent out of the area and still make the early deadlines of afternoon papers around the country.

There was another trove of information.

The Morning Union ran about nine separate editions to provide the many sections of Western Massachusetts with a local feel for the news. Often, there were nuggets of information in these local editions that either were not picked up for all edition use in the hectic pace of makeovers, or just had not been developed well by the reporters and editors.

It was a joy to turn one of these short items into a piece that got excellent play around the nation.

And it is a great pleasure to be one's own assignment editor, who can cover any story in an area with a population of half a million people.

There was a business beat, General Electric, Massachusetts Mutual, Monsanto, United Aircraft (across the state line in Connecticut), the American Bosch, the Springfield Arsenal, Smith & Wesson, Savage Arms, Fisk Tire (Uniroyal) in Chicopee Falls and dozens of smaller machine tool companies linked to the aircraft industry in Connecticut.

There were the college institutions, Springfield College and American International College in Springfield, Mount Holyoke in South Hadley, Smith at Northampton, Amherst and UMass in Amherst, Williams n Williamstown and a number of other smaller private, state and community colleges.

All this enticed a stream of celebrities beyond the political to the area: Jackie Robinson, Billy Graham, Wernher von Braun, Norman Rockwell (a fixture at Stockbridge), Joe Morello (Dave Brubeck's drummer, a

Springfield native), Charles Munch, Eugene Ormandy and all the visiting artists at Tanglewood in Lenox, which included comic Danny Kaye.

Only once in four years did any news source lay down a stumbling block to the coverage.

The name of the publicity staff member at Smith College escapes me, and it shall remain unpursued. But she insisted that it was not incumbent on the college to provide a ticket to a wire service reporter who desired to cover the first American tour of the Berlin Philharmonic since the end of World War II.

In fact, she did not wish the event to be covered and news reporters were not welcome.

What to do?

The best idea that occurred to me was to request the assistance of members of the orchestra themselves. As they were gathering their instruments to enter Greene Hall on the Smith campus in Northampton, I explained my predicament to a bass player and asked him if I might carry his instrument into the auditorium.

My German was fluent, his sense of humor was tickled and the concert was thoroughly enjoyed by all.

The four years spent in Germany at the end of the 1950s and into 1960 paid off one other time.

When Wernher von Braun arrived at Westover Air Force Base, he was pleased to be interviewed in his native tongue separate from the main news conference.

John Haigis, the owner of radio station WHAI in Greenfield, was so impressed that he allowed our sales representative in Boston, Bob Woodsum, to make a contract proposal to replace the Associated Press at the station. The day on which Mr. Haigis was to sign the contract, he asked Bob where I was. Bob told him that I was in Springfield. He said that he wouldn't sign the contract until I was invited up to Greenfield to join in the meal and the deal.

In fact, the entire news team, buttressed principally by a loyal and diligent group of stringers, was making so serious a run on the few remaining radio stations that were carrying the AP radio wire, that AP decided to send in reinforcements.

And it was significant competition.

George A. Higgins was assigned to set up an AP office in Springfield and did so, making a significant competitive splash before moving on to law studies, a stint in law enforcement and the creation of fiction works the likes of "The Friends of Eddie Coyle."

Ken LeMere was the rudder of the ship I steered through the journalistic waters of Western Massachusetts, and it was a joy to see him get the opportunity to broaden his appeal and his influence in television at WHYN.

It was a shock on being transferred to London to read of big news breaking in the Springfield area just after I had left it, the plane crash that injured the new Sen. Edward M.. (Ted) Kennedy in Westfield and the race riots in downtown Springfield.

But it was a worse shock to learn that Ken LeMere was suffering from a brain tumor. He was operated on in January, 1965, and died six months later.

JOSEPH COTTON

WILBRAHAM – Joseph S. Cotton, 71, of 136 Bartlett Ave., a retired night city editor for The Morning Union and The Sunday Republican, died yesterday in Baystate Medical Center, Springfield.

He retired in 1969.

Born in Montague, he lived in Wilbraham for 36 years. He graduated in 1936 from Harvard University, and had celebrated his 50th class reunion last week.

Before World War II, he was a reporter for the Greenfield Recorder and Gazette. He later ran a one-man newspaper, the Turners Falls Herald in Montague.

He served with the Army Air Force in Europe during World War II and was on the staff of Stars & Stripes.

He started as a reporter with The Springfield Union, as it was then known, and also worked for Time magazine and Life magazine as a local correspondent.

Jane Maroney, associate editor of The Morning Union, yesterday called Cotton "the quintessential reporter, editor and friend."

After his retirement from the newspaper, he became a teacher of English and journalism at Chicopee Comprehensive High School, retiring in 1977.

He was a member of the Valley Press Club, the American Red Cross, Friends of Origami of America, and the Newton Lodge of Masons, AF & AM.

He leaves his wife, the former Vivian Plouffe, two daughters, Jane C. Putnam of Manchester (Conn.) and Sarah Maciaszek of Easthampton; a brother, Bernard of Denver; two sisters, Yenta Kaufman of Salt Lake City, Utah, and Grace Wylie of Palm Bay, Fla., and a grandchild.

The funeral will be Monday morning at Byron's Funeral Home, State Street, with burial at the convenience of the family.

Memorial contributions may be made to the Pioneer Valley Chapter, American Red Cross.

Died June 12, 1986   **The** (Springfield, Mass.) **Morning Union**, *Friday, June 13, 1986*

JOSEPH S. COTTON
1915 – 1986

Joe Cotton was a night city editor, a colleague, a friend and finally a neighbor.

He was a member of the Valley Press Club, an organization of newspaper, television and radio news executives, editors and reporters of the Connecticut River Valley, from Springfield north to Greenfield, Mass.

That is where we met him and Vivian, his wife.

My wife and I had only recently arrived from Europe, so there was a quick affinity.

Joe had worked with Stars & Stripes in Europe, and was overflowing with anecdotes about Andy Rooney, Bud Hutton and Joe Fleming before many of us knew of their fame, and or notoriety.

It wasn't very long before we were invited to their cottage tucked in the woods in the bucolic village of North Wilbraham, a growing eastern suburb of Springfield.

The house was a magnet for all kinds of people, most of them interesting. And Joe made you feel as though you were too.

Soon, he was suggesting that we move from our apartment opposite the Springfield Armory (where at the time they were testing weapons for the helicopter gunships that would soon be flying over Vietnam) to a cottage down the road.

Warren Bennett, a character himself, was building a house up on Wilbraham mountain, and soon would be moving in.

His cottage, expanded from a former summer cottage, would be vacant, and Joe suggested we move in.

Warren, at $85 a month, was equally amenable to the arrangement, and we suburbanized ourselves.

In retrospect, those first four years in Greater Springfield flew by.

As manager of the Springfield, Mass. bureau of United Press International, most of my professional contacts were with the day people, the radio and television reporters preparing for the afternoon editions and the 6 o'clock broadcasts or telecasts.

But I did get to meet a number of the night people, the reporters and editors of the morning papers, first socially, and occasionally on the big stories.

One of the latter was the 1962 elections, the one at which Edward M. Kennedy was chosen as Democratic nominee and eventual senator from Massachusetts at the insistence of father Joseph P. and despite the reservations of brother John F.

I figured that one of the best ways to gain instant access to election results for relay to the Boston office would be to ask The (Springfield) Morning Union editor Paul Craig if I could work out of the Union newspaper office.

Craig gave me a quid pro quo.

Paul would be willing to give me space and instant access to whatever results or stories I wanted if I would take over one odious chore and relieve his staff of those obligations.

What was that, I inquired.

He asked me if I would be willing to provide The Associated Press, my competitor, with the election results that they wanted. I agreed, with one proviso. I asked if it would be all right if I waited a couple of hours after relaying my results to UPI before I did the same for the AP.

Craig, who apparently had had some flinty and perhaps uncooperative relations with the huge news cooperative AP, found the arrangement mutually satisfactory, if not slightly amusing.

Covering that election from The Union office gave me a chance to get much better acquainted with editors on that newspaper's staff, including Joe Cotton, Roger Sylvester and Larry DeBurro.

When the call came for my transfer from Springfield to London, it was Joe and Vivian who threw a going-away party at their house in Wilbraham, and took care of my wife and kids as they prepared for their ocean cruise across the Atlantic to join me.

Although we had purchased a house lot not far away just before leaving, we had no idea whether or when we would meet up with the Cottons again.

When the decision finally was made to return from Europe for the second time and finally settle down, I sent a telegram to Warren Bennett to find out if the old cottage was still available.

It had just been vacated, and by the spring of 1967, we were again neighbors to the Cottons.

And this time we were fellow Union staffers, because I had arranged to join the state copy desk of that morning paper.

Strangely enough, the change of ownership of which I had been briefed by UPI New England Business Manager Bob Woodsum seven years earlier had still not been consummated, if I may use that word in a proper context.

But the natives were restless, and many of the top news executives of The Springfield Newspapers who had fought the takeover of the papers by S. I. Newhouse, had bailed or were preparing to.

Paradoxically, these Saturday night massacres of the next few years, had a greater effect on The Union and the Sunday Republican staffs than that of The Springfield Daily News, although the latter served as the loudest and most strident trumpet of the dire effects the Newhouse takeover would have on the papers' employees.

This paradox is partially explained in the vignette on the late Springfield Daily News editor Richard Garvey.

Joe Cotton, as night city editor of The Union, was one of many editors uneasy over the future of the paper and their own.

Perhaps that was one of the reasons he obtained a rather ungenerous leave of absence from his superiors so he could re-matriculate at the university where the pressures of the depression had forced him to forgo obtaining his degree.

That institution was Harvard.

It had always nagged Joe that he had not finished his last year at Harvard.

He had studied there in 1932-33 and again in 1934-36, but things were tough during the depression and he could never manage, for economic, family and military reasons, to finish that final year.

It was not a matter of academics.

Harvard acknowledged that.

When Joe requested to finish his final year at Harvard three decades after his junior year, the administrative board agreed.

It was tough, Joe conceded later, but he persisted.

In June of 1966, Joe received his bachelor of arts degree in English with the Harvard Class of 1966 and simultaneously became a member of the alumni Class of 1936.

When Joe received his degree along with other residents of Dudley House, his classmates cheered when Master Thomas Crooks made an impromptu congratulatory speech.

There was a receptive audience too when Joe subsequently removed his gown and '66 cap and replaced the latter with a canvas one with "H '36" printed on it.

During festivities later, Joe referred to himself as a "Depression Dropout."

He also credited his wife with providing him with a Vivian Cotton Fellowship.

His wife had returned to fulltime teaching at Hampden Junior High School to provide the financial support needed for the final senior year.

But the best demonstration of Joe's creativity is contained in a bit of doggerel which the Harvard Class of 1936 saw fit to include in its Fiftieth Anniversary Report, a segment of which follows:

JOSEPH SIMON COTTON

Years in College: 1932-33, 1934-1936
Married: Vivian I. Plouffe (Westfield State Coll. '38)
Children: Jane Elizabeth, 1946 (Univ. of Massachusetts '67), m. Gary
     Putnam;Sarah Ann, 1951 (Univ. of Massachusetts '78), m.
     Stanley Maciaszek.
Grandchildren: One
Occupation: Retired Journalist, Teacher.
Home Address: 136 Bartlett Ave., Wilbraham, Mass. 01095
Principal Works: Making final revisions on satirical novel. TV director
     who read it says it has good potential for series.

(The Doggerel Follows)

It's pleasant nonsense to summarize the passing of fifty years;
The joy, the fears, the cheers, the jeers, the champagne and
     the beers.
Perhaps because of dead brain cells amassing in my attic
I tend to be, in these Golden Years, emphatically less dogmatic.

I smoke, I fuss, I drink, I cuss, unashamedly to excess,
And unrepentingly will do so 'til my last gasp, I guess.
I'm smugly pleased to boldly state I consider myself pragmatic,
Not morbid, contemplating Death and other things traumatic.

There isn't much to brag about under "Honors and Awards,"
But Vi and I take glowing pride in numbering friends by hordes.
Yes, when I think that I have filled my life's ambition greatly
My wife asks most disarmingly, "But what have you done
     lately?"

A porcine valve (aortic) for eight years has kept me supple,
Which, with my wife's hip-point implant makes us a bionic
     couple.
Of hobbies, I've a dozen, of interests, a score or more
I've written The Great Novel I now seek a publisher for.

As America's youngest editor, in '40 I got my kicks;
And as Harvard's oldest senior, I re-matriculated in '66.
For 40 years, I've filled the role of journalist and teacher.
(If the world's a stage and all men players, I played a double
     feature.

With hardened veins and softened brains, I review my days
     as predator
Exacerbating reporter cubs I brow-beat as a city editor.
Nostalgically I review those War II days in Paris
On Stars & Stripes with Jim Eathorne, Bud Hutton,
     Andy Rooney, Marty Harris.

I judge not man by face nor span. I count none enemy.
I still believe, though it seem naïve, that Truth will keep us free.
I owe no man, no bank, no clan, no finance company.
The ledger's balanced. The bill's marked "Paid" for my debt
     to society.

Joe Cotton was as an editor the kind of stickler that Lynne Truss, the 21st Century author of "Eats, Shoots and Leaves" would have been proud of.

It was so with the pig valve that doctors provided him in 1978, the one that gave him eight extra years.

I sat with him in his living room as he went over the hospital bills for which his generous medical benefits provided no responsibility.

He joshed about receiving a kosher pig valve, though not an observant Jew. He did not josh about the bills. He was upset.

As a student of the depression, he deplored waste and excess.

The doctors, when providing him with a pig valve, found an aneurism on the heart wall, and immediately repaired that defect as well.

Although appreciating the fact that the repair of the aneurism had saved his life, he nevertheless was upset by the billing.

The doctors had charged the insurance carrier and Medicare for two openings and two closings, one each for the pig valve and the aneurism. Joe insisted that they had only opened him once and closed him once, and shouldn't have charged double.

Joe had taught the last few years of his life because although not an observant Jew, he had a better understanding of the prophet Daniel than most observant Jews or Christians.
He had read the writing on the wall.

When Belshazzar had inquired of Daniel what MeNe, MeNe, Te Kel, u Phar Sin meant, Daniel had conveyed God's decision that the Babylonian kingdom's days had been numbered and its leadership found wanting (Daniel 5)

Many editors at the paper had got the same message. Many left before the takeover by the Newhouse regime and many more, among them Joe, did so shortly thereafter.

I'm not certain that Joe would have been among the casualties if he had not been the victim of an unfortunate incident near the end of his newspaper career.

Joe, a prankster and a wordsmith, frequently demonstrated one example of linguistic ribaldry which he held up as a warning to the unwary reporter and editor.

I quote the item in its entirety:

$58,000 Estate

"Stanley J. Pubick of 132 Winslow St. who died last December left an estate valued at $58,000, including real estate, personal property and livestock, according to an inventory filed in Probate Court Thursday.

Mr. Pubick left nearly $50,000 in bank accounts and in stocks, a house valued at $8,000, six prize Belgian hares and six recordings of songs he composed.

Mr. Pubick's will stipulated that the cash and house would be left to his wife, Stacia A. Pubick, while the Pubick hares would be left to be divided equally among other Pubick heirs. The Pubick airs were left to the City Library."

This piece of rough copy was left inadvertently on the city desk one evening while Joe Cotton was eating lunch.

It was swiftly and uncritically edited by an assistant untrained in probate matters and was sent up to the composing room to be set into type.

There, an observant proof reader spotted something amiss, and placed a red flag on the piece of copy. This flag was still waving up from the type after the story had been placed into the page for the stereotype machine.

I was unaware of any of this until I saw Joe vault out of his city editor's chair and gallop up the stairs to the composing room to get them to STOP THE PRESSES.

Before they could, 8,000 copies of The Morning Union with its report of the $58,000 estate of the fictitious Stanley J. Pubick had been printed.

Joe, not entirely guiltless, took the fall, and was suspended.

It took me years to learn who the guilty parties were.

The assistant who failed to edit the copy went unpunished.

And the superior who ended up suspending Joe for his misdeed, and possibly placing a blemish on his record that might preclude advancement under the new incoming regime, was the one who had removed the red flag from the page, and personally pushed it toward the stereotype machine, and the press, without correcting the error.

Joe soon left the paper.

Shortly thereafter, the guilty superior also retired, for other reasons.

Joe enjoyed the latter years of his life teaching at Chicopee Comprehensive High School. He was kind enough to invite me to address several of his classes, and eventually to read and critique his novel.

Although I did not share in some of his conclusions, I advised him to pursue a publisher.

He wasn't sure where to go.

I told him he had a shoo-in.

Who could that be?

Tom Wolfe, I said.

Long before the days of The Right Stuff, Bonfire of the Vanities, and I Am Charlotte Simmons, Tom Wolfe was writing news copy for The (Springfield, Mass) Morning Union.

The Union had been one of the few, if not the only newspaper to respond to the letter of application from the young Yale postgraduate from Richmond, Va.

He took the job and came to Springfield, working under the self-acknowledged browbeating city editor Joe Cotton.

Joe was one of the first to recognize the potential, and to seek to develop it.

The young reporter became a fixture at the Cotton house and even did his laundry there.

There had been a great rapport between them, and that was why I encouraged Joe to contact Tom about his novel.

Joe was reluctant to do so.

I asked for permission to do it for him.

He gave his OK.

Chapter 24

From Joe and Viv's kitchen, I called Tom Wolfe's publisher.

I left the message with a representative and she said she would get back to us.

Within 20 minutes, Tom Wolfe called himself.

He insisted that Joe send in his typescript.

As far as I know, he never did.

Perhaps he had the ultimate fear of every writer, not of rejection, but of rejection by someone who mattered.

But Tom Wolfe readily acknowledged his appreciation for the Springfield years a couple of decades later by accepting an invitation from Union managing editor Sax Fletcher to return and address the Valley Press Club at the Fort Restaurant's Heidelberg Room.

Joe was gone by this time, but the famous author was pleased that his widow Viv had been invited to the luncheon, and was placed beside him at the head table.

CHAPTER 25

WILBRAHAM MAN STRICKEN,
DIES WHILE DRIVING CAR

WILBRAHAM – An 82-year-old Wilbraham man died Monday while driving on Stony Hill Road when he suffered a heart attack and his car crashed into a tree.

Medical Examiner William Mosig ruled Monday that George Merwin of 93 Main St. died of a heart attack and that the injuries he received in the accident were not fatal.

Merwin, a semi-retired plumber, was driving south on Stony Hill Road at 8:42 a.m. when his car veered off the road near Blacksmith Drive, skidded about five feet and hit a tree, according to police.

His station wagon was extensively damaged in the accident.

Merwin was pronounced dead at the scene of the accident and transported to the Bay State Medical Center, Wesson Unit.

The (Springfield) ***Morning Union,*** *Sept. 15, 1981*

WILBRAHAM – The funeral of George P. Merwin, 82, of 93 Main St., who died Monday, will be Thursday morning at Beers & Story Funeral Home, Palmer, with burial in Hillcrest Park Cemetery, Springfield.

A native of Southport, Conn., he was an Army veteran of World War I, and lived here 35 years.

He leaves his wife, the former Susan E. Waugh; a daughter, Marilyn Hughes of Wilbraham, and a brother, Rodney, of Fairfield, Conn.

Donations may be made to the Heart Fund.

Died Sept. 14, 1981   *The* (Springfield) ***Morning Union***, *Sept. 16, 1981*

⌒

GEORGE P. MERWIN
1899 – 1981

"Did I wake you up, George?"

"No, Warren, I was just sitting here waiting for your call."

That was the response to the call from our landlord Warren Bennett at 3 in the morning one cold February morning in 1963.

There had been a sort of back blast of the furnace in the cottage on Bartlett Avenue in North Wilbraham, Mass., which left a good part of the cottage sooted and none of it heated.

Landlord Bennett, who had just recently moved into his newly constructed home up on Wilbraham mountain, thus opening the cottage to young rentals, responded immediately to the cry for help, and surveying the problem, called George.

George, then in his mid-60s, responded just as dutifully, making one suspect it was possible he was sitting fully clothed at 3 in the morning waiting for any emergency calls.

Before dawn, the problem had been alleviated and the house cleaned.

And George Merwin went on the list on the refrigerator to call in any future emergency.But we left Wilbraham for London a few months later, and had no need for George's plumbing and heating services until a number of years later.

It's funny when you build a house.

All of a sudden one is attracting visitors with every kind of specialty.

This happened five years later on our return to Wilbraham from three plus years in Europe.

One of the specialists was George.

George Merwin was not just, or merely, take your choice, a plumber.

He involved himself in heating and air conditioning, well drilling, and once acknowledged another sideline.

George also had a mortician's license, although no one in town ever confirmed his having utilized that talent or service.

There was another forte.

George was an intelligence specialist.

He lived in Wilbraham for 35 years, during a period when it blossomed from a farming community of 2,500 souls to a prosperous bedroom community for middle and upper executives of the likes of Massachusetts Mutual Life Insurance Co.; the Monarch life insurance company which Mass Mutual eventually swallowed and digested, Friendly Ice Cream Corp., which the Blake brothers, Curtiss and Presley, expanded to a regional power from one ice cream stand, the Monsanto Chemical Co., when it was still into chemicals, and a number of smaller machine tool companies that did subcontracting for United Aircraft, later United Technologies, in nearby Connecticut. There were also officers attached to Westover Air Force Base in nearby Chicopee Falls, which was a major Strategic Air Command bomber base for several decades and later a base for the giant C5 transport planes that would be utilized for Persian Gulf and Bosnian campaigns.

By the time we returned to Wilbraham to build our house in 1968, houses were sprouting up all over town, even on the mountain which had been considered unbuildable terrain.

George was one of the first specialists to turn up on the property up on Glendale Road. And learning that I was carefully following my father's pattern of not building before I had water and knew the cost of construction (Luke 14:28), he suggested how I should get some.

So long before any mortgage applications had been submitted or approved, George had one of his well-drilling associates at the site.

Before long, the price had been agreed upon, $3.50 a foot, and the drilling apparatus was operating.

George knew that I was serving as the general contractor for the construction, much as a lawyer representing himself has a fool for a client, and he had broadly hinted that I might turn over the heating contract to him.

The Melanson boys, Ed and John, had reservations about George, and probably allegiance to their own subcontractors. But on seeing the rough plans, noting that the water, 6 and 1\2 gallons at a depth of 120 feet was sufficient, and that Ed Ely, another neighbor, had already dug a cellar hole with his heavy equipment and smashed layers of ledge into pieces to make the foundation for a driveway, they were willing to take on the rest of the project if they could stipulate the sub-contractor for the plumbing and heating.

That, unfortunately, left George out in the cold, much as we had been by the furnace backup.

But to his credit, he never declared or exhibited umbrage, and when the floor-based heating unit froze one winter in the 1970s, George was able and willing to alleviate the damage at a reasonable price.

And as a newspaperman, it was always good to have George drop by and share some of his knowledge of the doings and undoings in town.

His Chrysler station wagon was as well known in town as any of the police cruisers. And when it crashed into a tree on Stony Hill Road after George suffered his fatal heart attack, it was still full of all the tools, and much of the infrastructure of his several trades.

CHAPTER 26

JUDGE FRANK FREEDMAN
EX-MAYOR, DIES AT 78

Known for bringing civility to the city
During a time of racial unrest, officials
Widely respected the judge and former
Mayor of Springfield

By BILL ZAJAC
Staff writer

SPRINGFIELD –U. S. District Court Judge and former Mayor Frank H. Freedman, 78, who died yesterday, was remembered as a hard working, kind person committed to justice and to the community.

"His legacy will be his civility and professionalism and the sensitivity to the community that he demonstrated throughout his life," said U.S. District Court Judge Michael A. Ponsor.

Freedman died at Baystate Medical Center from congestive heart failure after a short illness. He had worked at least 40 hours a week until two weeks ago.

His funeral will be Sunday at 1 p.m. at Temple Beth El, with burial in Beth El Cemetery. Harold R Ascher & Son Memorial Chapel is in charge of arrangements.

Mayor Michael J. Albano cited the respect Freedman earned through his public service and work on the bench.

"I can't think of anyone in our community who has the level of respect of Judge Freedman. I never heard anyone say a bad word about him. He was a real gentleman and class act," Albano said.

Freedman earned respect through his work and treatment of others, say friends and co-workers.

"I think he will be most remembered for his deep humanity, his consistent generosity, complete integrity and kindness to everyone," Ponsor said.

Assistant U.S. Attorney Kevin O'Regan, chief of the Springfield office, said Freedman was "consummately fair with an intrinsic sense of justice."

"In addition to understanding the seriousness of defendants' crimes, the judge was always very aware of the humanity of the defendants he sentenced and the effect that the sentences would have on defendants and their families," O'Regan said.

Freedman took office in 1967 and was serving his third term as the city's 46th mayor when he became a Nixon appointee to the bench in 1972.

He served as chief judge in the District of Massachusetts from 1986 to 1991. In 1992, he was given senior judge status that allowed him to cut his caseload. However, he continued to work full-time, often without vacations.

A flagship case for Freedman was a 1978 consent decree he signed to deinstitutionalize treatment of the mentally ill. It followed a suit filed by patients of the now-defunct Northampton State Hospital and opened the doors to people who languished in treatment centers for years.

Another consent decree signing was recalled by Albano as significant for Springfield. Freedman ruled that because the city was found to be engaging in discriminatory hiring practices, one minority job candidate would be hired for every white job candidate. The decree remains in effect today.

"It was a just decision that showed that he was ahead of his time, a progressive thinker," said Albano.

Freedman was also responsible for establishing the affirmative action policy for the state's fire departments. The policy remains in effect.

"He brought to the bench a humanity and humility that you can get only through being elected to a municipal office," said lawyer Christopher B. Myhrum, who served as a clerk under Freedman from 1980 to 1983.

Freedman's professional career was shaped greatly by racial strife. He was inspired to study law after learning about a young black sailor prosecuted and jailed for trying to buy a movie ticket.

He was mayor during racial unrest in the late 1960s following the assassinations of Martin Luther King Jr. and Sen. Robert F. Kennedy.

After two nights of rioting in Mason Square, Freedman imposed a curfew and enlisted the help of the city's clergy to defuse the unrest instead of bringing in the National Guard. He was praised for the handling of that situation by his successor, William C. Sullivan.

"After the riots, he got white and black groups working together to change things," said Sullivan, who served on a Freedman-appointed committee that included five business leaders and five black community leaders.

Charles V. Ryan Jr., who preceded Freedman as mayor, said Freedman was hard working, compassionate and honest.

"He was an outstanding citizen of this community and will be missed," Ryan said.

Ryan recalled Freedman's work on the City Council during Ryan's three terms as mayor between 1961 and 1967. Freedman served as City Council president in 1962.

U.S. Rep. Richard E. Neal, D-Springfield, said, "As one of over 50 individuals who has served as mayor of the city of Springfield, I was proud to call Frank Freedman a colleague.... He set the finest definition of the word citizen."

Until deciding to study law, Freedman thought he would become a sports journalist.

He never lost his passion for sports. In an interview marking his 30th anniversary on the bench last year, Freedman said he wouldn't leave the bench for any job except to become manager of the Boston Red Sox.

John C. Stuckenbruck, who worked with Freedman as clerk of the federal court here since 1979, said the only time Freedman's demeanor was anything but pleasant was when the Red Sox were losing.

Freedman served as a state assistant attorney general from 1963 to 1967. He practiced law privately from 1950.

The Frank H. Freedman Elementary School on Cherokee Drive is named after the judge and former mayor.

(Inserted from paid death notice: He was a lifelong resident of this area.

He was a graduate of Classical High School and a graduate of Boston University Law School. He had served in World War II as a naval officer.)

Freedman was married to the former Eleanor Labinger. He leaves three children, Joan Goodman, Wendy Mackler and Barry Freedman, and five grandchildren.

Died Aug. 21, 2003   *The* (Springfield, Mass.) ***Republican,*** *Aug. 22, 2003*

FRANK H. FREEDMAN
1915 – 2003

Frank Freedman was highly respected by my fellow journalists in Springfield, Mass.

So when I needed a lawyer for the first time in my life, it was easy to turn to him.

He would wander into the press room at the Springfield City Hall frequently, being one of nine members of the Springfield City Council.

Easygoing, friendly, and only as an afterthought, smart.

In the municipal elections in Springfield, he had gradually worked himself up the charts in the opinion of the electorate, and finally achieved the status as largest votegetter. He also gained the presidency of the Springfield City Council during the 1960s, before his run for mayor.

But in the summer of 1964, I needed a lawyer quickly, to help me conduct a title search on the property we had been offered in suburban Wilbraham. It was done with dispatch, as it needed to be, because I was scheduled to fly off to London and my new assignment with United Press International on June 4. I had first contacted him in mid-May.

He was very professional, but did chide me on one matter.

He said that I should have consulted him before I agreed to pay the surveying costs on the property on Wilbraham mountain that I had agreed to purchase from Henry and Freda Clark.

Freda had been adamant about that. The surveyor was a personal friend of the Clarks.

But I was still exuberant over the swift progress of the events in question and what I regarded as the generosity of Henry Clark.

The old man was not that well and in fact died less than two years later.

After agreement had been reached on the frontage for the lot, he asked me how deep I wanted to go.

I suggested we walk up the steep grade leading to one of the summits of Wilbraham mountain, and see.

Walk up as far as you want, Henry suggested.

I walked up as far as I dared.

As it was, I stopped too soon, because if I had gone a few yards further, I would have seen that I had the potential of owning the only piece of property on the mountain which had views in three directions, east, north to the Mount Holyoke range, and west over the Connecticut River valley.

As it was, where I decided to stop and not be too greedy, there was a very pleasant vista to Hovey Hill in Monson, Baptist Hill Road in Palmer, the Mount Holyoke range, and a lengthy stretch of: the Massachusetts Turnpike.

I acknowledged Frank's chastisement, but did not feel at all exploited, considering total costs of title search and surveying at less than $200.

My only other lengthy session with Frank was at a cocktail party at WMAS radioman Ken LeMere's house where I buttonholed him on the potential for development of the Connecticut River waterfront in Springfield.

I had already spent considerable time enjoying the benefits of the Rhine, the Danube and its two tributaries, the Inn and the Ilz, and could foresee similar development for Springfield.

Years later, having experienced the Thames, the lower Danube, the Sava, and riverside and lakeside development in Zurich, Geneva and Grenoble, I salute all the Springfield city fathers for having made such progress on the Connecticut River, with particular attention to the Basketball Hall of Fame.

Frank was elected mayor after my departure from Springfield, and elevated to a federal judgeship after my return.

I was only able to observe him on the bench in one case, that involving Heidi Hoffman, the infant daughter of a Jehovah's Witness couple from whom custody was seized by an overzealous medical staff in collusion with a hyperactive state judiciary.

The Hoffmans, supported by members of the Massachusetts bar from the Watchtower Bible and Tract Society, had filed suit to regain custody of the child.

The baby had not been weaned when the state seized custody, so the mother was required to be hospitalized with the child during the proceedings and transfusion of blood was forced on the child, who was suffering from acute leukemia.

The story was broken in The (Springfield, Mass) Morning Union in 1985, and quickly became fodder for television, the wire services and the national press.

Judge Freedman presided over the trial with a demeanor of fairness and patience which was in stark contrast to the helter-skelter defense of both the hospital legal representation and that of the Commonwealth of Massachusetts.

With custody of the child already returned to the Hoffmans, the case was declared moot, but the publicity of the case placed a much sharper focus on blood transfusions, acute leukemia, and hospital and judicial actions in such cases.

An attorney for the Witnesses told me years later that although the case created no new legal precedent, it was an important step in informing the general public of the issues involved.

One important result of the case was that journalists with young children in the Springfield area were much more aware of the dangers of blood transfusions and the powers of the medical establishments and judiciary in forcing them on patients.

As for the Hoffmans, they moved from Massachusetts to Greenville,

N.C., the home of East Carolina University Medical School, one of the few at that time which went out of its way to respect the wishes of parents in questions of transfusions.

There are now dozens, including the University of Massachusetts Medical School in Worcester.

Heidi survived, and shortly before this writing was reported to be a healthy and well-rounded teenager living with her father and stepmother in West Virginia. Her mother died earlier of cancer.

Frank Freedman had displayed the same humanity presiding over this case as I had seen as private attorney, city councilor and mayor.

But something jumped out at me on reading his obituary.

It was a fact that would stir the juices of such a conservative gadfly writer as Bernard Goldberg, who pilloried CBS long before Black Rock was splintered by the George Bush National Guard fiasco.

Not once in the obituary was it mentioned that Frank H. Freedman was a Republican. This Republican and observant Jew had climbed the political ladder in an overwhelming Democratic city, and this remarkable political achievement was not even mentioned.

In most red states, the rise of a star to the political pinnacle from the opposite party is an added credential marking his or her character.

In at least one blue state, it was a fact to be ignored, or censored.

FREDA P. CLARK

1905 – 2002

WILBRAHAM – Freda P. (Bennett) Clark, 97, a former resident of Crane Hill Road, died Wednesday at Wingate at Wilbraham Nursing Home. Born in Hampden, she had been a resident of Wilbraham for more than 85 years. She is predeceased by her husband, Henry J. Clark, 1966; her son, Wesley Clark, 1984; and her daughter, Wilma C. Beane, 1997. She leaves her granddaughters, Pamela Harris of Monson and Cheryl Page of Maine; and 7 other grandchildren, as well as many great grandchildren. A graveside service will be held Saturday November 23rd at 10 a.m. at the Glendale Cemetery, Glendale Road in Wilbraham. Lombard Funeral Home of Monson is in charge of arrangements.

Died November 20, 2002 **The** (Springfield, Mass.) **Union-News,** *November 22, 2002*

HENRY J. CLARK

1898 – 1966

Henry J. Clark, 67, of 431 Glendale Rd., North Wilbraham, died Wednesday in Springfield Hospital. He was born in Smith's Ferry, Northampton, Nov. 18, 1898, son of the late Charles H. and Cora B. (Reed) Clark and lived in North Wilbraham for the past 54 years. He was a grain salesman for the Cutler Grain Co., which was later sold to Wirthmore Feeds. He retired three years ago. He was a member of Glendale Methodist Church, North Wilbraham and the Wirthmore

Co. 25 Year Club. He leaves his wife, Mrs. Freda (Bennett) Clark, of North Wilbraham; a son, Wesley E. of Leominster; a daughter, Mrs. Wilma C. Beane of North Wilbraham; a brother, G. William of Ely, Vt.; five sisters, Mrs. Mabel Rohan of Ware, Mrs. Mildred Ellis of Bennington, Vt., Mrs. Harriet Burrows of this city, Mrs. Gladys Emery of West Springfield and Mrs. Ruth Scigowski of Rosedale, Long Island; seven grandchildren and several nieces and nephews. The funeral will be held at Graham – Wallengren funeral home Saturday at 2 p.m. Rev. Robert E. Morgan, pastor of Glendale Methodist Church, will officiate. Burial will be in Glendale Cemetery. North Wilbraham.

Died July 27, 1966   *The Springfeild* (Mass.) *Union, July 29, 1966*

THE EGG LADY

A Smith College student and her German law student husband from Bonn taught me something about freedom and the exercise thereof in 1963.

They, chafing under the same travel restrictions on naturalized citizens that affected our family, did something about it.

They sued. And by 1963, their arguments had wended their way through the federal appellate court system all the way to Washington, and the Supreme Court of the United States.

And they won.

That news story, that brought a certain measure of legalistic fame to the Connecticut River Valley, also released the shackles under which I had been operating for more than three years.

I had been resigned to remain in the United States for five years to comply with the restrictions on travel that might ensue if I were to take my German-born wife, my German-born son and my American-born daughter back to Europe in any conceivable foreign news assignment.

The Supreme Court decision broke those shackles and leveled the working field for natural-born and naturalized citizens.

One of the first orders of business was to obtain citizenship for my wife Maria, and that was accomplished quickly and efficiently with the assistance of the then U.S. Rep. Edward P. Boland, D-Mass., of Springfield, and Al Wade, my immediate boss at United Press International in Boston, who served as a witness.

The next thing was to wangle an assignment to London, from where all postings to the continent were made.

My efforts were rerouted through New York to Paul Allerup, the European news manager in London, and negotiations proceeded apace.

When agreement was reached on the conditions of a transfer from Springfield, Mass. to London, the news was sprung on a newly minted citizen-wife who I had always assumed would be thrilled to return to London where she would be much closer to her parents and siblings.

Not so.

This transplanted Bavarian, one of a regional breed well known for their stolidness, for want of a lesser term, was more concerned that the family, having finally found a hometown, had yet to make any progress toward a homestead.

I am not certain to this day how widely this disinclination to pull up roots again and move was shared with the young wives in the coffee klatsch group. The girls who met weekly in each other's homes to share their concerns had received the moniker the Stitch and Bitch Club by some of the spouses in the neighborhood.

But I know it was shared with Freda Clark.

Freda was hardly a member of the Stitch and Bitch Club, but instead delivered fresh eggs in the neighborhood.

The Clarks, she and her husband Henry, maintained a chicken coop up the mountain on Glendale Road which provided extra income as Henry, a grain salesman, approached retirement.

My spouse groused to Freda that her husband wanted to fly off to London, and the family didn't have a house, didn't even have any land.

"I have some land," interjected Freda.

Freda always liked Maria because she paid for her eggs in cash, and on time.

Maria cautioned Freda that she was sure the family didn't have any money to buy any land.

When that question came up, it was decided to determine how much cash had accumulated in a mutual life insurance policy that had been purchased from a faculty member at college a decade before.

We rode up to the Clarks, advised them it was possible a purchase could be made, and walked the property in question.

It happened to be the same hillside where the family had frequently picnicked during long hikes over Minnechaug Mountain.

It was swiftly determined that a hefty down payment could be made toward the land from the cash value of the insurance, and that a mortgage for the rest could be arranged.

Four weeks after Freda Clark said that she had some land for sale, the title search was completed thanks to Frank Freedman, who was later to become mayor of Springfield and a federal judge. The transaction was made, I was on a plane to London and the wife and kids booked on the Queen Elizabeth.

A few years later, a home was built on the lot and has remained in the family since.

As for Freda, her husband Henry died before our return from Europe, and after we built, she decided to sell her farmstead and chicken coop and build a more comfortable single-story home across the street.

Eventually, she moved in with her daughter, but upon the latter's death, was transferred to a nursing home.

Her obituary in the combined Springfield Union-News got nine lines, one less than the number of decades she lived.

This vignette is one acknowledgment that she deserved more.

DANIEL GILMORE, 66 DIES;
RETIRED REPORTER FOR UPI

Daniel F. Gilmore, 66, whose reporting career for United Press International spanned four decades and nearly every continent, died Aug. 7 at his home in Falls Church. He had emphysema.

He retired from UPI's Washington bureau, where he was a national security reporter, in July 1987. Since that time, he had been a senior correspondent for Maturity News, a Washington-based wire service covering the elderly for 80 newspapers in the United States.

Mr. Gilmore joined United Press, as the news agency was then known, in New York in 1941. Seven years later, he was assigned to UPI's London bureau, and subsequently served in Rome, Vienna, Frankfurt and Hong Kong; his work also took him to the Soviet Union, Eastern Europe, the Middle East, Africa and Indochina.

He was based in London again from 1962 to 1972, serving as European news editor. He then moved to Hong Kong to direct news coverage in UPI's Asia Division during the Vietnam War. He was transferred to Washington in 1973, when he became chief of the UPI team reporting national security affairs, concentrating on the State and Defense departments and intelligence services.

Mr. Gilmore was a native of New York City. He began his news career as a copy boy for the Associated Press news service and also worked for Time magazine while attending New York University.

He served with the Army Air Forces during World War II. He was a radio operator-gunner on a B17 Flying Fortress bomber when he was shot down over Europe in March 1944. He was a prisoner of war until May 2, 1945.

After the war, he resumed his career with UP, and helped cover such major stories as the Berlin airlift, the Hungarian Revolution, the Suez Canal crisis, the erection of the Berlin Wall, and meetings of U.S. presidents with European and Soviet leaders.

Survivors include his wife, the former Clare Lorene Brubaker, of Falls Church.

Died Aug. 7, 1988   ***The Washington Post*** *Aug. 9, 1988*

DAN

Dan was my immediate superior in London.

The London office of United Press International, or as our Commonwealth colleagues preferred to call it, British United Press, was at No. 8 Bouverie Street, just off Fleet.

It was an exciting place, full of interesting people of a number of nationalities.

And despite many travels on only two continents, it was the closest to the center of the world that I ever got.

Danny was the boss of the newsroom in London. As such he oversaw all the news that passed through that office from as far east as Karachi and as far south as Johannesburg.

Communications were relatively primitive at that time, the mid-1960s.

Occasionally the London desk would have to relay a lead from Vietnam that had been sent to Paris, because solid and reliable communication links had not yet been established during the early American intervention in that Southeast Asian nation.

Although there were radio links to certain centers such as Joburg, much of the news was sent to London by cable, and was written in that news shorthand called cabalese.

This required a great deal of rewriting on the London American and European desks, which sorted out the incoming news and processed it for their respective customer bases.

Danny was a wonderful boss in that sense, jumping into the breach whenever the news flow reached flood proportions, adding his experience and speed to the mix.

One example was the night of Oct. 14, 1964.

Danny and I were sitting on opposite sides of the rim amid the clatter of a dozen wire machines and our own typewriters.

"Do you know what, Tom?" Danny asked in one of those quick breaks between takes while inserting another book of copy paper into the machine.

"No, what?" I inquired.

"We've got four bulletin stories going at once. I've never seen this."

I focused quickly and realized he was right, and that I had been too busy even to notice.

It was a first, and a last that I never experienced again.

There were two ongoing stories that we had been concentrating on.

The British were having an election. We were chronicling the returns of the battle between Laborite Harold Wilson and Conservative Edward Heath to determine who was to occupy No. 10 Downing St. as prime minister for the next few months or years (Wilson eventually won).

And Bill Sunderland of the Rome bureau was accompanying the new pope, Paul VI, as he made the first Transatlantic flight of a reigning pontiff – to South America.

Two unexpected events interjected themselves into our labors.

Nikita Khrushchev, who had been battling in the presidium of the Communist Party of the Soviet Union for his political life after the Cuban missile crisis fiasco, had made a strategic mistake.

After drafting support from his military allies by flying Central Committee members favorable to him back to Moscow to overturn the vote of no confidence in the presidium, he went on vacation.

On Oct. 14, Khrushchev was ousted from power.

About the same time, cables starting coming in reporting that

Communist China had just exploded a thermonuclear device. Beijing had the H-Bomb.

A British election, an inaugural papal Transatlantic flight, a Kremlin ouster, and a Red Chinese H-Bomb.

Four bulletin stories, lead after lead, take after take, add after add, were marching onto the news wires, and Danny and I suddenly acknowledged that we were the drillmasters.

Years later, I encountered an excerpt from one of Boston Celtics basketball star Bill Russell's book "Second Wind."

In it, Russell had described two basketball teams reaching such a state of optimum performance that maintaining that level of performance became more important than the outcome of the contest itself.

I had played basketball myself and could only remember three instances, once in high school and twice in college, when I had had that experience.

In my news career, I can remember only one, that night in London.

Danny, at a more relaxed moment, related another memorable moment.

He described how he had been invited to one of those exclusive London clubs on The Strand or Fleet Street by an acquaintance.

In the club, his acquaintance left him at the bar for a few minutes to transact some business or other.

Danny, knowledgeable, experienced and engaging, struck up a fascinating conversation with two gentlemen at the bar.

He didn't think much more about it until he met his acquaintance some time later.

The acquaintance was exuberant.

Remember when I left you at the bar at the club the other night? his friend asked.

Of course, Danny replied.

Do you know who those two gentlemen were with whom you were having a conversation?

No idea, responded Dan.

That was J. Paul Getty and Nubar Gulbenkian.

He was referring to the expatriate American oilman and the Persian-Armenian merchant, two of the richest men on the planet.

And what's more, his friend gushed, they were delighted to meet you.

And another thing.

They were delighted that you did not know who they were.

They thoroughly enjoyed an animated conversation with someone who they knew was not trying to get anything out of them.

Danny stayed in London into the next decade, and eventually moved to Washington, where he covered the State Department for UPI, before its sale and eventual decline as a competitive news agency.

KAROL THALER

1910 - 1996

Karol Thaler, a diplomatic correspondent for United Press Inernational in London during the middle of the 20th Century, was a frequent conversationalist in the Bouverie Street offices of the news agency there. We worked only once together, in Belgrade in 1966. He died in London in 1996.

⁀

COURTLY KAROL

Karol Thaler was the London diplomatic correspondent.

As such, he covered the British Foreign Office and the embassy circuit in London for United Press International.

He was a courtly gentleman, very Continental in appearance and demeanor, and one of the most pleasant colleagues with whom to work and consort.

I would have liked to do have done more of both with him.

As it was, this was limited to discussing the copy which he submitted and that came over my desk in London, informing him of breaking news on the international wires that might affect his beat, or just engaging in pleasant discussions of affairs of state.

Opportunities to do the latter were few and far between in a busy newsroom.

In fact, there was only one opportunity in three years to do so with Karol.

After I had been in Belgrade for a time, he was sent on a swing of Eastern European countries to write a series of articles on that part of the world.

In the hours we had in Belgrade, at the office and over meals at the Metropol Hotel and in other Belgrade restaurants, we had opportunities to have lengthy conversations and make a thorough analysis of our respective jobs.

Sadly, we came to a mutual agreement.

On beats in totalitarian Communist societies like Hungary, Romania and Bulgaria or oligarchic socialist ones such as Yugoslavia, it was really very difficult to learn what was happening behind the scenes. We, like many of our readers, would have to wait for history to reveal many of the truths that we would have liked to report.

It is a fact that I learned a lot more about the societies in which I lived after I had left them, and could read up on their histories and put my own experiences in better perspective.

GEORGE H. PIPAL

1916-1996

Longtime newsman George Henry Pipal, who worked alongside Charles Schulz handling licensing and syndication of the famous "Peanuts" comic strip, died Wednesday at the age of 80.

For the past 20 years, Pipal worked for United Media Enterprises, owners of the copyright to "Peanuts." In 1979, Pipal moved to the Santa Rosa area from Old Greenwich, Conn., to work directly in Schulz's offices. He was getting ready for work when he died at his Kenwood home.

"He was extremely well liked. I was always impressed at how well he fitted in with the community. People took an instant liking to him," said Schulz.

For most of his life, Pipal was involved in the news – through college, newspapers, the wire services and as a naval aide and communications officer to Gen. Douglas MacArthur aboard the USS Nashville in 1944 and 1945.

"He took care of things like Yugoslavia wants 26 episodes (of the "Peanuts" cartoon show) dubbed into Croatian, that kind of stuff," said his son Frank. "But for the bulk of his career, he was in the news and met all sorts of movers and shakers of the day in ways that reporters can't do now."

A native of Lafayette, Ind., Pipal was editor of his student newspaper at the University of Nebraska. He began moonlighting for United Press – the forerunner of the United Press International wire service – in its Omaha offices in 1937, and then attended Columbia University School of Journalism. He served in the 7th Fleet, U.S. Naval Reserve, during World War II, attaining the rank of lieutenant. He was awarded the Bronze Star.

After the war, Pipal returned to United Press and was sent to London, where he met his future wife, Caroline Dunsmore of Scotland, whom he married in 1946. For the next several years, Pipal worked for the wire service throughout Europe, Africa and the Middle East. He was European business manager in London for United Press until 1966. After that, he was transferred to New York, where he worked for United Media Enterprises, a subsidiary of Scripps Howard Publishing Co.

Pipal was past president of the Sonoma County Press Club. An avid petanque player, he was a member of the Valley of the Moon Petanque Club.

He is survived by his wife, Caroline, of Kenwood; three sons, John Pipal of London, Philip Pipal of Irvine and Frank Pipal of Kenwood; one daughter, Suella Pipal of Copenhagen, Denmark, one brother; Frank Pipal of Teaneck, N.J.; and four grandchildren. A memorial service will be held at a later date.

Died Nov. 20, 1996   *The* (Santa Rosa, Ca.) ***Press Democrat,*** *Nov. 22, 1996*

STRANGERS ON A TRAIN

There were lots of ways to get to Fleet Street from the Old Kent Road in Bromley.

Our house was on Coniston Road just opposite the Bromley Court Hotel, the former estate of William Pitt the Younger (1759 - 1806).

It was parallel to the Old Kent Road, and just a few yards away from it.

One could amble over to that main link between London and Canterbury, and look back toward the center of Bromley to see if a No. 11 or No. 47 bus was in sight. If not, one could walk down the gently sloping hill toward the next stop, only a couple of hundred yards away.

If neither bus appeared, you were close enough to the Beckenham station to take the train in from there.

If a bus appeared immediately at the first stop, one could hop on for thrupence, or four pence (the fare rose during my London stay) and ride down to the Bellingham station, which was closer to the bus line.

On an especially warm and sunny day, one could forgo the bus hop, and start walking across the lush Bellingham green, a longer but pleasant stroll.

I researched several other ways to commute to London.

One of them was with Knut, a bearded Norwegian who prided himself on driving his Mini from Seven Oaks to London without ever stopping for a traffic light. In fact, he stopped barely long enough in Bromley to pick me up at the door.

Knut avoided lights by anticipating them and turning right or left as the case might be. He probably knew the London southeast section south of the Thames better than any cab driver, but it was not a relaxing ride.

It was just as well that I was moved off the night desk to the overnight, so that our shifts (he was on the European desk) no longer coincided.

One day, while studying my London map, I noticed that there was another train station not far away, but to the right of the Old Kent Road, not the left. I picked out a day when I had a little extra time, in case of a misconnection, and gave it a try.

When I opened the train door and entered the compartment, who should be sitting there but George Pipal. George was an executive upstairs with UPI, and I had never met him before, although we both knew who we were.

During the mutual interrogation session that ensued before the train arrived at Blackfriars Station, I learned that he had covered Czechoslovakia immediately after World War II.

I believe I learned that he was also of Czech descent.

George was not only knowledgeable about Eastern European operations, but was indeed responsible for them. He learned from me that my hope was for an assignment on the continent.

I confided my disappointment that having two children precluded any assignment to Moscow. It wasn't until a decade or more later that any American correspondents were assigned to Moscow who had families.

But before the commute ended, he had learned of my proficiency in German and acquaintance with a couple of Slavic languages and my willingness to work in Eastern Europe.

George then informed me that UPI was considering assigning native English speakers and writers, American, Canadian, British or Australians among them, to all the major European news centers where non-English reporters were now stationed. The goal was to cut down on the number of rewrites that had to be made in London.

He mentioned that one of those posts, which had not been manned by an American or Briton for several years, was Belgrade. I indicated a strong desire to be considered.

Not long after that, I was called in by Paul Allerup, the European news manager, and informed that I had been chosen to go to Belgrade. I was left with the impression that he was not overly pleased by the assignment, figuring that I was too inexperienced for the posting. There may also have been a suspicion that I had gone over his head to obtain this plum.

To exercise a semblance of fleeting control over my future in the distant Balkans, he strongly suggested that I go straight to Belgrade, and not go via Vienna. I neither concurred nor demurred.

But I had been reading copy out of the Vienna bureau headed by Franz Cyrus for 18 months, and regarded it as vital to get a briefing from Franz before heading for Yugoslavia. Besides, my wife's family lived in Passau, Germany on the Danube, and that route was the obvious one to take.

The Frankfurt Bureau had arranged for me to pick up a Volkswagen Beetle there, and we were now independently mobile for the first time in 18 months. After a short visit in Passau, it was on to Belgrade, via Vienna.

All thanks to a chance meeting on a train.

SIR PETER USTINOV, 82, WITTY ENTERTAINER WHO WAS A WORLD UNTO HIMSELF, IS DEAD

Peter Ustinov, the hair-trigger wit with the avuncular charm whose 60-year career amounted to a revolving series of star turns as actor, playwright, novelist, director and raconteur, died on Sunday at a clinic near his home in Bursins, Switzerland. He was 82.

Sir Peter had suffered for years from the effects of diabetes and, more recently, a weakened heart. His death was announced by Leon Davico, a friend and former spokesman for Unicef, for which Sir Peter had worked for many years.

A cosmopolitan, corpulent and full-bearded six-footer whose ancestors were prominent in czarist Russia, the British-born entertainer was a prodigy who began mimicking his parents' guests at the age of 2. He wrote his first play, "House of Regrets," in his teens; it opened in London to glowing reviews when he was 21.

As an actor, he won international stardom as a lanquid, quirky Nero in the 1951 sword-and-sandal epic "Quo Vadis?", gained increasing stature by playing sly rogues and became one of the few character actors to hold star status for decades, adjusting easily to movies, plays, broadcast roles and talk shows, which he enlivened with hilarious imitations and pungent one-liners.

His many honors included two supporting-actor Academy Awards for portraying a shrewd slave dealer in "Spartacus" in 1960 and a clumsy jewel thief in ""Topkapi" in 1964. He received three Emmys for television performances in the title role of "The Life of Samuel Johnson" in 1958, as Socrates in "Barefoot in Athens" in 1966 and as a rural shopkeeper who gains compassion from a youngster in "A Storm in Summer" in 1970.

He won a Grammy for narrating Prokofiev's "Peter and the Wolf" in a concert conducted by Herbert von Karajan and also directed operas and his plays in half a dozen European cities.

Reviewing "A Storm in Summer," Jack Gould of The New York Times praised Mr. Ustinov for shaping "an exquisite portrait of the individual who had known more than his share of sorrow yet in his disgruntled way clung to the noble values that are the mark of dignity and character." The critic lauded Mr. Ustinov's "incredible virtuosity" and hailed him as "one of the most gifted actors of our times."

Other reviewers occasionally accused the actor of approaching comedy more decoratively than genuinely, of overdoing mugging and mannerisms and of pretentiousness in playing historical figures.

In the last decade, he appeared in a half-dozen films for television or general release. Among them was "Luther," Eric Till's study of Martin Luther, that opened last fall. Sir Peter, who portrayed Prince Frederick the Wise of Wittenberg, said in an interview in The New York Times that he was surprised that the director had thought of him, at the age of 82.

"I didn't have anything against it, except that I can hardly walk," he said. "But we coped with that because I leaned on things and staggered through the film in some measure."

By late in the film, Sir Peter said, he understood why, during the 16th century, everyone died at the age of 40 or earlier: "Because having to dress up in curtains, which press the human body in all sorts of places where it's not usually pressed, was real agony."

He portrayed a doctor in the film "Lorenzo's Oil" (1992), and was the Walrus in Peter Postlethwaite's Carpenter in the 1999 television-film version of "Alice in Wonderland."

His more than two dozen plays included two spoofs of the cold war. One of them, "The Love of Four Colonels," won the New York Drama Critics Circle Award as the best play of 1953, and the second, "Romanoff and Juliet," received the British Critics' Best Play award for 1956. Other Ustinov plays included "The Banbury Nose," "Moment of Truth," "Photo Finish," "The Unknown Soldier and His Wife," "Halfway up the Tree" and "Beethoven's 10th."

His greatest film achievement was his co-adaptation, direction and production as well as his performance as Captain Vere in the 1962 film "Billy Budd," Melville's nautical allegory on good and evil.

Among other honors, Mr. Ustinov was appointed a Commander of the British Empire in 1975, elected to the Academie des Beaux-Arts in 1987 and received many honorary degrees on both sides of the Atlantic.

His film scripts and roles included "Private Angelo" (1949), which he helped to direct and produce and in which he starred as the protagonist, a bumbling Italian soldier; "Lady L" (as director and an absent-minded prince (1965), and "Hot Millions" (1968), in which he starred as a gentle swindler.

Other movie roles were in "Hotel Sahara" (1951), in which Mr. Ustinov appeared as a beleaguered Arab hotelier; "Beau Brummel" (1954), with the actor as a pompous Prince of Wales; "We're No Angels" (1955), where he played a slick convict; "Lola Montes" (1955), as a ubiquitous circus master; "The Sundowners" (1960), playing an Australian loafer. Later roles included his portrayal of a Mexican general in "Viva Max!" (1969), a fraudulent doctor in "The Treasure of Matecumbe"(1976), a sadistic sergeant in "The Last Remake of Beau Geste" (1977) and Charlie Chan in "Charlie Chan and the Curse of the Dragon Queen" (1981).

In later years he also stylishly portrayed Hercule Poirot, Agatha Christie's eccentric Belgian detective, in the films "Death on the Nile" (1978) and "Evil Under the Sun" (1982) and in a series of television specials. Also on television, he narrated many fantasy, historical and science programs and supplied a multiplicity of voices on many of them.

Admirers praised his talent, stamina and discipline in channeling his efforts despite an appearance of flitting among many projects that some friends likened to disciplined chaos. He rated his satisfactions in this order: 1) writing novels, 2) writing short stories, 3) playwriting, 4) acting, 5) directing and 6) producing.

"Writing has always been my deepest love," he said in 1982. "Acting is intrinsically easy. You're like a chameleon, adapting yourself to various circumstances and to what other people are writing. Writing is much more mysterious, and more personal." Among his novels were "The Loser" (1960) and "Krumnagel" (1971); his short stories included "Add a Dash of Pity" (1959) and "The Frontiers of the Sea" (1966). Other writings were "My Russia" (1983), "Peter Ustinov in Russia" (1988) and a 1977 memoir, "Dear Me."

He visited Russia often, before and after the breakup of the Soviet Union. In 1988 he flew to Leningrad, now St. Petersburg, for the opening of an art museum dedicated to his mother's family and housed in a building erected by one of his great-great-grandfathers. Also that year, he was host of a mini-series based on his book "My Russia," describing the changes to Soviet society under Mikhail S. Gorbachev thus: "It's been like an abscess bursting and health returning."

Sir Peter's writing was usually praised for wit, literacy and insights, but the consensus was that his work, though clever and diverting, suggested more than it accomplished. Reviewers agreed that his early plays showed great promise, but over the years they increasingly criticized his writing as that of an undisciplined jack-of-all-trades who frittered away his talents and was at times self-indulgent and verbose. Still, the critic John Lahr hailed the spiritual autobiography "Dear Me" as "an unusually graceful memoir whose wit bears witness to Ustinov's generosity and seriousness."

The entertainer maintained a frenetic professional pace for more than 50 years. Asked to explain his abhorrence of retirement, he replied, "I've always considered life to be much more of a marathon than a sprint."

Sir Peter was married three times. His first two marriages, to Isolde Denham and to Suzanne Cloutier, ended in divorce. He was married again in 1972 to Helene du Lau 'Allemans. She survives him, as do his four children: Tamara, in England, whose mother was Ms. Denham; and by Ms. Cloutier, Igor in Switzerland, Pavla of Los Angeles, and Andrea in Spain; and a granddaughter.

Peter Alexander Ustinov was born in London on April 16, 1921, the only child of Iona Ustinov, a journalist, and the former Nadia Benois, a painter. Both parents were half Russian with assorted parts French, Italian and German. Many of their forebears were prominent figures in czarist Russia, including a country squire with 6,000 serfs, the owner of the largest caviar fishery and a court architect.

The youth attended the private Westminster School in London until he was 16, when he began studying acting with Michel Saint-Denis as the London Theater Studio. Within two years he made his London stage debut and gained increasing notice by writing and acting in two reviews and writing five plays produced while he served in the British Army as a private in World War II.

In later years, he emphasized his nonconformance in school and the army with these anecdotes: one of his report cards warned, "Shows great originality, which must be curbed at all costs"; he told enlistment officers he preferred tank duty "because you can go into battle sitting down," and his superiors concluded, "On no account must this man be put in charge of others."

The actor's later observations included: "The theater is the place for the ventilation of doubts to make us more conscious of our humanity." "A politician is a man who reaches the top of the tree because he had no qualifications to detain him at the bottom" and "Humorists are the safety valves on the boiler.;"

He was for more than 20 years an unpaid roving ambassador for the United Nations Children's Fund, and for several years was a rector of the University of Dundee in Scotland. He also established the Peter Ustinov Foundation, which set up an international network of university scholars, politicians and others to examine the subject of prejudice. In separate initiatives his foundation sponsors medical clinics in underserved parts of the world.

Sir Peter, who once described himself as a "practicing European," spent as much time as possible aboard his ketch moored off Spain; he read voluminously, had interests in music and cars and varying command of eight languages; and he enjoyed tennis, squash and swimming. For many years his main home was a chalet outside Geneva with vineyards that produced 4,000 bottles of white wine a year. He had an apartment in Paris for a time and later had one in Boulogne.

When he was knighted by Queen Elizabeth in 1990, his main concern was how to reply to the invitation.

"The invitation said, 'Delete whichever is inapplicable: I can kneel – I cannot kneel.' But there was nothing," he said, "for those who can kneel but not get up."

Died March 28, 2004   ***The New York Times,*** *March 30, 2004*

THE WHIMPER AND THE BANG

London began with a whimper, and ended with a bang.

Between them, expatriate American poet Thomas Stearns Eliot died.

The whimper came when I found out that UPI gave me only a week to find housing for my family, which would soon be on the Queen Elizabeth heading from New York to Southampton.

It had been fun walking over to work off Fleet Street from the Waldorf Hotel on the Aldwych, and wallowing at night in one of those huge bathtubs in London hotels. And I had put aside Saturday for a full day of house hunting.

That's when I found out that Unipressers in London worked a 39-hour week, six 6 and ½ hour days with four weeks vacation.

I learned toward the end of the work week that I had received a plum assignment for Saturday, covering the film premiere of The Beatles' "Hard Day's Night."

The big boss didn't take too kindly to my whimpering that the Saturday assignment would force me to stay a few extra days at the Waldorf so I could find permanent housing. I got a couple.

I didn't care much for the Beatles.

I put them in a similar category with Elvis Presley, who had been romancing the colonel's daughter down around headquarters near Frankfurt a decade earlier while I was freezing my butt in bivouac on the Czech border with my Armored Cavalry Regiment buddies.

The Beatles, as far as I was concerned, were a quartet of crazy Liverpool kids whose raucous melodies, with one or two rare exceptions, were coupled with insipid, banal and, on occasion, even eschatologically unsound lyrics.

To be assigned to cover them seemed demeaning.

Nevertheless, off to the Odeon on Piccadilly we went, along with Princess Margaret, her then husband, Anthony Armstrong-Jones, and all the other notables of pop-rock.

The most interesting aspect of the whole show, in my view, was the aftermath, when a fleet of ambulances arrived at Piccadilly to cart off the swooning teen-age girls who had crowded against the grated fences set up outside the theater.

The doctors who treated the more than 130 poor wretches who were admitted to downtown London hospitals concluded that they were not necessarily victims of a paroxysm of idol worship.

Most of the penniless girls had traveled down to London from the Midlands overnight by train, had not had anything to eat or enough to drink for hours and hours, and had fallen victim more to exhaustion and dehydration than worshipful excess.

This made a better lead than the film itself and all the notables who attended it, and so it was written.

T.S. Eliot was not the sole icon to die during my stint in London, from June of 1964 until November of 1965, nor was he the most prominent.

An unsuccessful American presidential candidate, Adlai Stevenson, collapsed on Grosvenor Square near the American embassy during the period and died.

And I was also present for the death of one the most distinguished figures of the 20th Century.

Word filtered in from the Foreign Office and the Home Office in the middle of January that Sir Winston S. Churchill, lay close to death. Death's door was at Hyde Park Gate, his London home away from his country home at Blenheim Castle.

United Press International mobilized its finest writers from around the continent for what is indelicately regarded in news parlance as the death watch.

I was dispatched on regular shifts to Hyde Park Gate itself, first to establish a communications base from which we would have immediate telephone contact, a necessity three decades before cell phones.

The perch also enabled the assigned reporters to observe the arrival of notables and relatives for the great man's last hours.

And the Brits also gathered there, representing all strata, to honor the World War II prime minister.

Sir Winston's death on January 24, 1965 unleashed the greatest ceremony of the century.

An era had passed.

My era in London passed with my assignment to the Balkans in November of that year.

And my bosses, unlike with the Beatles assignment, sent me away from the British Isles with a bang.

The day before I was to leave on the boat train to the continent, I was assigned to cover the speech to be given by Peter Ustinov, not yet a sir, to the British Institute of Directors.

The great raconteur not only captured his audience, but his press.

More than 5,000 members of Britain's business and industrial establishment received a dash of spice with their annual ingestion of cold chicken at the biggest box lunch bash of the season.

Ustinov's principal platform plank at the gathering was an argument that both the British government and private industry ought to do more for the arts.

He did so in deftly political fashion, skewering the Big Powers in turn.

Ustinov:

—chided Americans for sending Peace Corps representatives to Athens to teach the "Greeks the meaning of the word democracy."

— urged the Russians, if they are going to have telephones, to print telephone books.

— lauded Britons for inventing new sports and games as soon as other nations became competent enough to defeat them in the old ones.

— acknowledged that the French nuclear force de frappe was here to stay and gave its owners "more than a sense of national arrogance."

— And he concluded with a serious warning to his Eurocentric audience not to accede to a gradual surrender to "the unfettered freedom of action" of U.S. finance, a warning applicable to a worldwide recession nearly a half-century later.

During a one-on-one interview after the speech, he concluded the lengthy convivial exchange of questions and answers with an invitation to attend a private party later in the evening.

I reluctantly explained that I had a story to write that night, and a family to gather in the morning for a move to the Balkans, and it would be prudent of me to decline the kind invitation.

It's the one party of my life that I truly missed attending. But the London stint, thanks to Peter Ustinov, ended with a bang instead of a whimper.

ON THE DEATH
OF FRANZ F. CYRUS

VIENNA – (The Editor) Franz Ferdinand Cyrus has died at 75 after a severe illness. After the war, he served as an editor at the "Vienna Kurier," and after that as bureau chief of the United Press International wire service for Austria, Southeast Europe and Switzerland. He subsequently served for several years as press secretary at the Austrian embassy in Washington. Austria loses in Franz F. Cyrus a tireless representative who provided an accurate reflection of Austria in the American media.

Wiener Kurier   *Feb. 9, 1995*

(Translated from the German by the author)

FRANZ CYRUS
1920 – 1995

I had been advised by (European news chief) Paul Allerup in London to proceed directly to Belgrade after my appointment as chief of the Belgrade bureau of United Press International.

Paul felt there was no need to take a detour to Belgrade via Vienna, where Franz Cyrus was in charge of the entire Balkans news operation.

But I not only regarded Franz highly after reading the dispatches from his and other southeastern bureaus for the past 18 months, but felt that he, as an Austrian, could serve as an important mentor to a rookie covering that region.

Another consideration was the fact that I was depositing my family in the Bavarian Danube River city of Passau for a period while I sought housing in the Yugoslav capital.

The Frankfurt bureau had arranged for me to pick up my Volkswagen Beetle, the third of 11 that passed through the family over a quarter century, and I stayed overnight at Dick Growald's apartment to make the transaction.

Dick, the peripatetic foreign correspondent who proceeded from Frankfurt to Moscow to White House correspondent in Washington before settling down with the San Diego Union, was off somewhere and had left the keys for me.

This was just one other way to keep the expenses down under the watchful eyes of the Unipress accountants.

From Frankfurt, I proceeded on to Passau, and then Vienna.

Franz was a gracious host.

He was pleased that UPI had sent in a correspondent who not only was interested in Slavic, Finno-Ugric (Hungarian) Romanian and Ottoman Turk history, but also was fluent in German, a lingua franca in much of Eastern Europe.

He was also aware of the state of the Belgrade bureau, which was manned by two Serbs, one elderly and failing, and the other with little English capability.

The bureau, in fact, was useful for little else than forwarding accounts of international soccer matches and their results and as a communications base if foreign correspondents had to be sent in to cover major breaking news.

Franz was also aware of its limitations as far as equipment was concerned.

That was best exemplified by the teletype machine used to send out dispatches. I later determined that it had been manufactured by Siemens in 1927.

Franz housed me at the Bristol, a Ritz-owned and styled hotel on the Vienna Opernring across from the UPI office.

He also lent me a proper suit jacket to wear to the Vienna State Opera. I had noticed while reading the Vienna papers that a tremendous storm was brewing over the attire of the young soprano who was singing the part of Salome in the famed Richard Strauss opera.

The staid Viennese opera crowd was appalled that the Dance of the Seven Veils apparently was being performed without the veils.

This compounded the cultural felony that the singer, Anja Silja, was linked romantically with Wieland Wagner, the grandson of the famed composer and the impresario of the opera performance.

I immediately dashed off a piece in English on the furor, which not only revealed the trove of material in any European capital for the energetic newcomer, but made it quite obvious that I had not gone directly from London to Belgrade.

But it also enabled me to see one of the great performances of the Strauss opera, and the image of John the Baptist as played by Eberhard Waechter remains with me to this day.

Franz also generously offered to provide me with materials which he knew would be in short supply, and perhaps unobtainable, in Belgrade.

The next morning, I headed out of Vienna and toward the Alps toward Slovenia, the most northern republic in Yugoslavia.

I passed through Vienna twice more during my Balkans assignment, once to pick up my family and secondly during a vacation trip up to Germany and Austria.

Many members of the diplomatic and military staff at the U.S. Embassy , and particularly their wives, regarded Belgrade as a hardship post during those years, the mid-60s.

But certain thoughtful members of the embassy staff gave us limited privileges and access to the small commissary at the embassy, and that was plenty for us.

And Franz gave us more than enough professional support.

That was made evidence during my second passage through Vienna.

Franz asked me whether I planned any coverage of other countries in the region, focusing primarily on Hungary, Romania and Bulgaria, all then solidly behind the Iron Curtain and under the control of the Soviet Union.

I told Franz that would depend entirely on breaking news.

That was when he did me a huge favor.

UPI had been providing news service to all the countries in eastern Europe for a number of years, and receiving compensation for it in local unconvertible currencies plus reciprocal news and communication access.

Those currency balances had been building up for years in the banks of the respective capitals, and were utilized infrequently when Franz or other foreign correspondents passed through.

Since the crushing of the Hungarian revolution in 1956, those trips had been rare.

Franz offered me letters of access to those accounts, and invited me to use them any time I had a breaking story in the region.

When I was given the opportunity to break two of my own the following year, the access proved invaluable.

I was never able to thank him enough.

MILOVAN DJILAS, YUGOSLAV CRITIC OF COMMUNISM, DIES AT 83

By Serge Schmemann

Milovan Djilas, the Yugoslav Communist revolutionary whose denunciation of his former comrades in 1957 as a privileged and self-serving "new class" became an early banner of dissidents and anti-Communists, died in Belgrade yesterday. He was 83.

His son, Aleksa Djilas, a historian, said Mr. Djilas was treated Wednesday night for a heart complaint and died at home on Thursday. The elder Djilas had been increasingly weakened by age and heart problems in recent years, but he remained intellectually active to the end.

A revolutionary, soldier, political leader and writer, Mr. Djilas, in his own phrase, "traveled the entire road of Communism," from Partisan guerrilla fighter against Nazi occupiers of Yugoslavia and ardent believer in Stalinism, through disillusionment and revulsion at the "all-powerful exploiters and masters" it had brought to power—Stalin first among them.

Mr. Djilas was the closest lieutenant to Tito in the resistance to the Serbian monarchy, in the Partisan struggle against German and Italian occupiers and in the creation of a Yugoslav Communist state. It was he whom Tito sent to Moscow in January 1948 to tell Stalin that Yugoslavia intended to pursue its own national development, independent of Moscow.

The divorce was made public in June 1948, and Yugoslavia became the first Communist state to break with the Kremlin, a move that gained it respect and assistance from the West and a leading role among nonaligned nations.

But Mr. Djilas (pronounced GEE-lahss) soon began to voice disenchantment with his own party, and in 1954 Tito expelled him from its ranks and from his Government posts. Mr. Djilas spent much of the next 36 years in prison or in official disgrace.

In January 1955 he was put on trial for "hostile propaganda" over an interview with The New York Times, and received a suspended sentence. It was at this time that he began work on "The New Class," as well as "Land Without Justice," a history of his native Montenegro. In December 1956 he was imprisoned for "slandering Yugoslavia" in statements made to a French magazine and in an article for The New Leader in New York.

The prison to which he was sent, Sremska Mitrovica, was the same in which he served three years as a young revolutionary, fresh out of law school, when he was arrested for organizing demonstrations against the monarchy. It is a reflection of Mr. Djilas's political development that during the first incarceration he learned Russian and in the second he studied English.

With prison imminent, Mr. Djilas managed to smuggle the manuscript of "The New Class" abroad. Its publication in 1957 was an immediate sensation.

Though the cold war was at its zenith and denunciations of Stalinism and Communism were common, the prevailing image of Communist leaders was of ruthless ideologues. "The New Class" was the first exposure from within a Communist state of leading Communists as a new elite dedicated to its own privileges and power, and the first denunciation of the system from an unimpeachable source.

"Membership in the Communist Party before the Revolution meant sacrifice," Mr. Djilas wrote in "The New Class." "Being a professional revolutionary was one of the highest honors. Now that the party has consolidated its power, party membership means that one belongs to a privileged class. And at the core of the party are the all-powerful exploiters and masters."

The criticism was devastating for Communists. Foreign and domestic attacks until then had focused on the ideology and the system, which Communists could rebuff as class warfare or ideological sniping. But Mr. Djilas accused the Communists of the highest hypocrisy, of living and acting like the "exploiters" they had fought against.

Among dissidents and critics of Communism, Mr. Djilas became a symbol of resistance, and "new class" entered their vocabulary as a synonym for the secretive and devious Communist ruling elite. Mr. Djilas's book became taboo in all Communist states, and it was not published in Yugoslavia until 1980.

"The New Class" resulted in another trial for Mr. Djilas on charges of being " hostile to the people and the state of Yugoslavia," for which he was given a seven-year sentence. After the appearance of another book, "Conversations with Stalin," in which he branded Stalin "the greatest criminal in history," five years were tacked on to his sentence.

After he had served nine and a half years, Tito set Mr. Djilas free, and he left on visits to Britain, the United States and Australia. "Prison transformed me," he said in an interview many years later. "It transformed me from an ideologist into a humanist."

He was a visiting professor at Princeton in 1968 when the Soviet Union led an invasion of Czechoslovakia. His criticism of that invasion and other interviews led to the revocation of his passport on his return, and it was not returned for 18 years.

Mr. Djilas spent most of the last decades of his life in Belgrade, writing commentaries, histories and novels.

Watching from afar the attempts of Mikhail S. Gorbachev to reform the Communist system in the Soviet Union, he predicted that the Soviet system would not survive the lifting of centralized control.

In 1988 Mr. Djilas told an interviewer who asked about Mr. Gorbachev's efforts that "his difficulties will begin in three or four years when decentralization, privatization and self-management will confront him with the painful fact that none of these reforms can be made really effective without revamping the political profile of Soviet society."

The collapse of Communist regimes across East Europe confirmed Mr. Djilas's critique of the system. But in his last years, Mr. Djilas seemed to move from satisfaction at the defeat of Communism in Yugoslavia to dismay at the ethnic violence that emerged in its aftermath.

He welcomed the first wave of anti-Communist demonstrations in Belgrade in March 1991, which he said reminded him of uprisings 50 years earlier against Prince Paul, who had attempted to align Yugoslavia with the Nazis.

But he opposed Belgrade's war against Croatia, gaining the opprobrium of the former Communists who had emerged as Serbian nationalists. The old Communist daily, Borba, accused him of betrayal.

In an interview with David Binder of The New York Times two years ago, Mr. Djilas said he could see "no way out" of the violence.

Nationalism, he said, had replaced Communism as the main ideological currency in the Balkans. And his life had taught him that "you cannot reform an ideology."

Mr. Djilas's pessimistic view of the Balkans came with his descent "from an ancient tribe of peasants and shepherds" in the mountains of Montenegro, in southern Yugoslavia. From his birth there on June 12, 1911, one of seven children of a Montenegrin officer, he wrote in his biographical book, "Land Without Justice," he was immersed in clan feuds.

His mother was from a Serbian clan that had settled in the area, but kept its Serbian identity. Leaving home at the age of 10, Mr. Djilas attended school in nearby towns and, at 19, enrolled at the University of Belgrade to study philosophy and law. Already drawn to Communism, he became a student leader .

His first arrest came in 1933. On his release he returned to the fray and, in 1937, met Josip Broz, head of the clandestine Communist Party, who went under the nom de guerre of Tito. Tito charged Mr. Djilas with finding volunteers for the Spanish Civil War and assigned him to the party's Politburo.

World War II claimed the lives of Mr. Djilas's father, two brothers and two sisters. He himself held key positions with the Partisans and their political arm.

Mr. Djilas made his first trip to Moscow in 1944 as the head of a military mission, and there he held the first of the meetings with Stalin that he subsequently described in "Conversations With Stalin." Though he arrived "totally loyal" to the Soviet leader, he wrote, he developed doubts that grew in subsequent visits to abhorrence.

Mr. Djilas's strongest differences with the Soviet leadership developed over the systematic looting and rape of Yugoslav civilians by the Red Army, and the reaction of Stalin and other Soviet leaders to his complaints. At a meeting in Moscow, Stalin ridiculed Mr. Djilas and demonstratively kissed his Serbian wife while accusing Mr. Djilas of ingratitude.

Mr. Djilas was instrumental in Tito's break with Stalin and the international Communist movement that Moscow dominated. He defended Yugoslavia's national Communism as editor and contributor to Communist, the theoretical journal, and to Borba, the party daily.

But by the early 1950s, Mr. Djilas was growing increasingly disenchanted with the course of Communist development, in Yugoslavia as elsewhere, and his writings became increasingly critical.

Ousted from the party in 1954 and under a suspended sentence, he lived jobless and under surveillance in Belgrade until the publication of an article, "The Storm in Eastern Europe," appeared in The New Leader in New York in 1956. The article welcomed the Hungarian uprising that year as the beginning of the end for state Communism. But it took three decades of prison and isolation before Mr. Djilas's prophecy came true.

In those years, Mr. Djilas completed many works of fiction, biography and history. He wrote a major biography of the Montenegrin prince-poet, Njegos, a translation of Milton's "Paradise Lost," and a classic about the partisan struggle entitled, "Wartime."

Mr. Djilas is survived by a daughter from his first marriage, Vukica, his son Aleksa, and a grandson, all of Belgrade. His second wife, Stefanija, died in 1993. His first wife, Mitra, survives. Both were Partisan fighters.

Died April 20, 1995   ***The New York Times**, April 21, 1995*

THE REVOLUTIONARY SEER

I met Steffie first.

A woman, ostensibly a stringer for Time magazine, called me shortly after my arrival in Belgrade as bureau chief with United Press International.

She wanted to introduce me to Stefanija Djilas, the second wife of the Yugoslav Partisan leader and later dissident who was serving a lengthy prison term for publicizing hostile propaganda against the state.

It was agreed we would meet in the Excelsior Hotel, one of several World War I and older vintage hotels in the Yugoslav capital.

The woman was obviously a link between the Djilases and the western world, and I did not delve any further into that.

It was agreed that if Mrs. Djilas had any news to convey to the outside world about her husband's fate, she could do so through me. We exchanged addresses and telephone numbers and took our respective leaves.

The Yugoslav security services obviously knew more about our Western friends than I did, because they did not remain in Belgrade very long.

It was the practice in Eastern Europe to submit your passports at hotels for verification. When the two visitors received their passports back that evening, they had, unbeknownst to them, been stamped with visas limiting their stay to 24 hours.

Since the stamps were in Serbo-Croatian, a language they could not read, they thus found themselves in violation of the visa stays and were expelled from the country before I could see them again.

Mrs. Djilas never found cause to call me, and I didn't see her again until her husband was released from prison with an early amnesty in January of 1967.

It took her husband a period of time to get away from the prison regimen. At our first meal together, he had to excuse himself for his eating habits. The authorities at the Sremska Mitrovica prison, up the Sava River from Belgrade, had only given the inmates 20 minutes per meal.

He apologized a couple of times for eating so fast.

We did several interviews, print and film, before I left Belgrade in March, but we were to meet again shortly thereafter.

The Yugoslav government also had returned his passport, and agreed to allow him to travel abroad.

He took advantage of this to accept a visiting professorship at Princeton in 1968, the alma mater of his publisher, William Jovanovich, who was also of Montenegrin extraction.

We met again there shortly after his arrival.

He invited us to the home that Princeton had provided him and his wife during his stay, and we were not surprised to be checked by security personnel before we were admitted.

What we did not know, and learned through Milovan and Steffie, was that there was another famous figure right next door, who also warranted security attention.

It was Svetlana Allilujeva, Stalin's daughter, a recent defector from the Soviet Union.

It was a failing on my part that I never asked Milovan whether he, the author of "Conversations with Stalin," had ever had any serious conversations with Stalin's daughter.

It was another failing not to have suggested a meeting between Milovan and another dissident, Alexander Solzhenitsyn, who by this time was ensconced protectively in the mountain isolation of Cavendish, Vt.

That would have been a conversation on which I would have loved to eavesdrop.

Milovan Djilas's criticism of the crushing of the Prague spring by the Soviets in 1968 resulted in the withdrawing of his passport, and he did not get it back until the late 1980s.

But in those two decades, he continued his writing of history, novels and articles from his comfortable apartment at Palmoticeva 8 in Belgrade.

I didn't return there until the summer of 1989.

I had timed my visit to the Balkans around June 28 because of the historical implications of that date, not only for the Balkans, but for the world.

That was the date of the Battle of Kosovo, the defeat of the Serbs by the Turks in 1389 which opened the floodgates to southeastern Europe for the Ottoman Empire.

It was also the date for the start of World War I.

The Austrian archduke was warned by his own military intelligence not to parade through Sarajevo on June 28, 1914, because it would invoke the memory of the occupation by another occupying power, the Ottoman Empire.

Franz Ferdinand ignored the warning, and was assassinated by a small group of Bosnians – Serbs, Croats and Muslims – who were reacting against this new imperial power, Austria-Hungary.

Sir Winston Churchill once remarked that the Balkans have experienced more history than they can consume.

The most recent Balkan wars, of the 1990s , are another confirmation of this.

The new leader of post-Tito Yugoslavia, Slobodan Milosevic, was turning the 600th anniversary of this defeat at Kosovo Polje, the Field of the Blackbirds, into a nationalistic orgy of celebration. Some press estimates indicated that as many as 2 million Serbs in exile, from as far away as Australia, were coming to participate in the pilgrimage to the battle site on June 28, 1989.

My other Serbian acquaintances in Belgrade were unsettled by this outpouring of chauvinism, and anxious over what it might portend.

They were not even considering attending the premiere of the film that Milosevic had commissioned, Boi Kosovo (The Battle of Kosovo), to celebrate it.

But they were able to obtain tickets for the showing of the film for me. It was not dissimilar from "Braveheart" or "The Battle of the Bulge".

I saw the film twice, the first time in Belgrade and the second in Kolasin.

Kolasin was the birthplace of Milovan Djilas in the mountain fastness of Montenegro. It was only coincidentally one of my overnight stops on the itinerary I had crafted for the trip.

I had spent months setting up the itinerary of my six-week trip to Europe, and the smoothness of the transition paid for every second of preparation.

The Balkan portion began in Belgrade for a four-day stay, a flight to Dubrovnik for two nights, and then a trip by van up into the mountains of Montenegro and across to Peč in Kosovo, the poorest region of Europe. From there, it was to proceed to Ohrid, in Macedonia, over to Skopje, and back to Belgrade.

Friends in Dubrovnik tried to persuade me to buy a villa there and stay, and I was tempted to consider it, especially after climbing the hills above it to a vista reminiscent of my year in Carmel Highlands in California.

A couple of years later, I reflected on such a move, with many of the villas and the hotel I had stayed at in Dubrovnik in ruins from Serbian guns.

But none of my friends and colleagues, east or west, anticipated such excess in the summer of 1989.

Even though the seeds of such excess were sprouting, even in the mountain isolation of Kolasin.

The town had been mobilized for a showing of Boi Kosovo on the night that I stayed at its modest and only hotel.

It was to be shown on a large screen in the hotel lobby, and everybody was there.

It gradually became obvious what was afoot.

When I had served as a foreign correspondent in Belgrade in the mid-60s, Kosovo-Metohija as it then was called, was a provincial backwater in the bowels of the Balkans.

Its population of 1.5 million already consisted of 900,000 Albanians and 600,000 Serbs.

By the time I visited the region for the first time in 1989, the exodus of Serbs and a surging Albanian birth rate had reduced the Serbs to 300,000 and raised the Albanian population to more than 1.2 million.

Milosevic already had reversed the measures of autonomy granted by Tito before his death, and cries of the right of return could be heard throughout the Serbian nation.

Nowhere was this more stark than in Kolasin, a mountain den of warriors and patriots, whether to clan or tribe or nation.

Years later, when my Bible studies finally began penetrating into the original Hebrew, Aramaic and Greek, I ran across the Greek word kolasin in the Gospels.

How apt that word was for that mountain village.

The passage is from Matthew 25.

Matthew quotes Jesus describing what is going to happen at Judgment Day:

"When the Son of Man arrives in his glory, and all the angels with him, then he will sit down on his glorious throne. And all the nations will be gathered before him, and he will separate people one from another, just as a shepherd separates the sheep from the goats. And he will put the sheep on the right hand, but the goats on the left." Matthew 25:31-33. NWT Jesus subsequently explains what will happen to those, upon his arrival, who do not treat his true servants just as they would him.

"And these shall go away into eternal punishment: but the righteous into eternal life." Matthew 25:46 ASV

The Greek word in the last passage, for eternal punishment, or everlasting cutting-off, is kolasin.

Kolasin was an isolated mountain hamlet, cut off from the world, to the point that the only way Milosevic could reach it was via a televised broadcast to one television set set up in the village hotel.

Milosevic was mobilizing, but for what – war.

The issue came up upon my return to Belgrade, and a long chat with Milovan about the future.

He was uneasy about the nationalistic fervor.

So I asked him if such Serbian nationalism would have ever developed if his Serbian Partisan colleague Aleksandr Rankovic had managed to gain power after Tito left the scene.

Even though Tito had removed Rankovic from power during the 1960s because of alleged excesses by the security apparatus under Rankovic's control, Djilas demurred.

He was Tito's right-hand man, his hammer, Djilas said.

He would never have submitted to nationalistic excess, and endangered the united Yugoslav state.

As it was, Tito, like many chief executives, of state, church or corporation, never prepared well for his succession.

He outlived or outmaneuvered all his deputies, Edvard Kardelj, Milovan Djilas and Aleksandr Rankov, and never groomed anyone to take their place.

Thus the Serbs, the Balkans, and the world, got Milosevic.

One can only speculate what might have happened if Milosevic had allowed the Slovenians and Croatians to separate from Yugoslavia without retaliation.

Bosnia had historically been a territorial disaster for all conquerors, military or religious

It had resisted Rome and Constantinople, and their competing doctrines of Christianity. It had accepted Ottoman Turkey's promise of autonomy if it allowed the Turks to advance toward the north, and Vienna. It gave Islam a very loose embrace and allowed its progeny to proceed to Istanbul in the elite Janissary officer corps.

And it had welcomed many of the Serbian and Croatian fellow citizens to Sarajevo over the years to a more open and less nationalistic atmosphere than within either the Ottoman Empire, the Kingdom of the Serbs, Croats and Slovenes or the Socialist Federal Republic of Yugoslavia.

It was this kind of atmosphere that welcomed the world at the 1984 Winter Olympics.

And when a New York Times correspondent asked the chairman of the Olympics that year, Pavle Lukac, whether he was worried that there wasn't any snow, he replied with Bosnian aplomb, although he himself was a transplanted Serb from Belgrade of Hungarian extraction.

Don't you want the athletes to all arrive here? he asked in reply.

Of course.

Don't you want all the spectators to arrive here? he went on.

Of course, was the answer.

Then as soon as they are all here, the snow will come, Pavle assured his questioner.

And come it did, to the point that some of the early events had to be postponed because of the excess of snow.

What would have happened to Bosnia if so much of the world had not been exposed to its beauty and nonchalance at the 1984 Olympics?.

And what would have happened to Kosovo if Milosevic had not been so foolish as to turn his attention to Bosnia instead of his initial concern, Kosovo?

As it was, a quarter of a million people died and 2 million were displaced in Bosnia and other parts of Yugoslavia before the battles ended.

If Milosevic had concentrated on Kosovo first, it most assuredly would have been worse. And the world might have cared even less.

As for Milovan Djilas, he was still railing at such injustice and criticizing his old Communist colleagues turned nationalists to the very end of his life.

And always had been willing to pay the price.

CHAPTER 34

PAVLE LUKAČ

1929 - 1988

Pavle Lukač, former correspondent for Yugoslav newspapers and spokesman for the Winter Olympics in Sarajevo in 1984, died in 1988. An obituary was not available at this printing.

PAVLE

Pavle Lukac was a dynamo.

When I first met him, he was a reporter for Vecernje Novosti,, a Belgrade tabloid comparable more to the The Daily Sketch of London and the old Boston Record and New York Daily Mirror than the gray and staid Communist Party and Yugoslav government papers in the capital, Borba and Politika.

We first began to work together when the report of the ouster of Vice President Aleksandr Rankovic leaked out.

I had been warned by one of my contacts at Tanjug, the Yugoslav news agency.

I was not advised what was happening on the morrow, but was told to stay by my machine because a big story was breaking.

So I was all ready with translator handy when Tanjug broke the story.

President Josip Broz Tito alleged that Rankovic, in charge of security for the Yugoslav state, had had Tito's private quarters bugged, ostensibly to assure himself that he, Rankovic, was not the target of any plot.

The ouster of Rankovic, and an underground swelling of support for the Serbian strongman via fax and gossip, led to rumors of coup and countercoup throughout the six-member federal republic for weeks, and Pavle was in the vortex.

Both of us had received mysterious faxes on our office machines, and soon he, I, and representatives of the East German, Czech and Russian press and diplomatic corps were comparing our faxes and notes to determine whether the Rankovic ouster was going to be the end of political turmoil in that part of the Balkans.

I had inquired of the first secretary at the U.S. Embassy as to what he knew of the Rankovic affair and what was boiling beneath the surface.

But Adolph (Spike) Dubs was less than forthcoming with me. He gave me nothing, although he was too competent not to have had anything.

But when I started to mine nuggets of information about what was going on from my underground shafts that stretched beneath the Iron Curtain, I got a call from Spike.

I just told him to read my wire dispatches.

The crisis eased, Tito weathered the storm, and Rankovic, who had been the right arm of Tito's power for two decades, slipped into ignominious retirement.

"Spike" Dubs, an able diplomat, was later posted as first secretary and then chargé d'affaires in Moscow, before being appointed ambassador to Afghanistan.

"Spike" was a victim of perhaps the first shot in the modern jihad of Islamic terrorism, even if that shot did not resound around the world at that time.

He was shot dead in Kabul in February of 1979, a victim of elements then backed by the Soviet Union in its long and failed attempt to rule there.

Pavle played a more favored role in international affairs.

By 1984, he had been appointed chairman of the International Winter Olympics at Sarajevo.

His tutelage remained a fond memory for all who participated or attended those games, and left them horrified at the civil war that destroyed that beautiful city in the early 1990s and cost so many lives. Those memories also galvanized their efforts to put pressure on all elements to bring the ethnic cleansing to a halt, after the death of a quarter million and the displacement of eight times that number.

Pavle also left a legacy of unflappability with the press. Correspondents were pressing Pavle about the lack of snow as the day of the opening ceremonies approached, and the mountain slopes lay barren of snow.

Don't you want the athletes all to get here? Pavle would ask the foreign correspondents.

They of course would agree.

Don't you want all the spectators to get here? Pavle would ask.

Again they would affirm that that would also be desirable.

Then let the planes all come in with the athletes, Pavle assured them.

And then the chartered planes with all the spectators will arrive, Pavle said.

And then the snow will come. The correspondents, dubious, waited. The planes came in. And then came the snow, just as Pavle had predicted.

So much, that several of the early events had to be postponed so it could be cleared.

Pavle was a dynamo.

JOHN A. DONATI, 71,
WAS FOOTBALL COACH

WILBRAHAM – John A. Donati, 71, of 250 Mountain Road, a former standout athlete and Springfield football coach, died Wednesday at Baystate Medical Center in Springfield.

He taught biology and physiology and was a guidance counselor at the former Technical High School in Springfield. He also was a guidance counselor at Central High School in Springfield. He retired in 1989.

He coached football at Springfield's Cathedral High School in the early 1960s and was the third coach in the school's history. He entered the Springfield school system in 1958 at Duggan Junior High School and was an assistant coach at Classical and Tech before taking the Cathedral post in 1962.

He was previously a physical education instructor at Cortland (N.Y.) State College.

Born in New Britain, Conn., he graduated from New Britain High School, where he was a standout football, baseball and basketball player. He captained the football team and was named its most valuable player.

He attended prep school at LaSalle Academy in Oakdale, N.Y., and then entered Syracuse University, where he earned bachelor's and master's degrees.

He played three years as both fullback and quarterback at Syracuse and earned the Outstanding Player Award in 1951. He also helped coach the freshman football team at Syracuse for several years.

He was an Army veteran and a communicant of St. Cecilia's Church. He lived in Springfield before moving here in 1965. He was a member of Phi Gamma Delta and a past member of the Elks Lodge in Springfield.

He leaves his wife, the former Gloria Vosburgh, two sons, William S. of Wilbraham and James A. of North Grafton; a brother, Richard of Old Saybrook, Conn.; two sisters, Nora Guenther of New Britain and Ann Cimadon of Enfield, and two grandchildren.

The funeral will be at noon Monday at Sampson's Chapel of the Acres in Springfield with burial in Adams Cemetery. Calling hours will precede the funeral. Memorial contributions may be made to the American Diabetes Association Massachusetts Affiliate, 2348 Post Road, Warwick, RI 92886,

Died September 22, 1999   ***Union-News*** *(Springfield, Mass.) September 25, 1999*

JOHN A. DONATI
1928 – 1999

John Donati was a member of the round table.

In fact, he was the only member of the round table with whom I was acquainted the Friday night that I walked into Santi's, in what was then Springfield's Italian South End.

It was the early '70s, and things had changed a lot in seven years.

In the early '60s, I had worked from early morning until mid-afternoon on the United Press International radio wire, and then enjoyed an occasional moment relaxing at Jimmy Shea's, an Irish pub on Worthington Street, where I could quaff a 10-cent beer before going home to supper. (I eventually could afford the 20-cent glass).

But by the early '70s, after a stint in Europe and repatriation, I was working nights at The Springfield (Morning) Union and and needed a bite and a beverage late at night, after the early editions.

One night, I tried out Santi's.

John hailed me over to the round table from the bar, and began introducing me to the other knights.

There was Bob Ryan, the pharmacist, Ed Shea, an assistant principal at a junior high school, George Lawler, the fireman, Pete Gagne, another pharmacist, Al Veronesi, the 7-Up bottler, and Julio Nozzolillo, the grade school teacher.

They were wont to meet at Santi's Friday nights for pizza and an evening of lively banter.

Ryan took an instant shine to me because I was in the Ballantine Ale phase, a very early one I might add, of my brewing connoisseurship.

His father, a popular and respected pharmacist in Springfield's North end, had been a Ballantine Ale drinker.

From then on, for a number of years, the minute I walked in the door on Friday night, there were instantly two bottles of Ballantine Ale on the table for me.

Notice had immediately been taken of my capacity, developed in Bavaria, one which fortunately has diminished with the years.

It was difficult to get a word in with this bunch, and even harder to buy a round.

During my social career, I had subscribed to my father's doctrine, developed at the Gray Barn in Whitinsville, Mass., of never accepting or buying rounds.

He, as a member of the Board of Assessors, did not want to be beholden to any property owner in town, and in fact often dropped in to his local after an evening of work for one lone beer before going home.

At Santi's, this was an impossible regimen to follow. One had to fight to buy a round, and seldom caught up.

I eventually became close friends with two other members of the round table, Ryan and Veronesi, and have John Donati to thank for that.

John and I recognized each other that night at Santi's because we were neighbors.

John lived up on Mountain Road in Wilbraham, overlooking the Mount Holyoke range and Westover Air Force Base to the north and west. It was a beautiful piece of property.

I had envied those living in the neighborhood when I first was invited to move out there, and my wife and I had met John and Gloria socially in Wilbraham.

John also had introduced me to his next door neighbor Waldemar

Chapter 35

Donner, a fascinating character whose career ranged from being an engineer at Radio Kiev in Ukraine before World War II to designing tuners for Cadillac cars for F. W. Sickles, a Chicopee Falls electronics firm, in the 1970s.

If there were no life in a party, John would resuscitate it.

He was not a raconteur.

It was just that John had never heard a joke he didn't like.

Joketellers gravitated toward John, and he not only emboldened them, but made them better in the telling.

We had been a welcome young addition to the older mountain gang during our first two years in Wilbraham.

A decade later, the older folk were slowing down, and we moved into our own, younger crowd.

It eventually seemed incumbent to invite several of the Santi couples to mingle with some of our new Wilbraham neighbors.

Freda Clark had sold her farmhouse, land and chicken coop shortly after we had built our house on land that we had purchased from the Clarks several years before. She had then built a smaller one-story house across the street

The Bolduc family had bought the Clark house, and we decided that the chicken coop, now cleaned up from various detritus and with a new coat of paint, would be the perfect place for the party.

The Donatis and the Ryans accepted invitations.

Mary Ryan was just beginning to enjoy an active social life.

Not only was she a nurse.

She had borne, nursed, and was in the process of raising eight children of her own. And looked as though she hadn't had any.

Bob could not have been easy to live with, although you couldn't tell it by Mary.

If it had been a long time since the pizza disappeared when the bar closed at 2 p.m., it was not above Bob to invite stragglers home for breakfast.

I allowed myself that indulgence just once, and was amazed at Mary's easy hospitality.

I tried emulating Bobby once after a bowling banquet. We had played cards for several hours after the meal at the Polish-American Club and several of us were hungry again. Butch Opalinski, the local butcher for the Indian Orchard section of Springfield, offered several of what he regarded as the best steaks around that were hanging in his shops. It was generally agreed by fellow bowlers Jim Adam and Bill Garvey that they would taste delicious at 3 in the morning. When we arrived at my house for the feast, the reaction was not quite so warm as that generally accorded her spouse by Mary Ryan. But that is another vignette.

Mary had taken up golf, was getting out socially, and it was doing both her and the people who loved her much good.

In fact, at the chicken coop party, as it came to be called, she enjoyed herself immensely, and even managed to overimbibe a little.

That was something she immediately recognized. It was at that point that she lurched toward John Donati and me.

"What am I going to do?" she pleaded. "Bobby is going to kill me."

John and I gaped at the incongruity of it all.

Each of us grabbed one arm and sturdily guided Mary to her mode of transportation.

Bobby isn't going to do anything. He won't dare, we assured Mary.

Not that he would have anyway.

Nevertheless, John and I felt like Sir Galahads.

Mary was like a feather to John.

His obituary noted his athleticism

That athleticism was understated.

He never talked much about it himself.

One time, he did mention that the Syracuse football team had gone to the Orange Bowl one year after his playing days, when he was on the team's coaching staff.

He didn't leave out the fact that Alabama whomped his Orangemen.

Or that Alabama had a pretty good quarterback that year.

His name was Bart Starr.

The wounds from that defeat hurt less through the years as Starr's star climbed higher in the football heavens.

John preferred to talk about others.

One of the others was Jim Brown, who was just starting his athletic career at Syracuse as John was finishing his, and joined the coaching staff at Syracuse.

John would get excited describing Brown's accomplishments on the lacrosse field, which other athletes also marveled at.

Jim Brown was a two-way All American.

John Donati may not have been an All-Ameican, but he certainly had a way about him.

ALBERT C. VERONESI

1919 – 2004

AGAWAM – Albert Veronesi of Agawam entered into eternal rest on Monday, August 16, 2004, surrounded by his family.

Born in Springfield, he lived in Agawam for the past 45 years. He was president of the 7-UP Bottling Co., retiring in 1988. His son, Paul Veronesi, who passed away March 17, 2004, joined his dad and his dad's partner, Richard Torrey, working for the 7-UP franchise in Hampshire and Franklin counties.

Albert was a communicant of St. John the Evangelist Church. Albert was a veteran of World War II. He spent three years in New Guinea as a member of the 565th Signal AW Bn 5th Air Force. He was a radio operator attached to a radar outfit. He worked with a radar outpost whose primary job was interception and notification of approaching enemy aircraft.

He was a lifetime member of the Springfield Elks and a fulltime member of the Elmcrest Country Club for 30 years.

He was a loving husband, father, brother, and a friend to all who knew him. He was always willing to lend a helping hand to anyone who asked. He loved a good joke and had a wonderful sense of humor. He enjoyed sports, especially baseball and the Yankees.

He was the son of Giacomo and Palmira Veronesi. He is survived by his wife Estelle (Stachowicz) Veronesi, predeceased by his son, Paul Veronesi, and his daughter Diane Veronesi. He leaves a sister, Mary (Veronesi) Anderson, several nieces and nephews and his godchildren, John W. Anderson, Gary Mayotte and Dr. Paul Rigali, Jr. He also leaves his best friend of 70 years, Paul Rigali, Sr.

Funeral services will be held Thursday, August 19, 2004, at 9 a.m. from the Colonial Forastiere Funeral Home, 985 Main St. Liturgy of Christian Burial at 10 a.m. in St. John the Evangelist Church, Main St., both in Agawam. Burial will follow in St. Michael's Cemetery, 1601 State St., Springfield. Calling hours are Wednesday from 2 p.m. to 4 p.m. and 6 p.m to 8 p.m. In lieu of flowers memorial donations may be made to St. John the Evangelist Church or to the Baystate Visiting Nurse Association and Hospice, 50 Maple St., P.O. Box 9085, Springfield, Ma. 01102-90584

Died Aug. 16, 2004   *The* (Springfield, Mass.) ***Republican,*** *Aug. 17. 2004*

A LEGACY

Very nice guy.

That's how the name Albert C Veronesi translated for retired Massachusetts State Police Lt. Roy Anderson, one of his many friends.

His best friend, Paul Rigali, shared Albert's legacy at his funeral.

"I set out to find a friend but couldn't find one.

I set out to be a friend and friends were everywhere."

Al was a member of two tables at Santi's restaurant in Springfield's South End, and it was difficult to get a seat at either one.

The Knights dominated the Friday night Round Table next to the bar. (See DONATI)

The days dominated the table in the restaurant for lunch.

After years of humping as a deliveryman for the 7-Up franchise in Hampshire and Franklin counties in the Connecticut Valley of Massachusetts, Al was offered a share of the franchise at his boss's retirement.

He and his junior partner maintained and built up the very successful business, which gave Al more and more time for relaxation and golf.

Lunch at Santi's was the most relaxed time of all.

The table had eight seats, and Al owned the one next to the kitchen.

Often, the eight were filled, and the overflow filled an adjacent table and booths.

The gathering attracted business and professional men, lawyers and politicians, policemen and city officials.

Al had not had it easy.

Although he was born in the United States, the family went through some very difficult times, and Al returned to Italy at the age of six.

Years later, at the 19th hole of a golf course, it came out what he was doing there.

George Wegman of Wilbraham, father of the portraitist William Wegman, was describing how his B-24 had crashed while on a bombing run over Italy during World War II.

During the narrative, Al interrupted Bill to have him repeat the name of the village into which he had parachuted.

"That's where I picked olives," Al interjected.

The two men then conducted a lengthy dialogue on that little mountain village that had provided a safe haven for both men, from war and an economically perilous peace.

Paul related how Al returned to the States in 1934 and was placed in 7th grade at the age of 16.

Rigali took the ruddy older *paisano* under his younger wing, and the two remained friends for seven decades.

Both entered the military during World War II, Rigali being assigned to a minesweeper in the North Pacific, and Al to a 5th Air Force signal outfit in the South, on New Guinea.

During one of our somber moments together many years later, Al described a letter he had written to his older brother serving in the Army in France.

It came back to him marked deceased.

Albert survived both that shock and the war and returned home safely to begin his professional life, marry and start a family.

He and Estelle had two children.

The oldest was Diane and the youngest Paul.

Diane died in 1957, a blow from which Al never fully recovered.

An unfeeling clergyman had explained that God had taken his daughter. It was an accusation that Albert never accepted.

He was not inclined to attribute the taking of his daughter to God, nor to blame him for it, and was open to considering other possibilities.

He accepted the argument that God knew the DNA of every human being ever born, (Psalm 139:16) and had extended the promise of a resurrection of both the righteous and unrighteous (Acts 24:15).

Although he was not prepared to act seriously on the possibility that his daughter might be reunited with him on this planet earth, he intellectually left the door open for the eventuality.

Tragically, this was to apply also to his son Paul, his pride as a student and athlete, and a loyal son to his father and mother at home.

Paul contracted a serious kidney disease in his early 50s, and after a long and difficult period at home and in hospital, died at the age of 53.

That was on March 17 of 2004. Less than five months later, after battling cancer that had invaded many of his inner organs, Al confided to his best friend Paul that he was ready to go, and did so on Aug. 16.

It turned out that when Al Veronesi no longer occupied a seat, all the rest of them in that corner of Santi's restaurant were also empty.

MRS. ROBERT RYAN

Mrs. Mary (Martin) Ryan, 40, of 30 Spruceland Ave., Springfield, died Monday in Springfield Hospital Medical Center. She leaves her husband, Robert M. Ryan; two sons, Robert and John Ryan; six daughters, Misses Kathleen, Marie, Maureen, Elizabeth, Julia and Linda Ryan; and a brother. The funeral will be Thursday morning at the Hafey funeral home with services in Holy Name Church and burial in Gate of Heaven Cemetery.

Died Nov. 26, 1973   *The* (Springfield, Ma.) ***Daily News,*** *Nov. 28, 1973*

MARY (MARTIN) RYAN
1933 - 1973

Memory refuses to cooperate as to when I found out about the three German sailors.

Bobby Ryan, a drinking and later a golfing buddy, may have told me about them at Santi's, a popular restaurant and watering hole in the Italian South End of Springfield, Massachusetts.

John Donati, a suburban neighbor, former Syracuse University quarterback and later high school coach in Springfield, was responsible for making the connection.

He was sitting at the round table that Friday night in the early '70s when I walked in around 11 p.m. for a lunch break

If that sounds a little late for lunch, we are talking about newsmen here, editors who have worked all evening putting to bed the first editions of a middle-size metropolitan newspaper. Eleven was the perfect time for a leisurely lunch before returning about midnight to update the latest breaking wire stories and put to bed the final city editions.

I had met the Donatis in suburban Wilbraham, and he was the only one I recognized at the Round Table on that particular evening.

He quickly introduced me to the rest of them: Bobby Ryan, a pharmacist, son of a prolific pharmacist who produced a very political family in the city of Springfield; Ed Shea, then a school vice principal (I never did like that job description) and a Ryan buddy; Al Veronesi, a 7-Up bottler from across the river in Agawam; George Lawler, a Springfield fireman; Pete Gagne, another pharmacist; Julio Nozzolillo, an elementary school teacher, all regulars, and several other part-timers who would fill the remaining chairs around the *Stammtisch,* a wonderful German word describing a reserved table for regular guests.

Presiding over it all and a frequent participant in the lively banter was Al Santi, the owner and an imposing man about Avellino, whose forebears had deserted Calabria only as recently as most of the forebears of the others at the table had deserted their disparate homelands.

Last call was 2 a.m., and it was strictly enforced. But that wasn't necessarily the end of the affair. Al Santi's brother Ray had a restaurant without a liquor license just down Main Street that catered to the after-hours crowd that had nothing more to drink but plenty still to say.

They would gather at Ray's Grinders from 2 a.m. on for coffee, a late bite or even an early breakfast.

But every once in a while, Bobby Ryan would decide that Ray's Grinders wasn't good enough and would invite one or two of his closer friends home for breakfast.

And the cook?

Invariably it was Bobby's wife, Mary, a professional nurse and the mother of eight, who would be either awakened or summoned, or both, to cook breakfast for the invited guests.

And miracle of miracles, she would.

It was as though she had spent a considerable time, despite the hour, preparing to be the happy hostess.

Dressed, coiffed, bright, gracious, whatever.

And pleased to see Bobby's longtime friends, who early on learned not to abuse the invitations, and any new ones.

I couldn't believe it the first morning I accepted, with trepidation, the invitation.

Mary seemed to be the wife that any and every man would treasure.

And she became a linchpin in a small circle of couples which developed from then on as she slowly moved into a social circle of parties and golf from her dedicated domesticity.

We had been a welcome young addition to the older mountain gang during our first two years in Wilbraham.

A decade later, the older folk were slowing down, and we moved into our own, younger crowd.

It eventually seemed incumbent to invite several of the Santi couples to mingle with some of our new Wilbraham neighbors.

Freda Clark had sold her farmhouse, land and chicken coop shortly after we had built our house on land that we had purchased from the Clarks several years before. She had then built a smaller one-story house across the street

The Bolduc family had bought the Clark house, and we decided that the chicken coop, now cleaned up from various detritus and with a new coat of paint, would be the perfect place for the party.

The Donatis and the Ryans accepted invitations.

Mary Ryan was just beginning to enjoy an active social life.

Not only was she a nurse.

She had borne, nursed, and was in the process of raising eight children of her own. And looked as though she hadn't had any.

Bob could not have been easy to live with, although you couldn't tell it by Mary.

Mary had taken up golf, was getting out socially, and it was doing both her and the people who loved her much good.

In fact, at the chicken coop party, as it came to be called, she enjoyed herself immensely, and even managed to overimbibe a little.

That was something she immediately recognized. It was at that point that she lurched toward John Donati and me.

"What am I going to do?" she pleaded. "Bobby is going to kill me."

John and I gaped at the incongruity of it all.

Each of us grabbed one arm and sturdily guided Mary to her mode of transportation.

Bobby isn't going to do anything. He won't dare, we assured Mary.

Not that he would have anyway.

Nevertheless, John and I felt like Sir Galahads.

The two of us escorted her to her transportation home and safety.

Only after having experienced Mary's hospitality firsthand could I understand the story of the three German sailors.

As I best recall, it happened this way.

Three German sailors with a pass from their vessel in Boston probably didn't know who Horace Greeley was, but decided to go West anyway.

They, for some unexplained reason, hopped on a bus and traveled the 90-odd miles to Springfield, the third largest city in Massachusetts on the banks of the Connecticut River.

There, they undoubtedly experienced the architectural delights of The Municipal Group, comprising City Hall and Symphony Hall flanking the Campanile, the replica of St. Mark's in Venice which at that point was the tallest structure in the city.

They also had the opportunity to view the imposing Springfield Municipal Library, and the adjacent Quadrangle off State Street with its attendant museums.

But walking back down State Street toward Main, and querying after their wanderings which direction the bus station was, they somehow were guided "links" instead of "rechts".

After about five blocks hoofing in the wrong direction, they stopped in at Santi's to verify their directions.

Their first contact at Santi's was the Round Table.

By that time, it was late in the evening, and the question arose whether there were any more buses back to Boston.

Bobby Ryan resolved that quickly, after a sociable quaffing of beers to get better acquainted.

The three German sailors would stay the night in Springfield, and return to Boston in the morning.

And where would they stay? At the Ryans, of course.

In some quarters, such a maneuver might be enough to sink the Graf Spee, but not at Mary's house.

The German sailors were received, bedded and breakfasted with the same patient, gracious hospitality as all previous unexpected guests.

And what happened the following Christmas. Gifts flowed in a reverse Marshall Plan from Germany to the eight Ryan children. And for several Christmases thereafter.

One year, the gifts came in the form of taped music and messages, all in German.

My wife, a Bavarian, and I, with a degree of fluency in German, volunteered to translate.

Joy to the world.

"Cast thy bread upon the waters," the mighty congregator said in Ecclesiastes, Chapter 11, Verse 1, "for thou shalt find it after many days."

The Ryans cast their bread upon the waters, and it came back soaked in goulash.

Until 1973.

There were late Indian summer days in November of 1973. Bobby and three of his friends were golfing at Elmcrest Country Club in East Longmeadow when the telephone call came in.

Mary had fallen on her driveway at home and had broken a bone. The foursome broke off the match immediately and Bobby headed to the hospital.

The first queries, though sincere, were informal and almost matter-of-fact. But with each passing hour, the concerns deepened.

Mary, in breaking a bone, had released a latent villain in her body.

This was quite early diagnosed as acute leukemia.

Two days after the fall, Mary Ryan confided to her female friends during telephone conversations that she was going to die.

Death came swiftly.

Mary Ryan died on Nov. 26, 1973, a few days after her fall.

It was a very large funeral at Holy Name Church in the Forest Park section of Springfield on Thursday, Nov. 29, 1973.

An epilogue appeared at the close of the Academy-award winning film "Chariots of Fire" about the Olympic runner and Scottish missionary Eric Liddell, who died interned by the Japanese in China in 1945.

It said: "All Scotland Mourned."

On that last week of November of 1973, it seemed as though "All Springfield mourned."

ROGER E. SYLVESTER

1911 – 1989

SOUTH YARMOUTH – Roger Ellis Sylvester, 78, of South Yarmouth, a retired managing editor for the Springfield newspapers, died Tuesday in Cape Cod Hospital, Hyannis.

He joined the staff of The Evening Union in 1935, and then was transferred to the copy desk of the morning paper in 1939. In 1950 he was named news editor, and served in that capacity until being appointed managing editor of The Springfield Union and Sunday Republican in 1969. He retired in 1970.

Born in Springfield, he was a 1929 graduate of the former Technical High School, and a 1933 graduate of Dartmouth College.

He was a six-year treasurer of the Dartmouth Club of Cape Cod, and served two terms as president of the Senior Citizens Social Club. He was also a member of the Retired Mens' Club, the FISH organization, the Springfield Newspapers 25 Year Club, the Alpha Sigma Phi fraternity and the Pemaquid Contract Bridge Club.

He enjoyed gardening and raising tropical fish.

His former wife, Adeline (Hewitt) Sylvester, died in 1984.

He leaves his wife, the former Helen Hancock, and a daughter, Helen Curtis of Lake City, Ga.

A graveside service will be Thursday morning in Ancient Cemetery, Yarmouthport.

Hallett Funeral Home is in charge.

Memorial contributions may be made to the Dartmouth College Alumni Fund, 103 Main St., Hanover, N.H., 03755, or to any charity.

Died June 27, 1989   *The* (Springfield, Mass.) *Union-News, June 28, 1989*

⌒

MIXED EMOTIONS

It always amazed me how Roger Sylvester could remain so tranquil amid the flood of news copy.

Roger was the news editor of The (Springfield, Mass.) Morning Union when I arrived back in Springfield from Belgrade, Yugoslavia in 1967.

The Union was one of the few newspapers in the Northeast which subscribed to all of the major news services, The Associated Press, United Press International, The New York Times Service and the combined Washington Post-Los Angeles Times news service.

Even though The Union and its Sunday Republican edition had large news holes, there was a tremendous pile of copy to go through.

Yet every evening, at 9:30 p.m., Roger would stand up, pick up his brown bag, and retire to the morgue (newspaper argot for library) for lunch.

Most of his decision-making had been made, and if any changes were later dictated by late-breaking events, he calmly adjusted to it.

I envy that still.

Because not only did he handle the job with a pacific equanimity, but with consummate skill and judgment.

As I was assigned more frequently to the Page 1 desk just under Roger, I began to appreciate that more and more.

Invariably he chose the best story of the major ones that were going on Page 1 of all those that had been provided by the various services.

In many cases, it was not only the better story, but also the shorter.

And my respect, and my effort to emulate his judgment, intensified.

I could not even try to emulate his calm.

As a series of Saturday night massacres decimated the newsroom as part of the ownership changeover in the late 1960s and early 1970s, it became obvious that Roger was getting close to retirement.

Management was kind enough to honor him with an appointment as managing editor. It was an appointment that previous superiors would have been wise to have done much earlier.

But Roger, a gray-headed gentleman with a wry smile, was ready for his beloved Cape Cod.

At his retirement dinner across the Connecticut River at the Storrowton Tavern on the Eastern States Exposition grounds in West Springfield, Roger stood to deliver his farewell.

He said he was leaving with mixed emotions, joy – he hesitated – mixed with rapture, mixed with ecstasy, mixed with exhilaration.

The audience roared.

HARRY CHARKOUDIAN, 84
WAS OWNER OF DRUGSTORE

Harry N. Charkoudian, 84, of 935 Roosevelt Ave., founder and former owner of Charkoudian Drugs, died Sunday in Ludlow Hospital.

Charkoudian was a member of the Springfield Rotary Club since 1957 and he was recipient of the Paul Harris Fellow Rotary International Award in 1983.

He was a 32nd degree Mason of the Hampden Lodge of Masons.

He was past president of the Springfield Druggists' Association and former director of Cooperative United Bank

Born in Marash, Turkey, he had lived in this city most of his life.

Charkoudian was graduated from Mount Hermon School and the Massachusetts College of Pharmacy, He received an honorary bachelor of science degree in pharmacy from Hampden College of Pharmacy in 1973.

He was a member of Melha Temple Shrine and Springfield Lodge of Elks Lodge and a life member of the Massachusetts Pharmaceutical and American Pharmaceutical Associations.

His first wife, Grace (Elgin) Charkoudian, died in 1966.

He leaves his widow, Rose (Karakian) Charkoudian, and a brother, Edward of Centerville.

The funeral will be held Wednesday at Dickinson-Streeter Funeral Home with services in St. Gregory's Armenian Church. Burial will be in Hillcrest Park Cemetery. Memorial contributions may be made to St. Gregory's Church or First Baptist Church of West Springfield;

Died Aug. 26, 1984   *Springfield* (Mass.) ***Daily News****, Aug. 28, 1984*

HARRY CHARKOUDIAN
1900 – 1984

Harry Charkoudian was introduced to me by Jimmy Guarnera.

Jimmy was one of those oldtime pharmacists who spent almost as much time behind the soda fountain as in the pharmacy.

His drug store on Boston Road in North Wilbraham, Mass., on the same path General Knox took to get his guns from upper New York State to Dorchester Heights during the Revolutionary War, was a social center during the early 1960s.

North Wilbraham was still a village then, distinctive from the growing larger center, which was becoming a suburban boom town. It had its own small post office, a small grocery run by a popular Lebanese family, a bar, and several stations, two for gas and one for fire.

Everybody knew each other, and cared.

By the time we returned in the late 1960s, things were changing swiftly. Jimmy was preparing for retirement and sold the business, but kept the building, which was divided into two, a drug store and a package store.

Jimmy, despite being one of the most generous persons in town, and as a businessman, one of the least demanding, nevertheless was able to retire and utilize his membershjp at the Country Club of Wilbraham, a nine-hole facility with too few holes and too many members.

He encouraged me to come out to play on Mondays, when townies were allowed to golf at very reasonable rates.

Residents of Wilbraham were allowed to play on Monday mornings for only $10 a round, which was considered a bargain for a semi-private course. The rates at the time for Chicopee Country Club and Franconia Golf Club, public courses in Chicopee and Springfield respectively, were $2 to $3 a round.

I finally had overcome my longtime antipathy to the sport.

Despite my early introduction to golf by my late Uncle Chick and a brief fling one summer during college at the Milford, Mass., golf club with Herman (Pinky) Roche and Jack (Mull) Mulligan*, I had harbored a reverse snobbism toward golf which blossomed during adolescence.

There were three ways to earn money in Whitinsville as a kid before the supermarkets moved in and made a fourth, for bag boys and stock boys.

*Pinky was Herman Roche, a school classmate for 12 years and fellow graduate and basketball teammate at Northbridge High School. He later graduated from the University of Massachusetts and went on to a successful business career in Chicago. Mull was Jack Mulligan, another schoolmate for 12 years, another basketball teammate and later graduate of Georgetown who remained in Washington with the General Services Administration.

One was as a caddie at the Whitinsville Golf Club. That milieu included the executives of the Whitin Machine Works, and the professional people in town. There was no room for anybody else, and the waiting list for even the elite in town to join was long. The only member I excluded from the category of swells was my minister at the United Presbyterian Church, Dr. Orville J. Fleming.

He was absolved of two vices, golf membership and his subscription to the Sunday New York Times, which although produced on Saturday, lay respectfully at his front door until Monday before being retrieved.

The second level of adolescent employment, one step down the social ladder from caddies (some of whom were recruited to Wiano on Cape Cod during summer vacations) were newspaper boys.

There were two groups of newsboys, the ones who delivered The Worcester Telegram in the morning and those who delivered The Evening Gazette in the afternoon. A few Boston papers were thrown in, but just a few.

Bobby Bergquist, a neighbor who had one of the routes operated out of Mame Sherlock's news store on Prospect Street, enlisted me to sub for him when I was 10, and when Berkie, who later married the daughter of a West Point graduate and himself became a general, moved on to better things, I took over his route.

The job at the bottom of the pecking order was that of pinboy. It was hot, physical, seasonal and smoky. And although there were respectable bowlers in town, even church leagues, there was something déclassé about setting up pins.

This avocational prejudice lingered through the years, and militated against even a visit to any of the golf courses on the Monterey Peninsula in California despite an otherwise full year spent in that idyllic setting while attending the Army Language School.

Jimmy Guarnera broke down the prejudice, although I still entertained a jaundiced attitude toward many of the members of the country club, until I got to know them better over the years.

I became a swing member of a foursome that included Jimmy, Harry Charkoudian, Joe Donelli and occasionally Phil Murphy, my optician.

Harry, of course, was an Armenian, or to be politically correct, an American of Armenian extraction. Or to be more specific, an Armenian born in Turkey. Or it could be phrased, born in Turkish Armenia, when there was one.

All this was instantly recognizable by the name ending in ian, meaning son of, and the swarthy complexion.

I knew a lot about Armenians, having grown up in a town that accepted many of these refugees from Turkish pogroms before, during and after World War I.

The Whitin Machine Works employed many of them in the toughest, and some of the best paying jobs in the shop, in the foundry and cast iron room.

My father was a paymaster at the factory, and he paid those workers.

An indelible image is the day he took me as a little boy to the platform overlooking the molders in the foundry and explained how difficult the work was.

He also explained that many of those workers were unfortunate refugees, many forced to do that back-breaking work because, even though highly educated, they had not been in the country long enough to learn English well.

Jimmy, Harry and Joe were not the best of golfers, but they were great company.

And I, being younger, bigger and stronger than any of them, was soon boondoggled (I thought boonswaggled was a word) into giving them two strokes on the par fives and one on too many other holes.

Monday mornings became a regular golf day for a couple of years, the younger guy playing with the old men.

Jimmy then suggested that I join the club, and offered to be my sponsor. Payment of a fee at the end of the golfing year led to a waiving of the initiation fee, and my antipathy toward golf morphed into addiction.

One day, Harry told me that he had pieced together a short history of how the members of the family had arrived in the United States. He said that his English was not very good, mentioned that I was a writer, and asked if I would be willing to help him.

I agreed, but on one firm condition.

"What is that?" Harry asked.

That we don't start until after golf season.

We began in November.

It took just two hours a week.

I would visit Harry and his second wife Rose at their comfortable home on Roosevelt Avenue in Springfield for one hour in the middle of the week to interview Harry and gather information.

It would take me about one hour to write it up at home.

The winter weeks rolled by, and the project got more interesting by the week.

I asked Harry about letters, passports, mementoes.

He would come up with things he didn't know he had.

I came up with the realization that I knew some Armenians but not much about history.

I began reading histories of the Ottoman Empire, and before.

By March, Harry and I had copy and proofread a family history that had grown to more than 100 pages.

I told him that if we were going to print enough copies for all the members of the family, it would be best to put it on a computer.

I found a computer store that would allow me to use an Apple II there for a fee, and Harry agreed to advance the $300 to cover that cost.

That was a subject we had never discussed.

Harry had said at the outset that he would compensate me for the work, and that was good enough for me.

Neither of us had anticipated that we were going to write a book.

But it had been completed before another golf season had rolled around, and that was the main thing.

Finally, after a delicious lunch of grape leaves and other kevap dishes, we got down to the issue of compensation.

I had made out an expense voucher.

I handed it to him.

Harry blanched.

I asked him to turn it over.

On the reverse side of the voucher was the rate I was paid per hour at the Springfield newspapers (I was a news editor with double bonuses, regular and executive, which I did not include) and the number of hours that I had worked on the memoir.

He showed both sides to his wife Rose.

She studied it, touched Harry on the arm, and guided him to the next room.

When she brought him back, he had a check in his hand.

It was for the amount requested, half of what was listed in the detailed voucher on the reverse.

I invested it – bought my first computer with it, a DEC (Digital Equipment Corporation) behemoth which I used for a number of years, and wrote a novel on it.

When Harry died, the family members invited me to the funeral, and to the family gathering at an Armenian restaurant in Springfield.

On the morning this piece is being was written, 20 years after Harry's death, I read a piece in The New York Times about Armenians, now relatively free, but still struggling as a nation of 3 million in a very troubled part of the world, the Caucasus.

Scattered around the world are the progeny of those who survived and fled, 4 million.

ROBERT W. MUIR STRICKEN, CO-OWNED REPAIR SHOP

HAMPDEN – Robert W. Muir, 40, of 9 Mountain Drive, co-founder and co-owner of Bob and Paul's Little Workshop, died Wednesday in Baystate Medical Center, Wesson Unit.

He suffered an aneurism on Monday.

His partner, also an auto mechanic, was Paul J. Stasiak of Springfield.

They converted an old (Railway Express) truck into a traveling auto repair shop and their service was increasingly in demand, according to a neighbor.

Born in Springfield, he lived in Hampden 18 years and was a member of the Jehovah's Witnesses.

He leaves his wife, the former Carol Svec; three sons, David R., Eric D. and Timothy J.; two daughters, Kathy J. and Sarah M., all at home, and three sisters, Beverly Brown of Pottstown, Pa., Barbara Grant of Scituate and Nancy Weston of Centerville.

Burial will be at the convenience of the family. Toomey-O'Brien Funeral Home, West Springfield, is in charge.

Died June 17, 1981   *The* (Springfield, Mass.) ***Morning Union***, *Friday, June 19, 1981*

⌒

DUST

Robert W. Muir

Bob Muir was the first Jehovah's Witness I ever allowed into the house.

He had asked one question.

"Are you interested in the Bible?

"Yes," I answered.

"I'll show him," I thought.

"Come on in," I invited.

And he and his companion, Dave Stoddard, walked from the deck into the living room.

I urged them to make themselves comfortable, and headed to the bedroom for my Bibles.

Eleven years after having moved into our new home on Glendale Road in Wilbraham, Mass., an eastern suburb of Springfield, I still didn't have a library, an office, or even shelving for books collected in a number of states and foreign countries.

Most of the books were still in foot lockers.

The Bibles were in one of the bedroom closets.

But it took a while to get them together and show them to my guests.

The main problem was dust.

The Bibles, several in English, one in Russian, one in Ukrainian and a couple in German, both Luther and Zwingli, had lain in the closet for years without ever having been opened.

It was an embarrassing few moments to get them all dusted off before the display,

But display them I did, and seemed to have made an impression on our guests, who probably felt ecstatic about having made contact with a neighbor who had respect for the Holy Word of God.

We engaged in a friendly conversation about where the Bibles had been obtained, our respective interests and occupations.

It turned out Bob was a jack of many trades, including auto mechanic, specializing in Volkwagens.

That may have been another reason he had taken his turn at our door, because there may have been as many as four Volkswagen Beetles in the yard and garage at our house at the time.

The two Witnesses were veterans. They were unobtrusive, friendly and did not overstay their welcome.

And Bob, seemingly impressed by the pile of Bibles on the coffee table, asked whether he could return with a friend.

A couple of weeks later, Bob returned with the friend, who turned out to be Stormin' Norman Miller, a former U.S. Marine and Teamsters union official who had been figuratively dragged into Christian belief by a loving wife who exercised that wonderful Scripture in First Peter, third chapter, first verse:

"In like manner, ye wives, be in subjection to your own husbands; that, even if any obey not the word, they may without the word be gained by the behavior of their wives."

American Standard Version.

After that, it was just like the ancient pitching legend Satchel Paige suggested, that there is no looking back, because the Devil may be gaining on you.

But that's for other chapters.

As for Bob, he and his colleague and co-religionist Paul Stasiak became more than friends.

They became my Volkswagen mechanics, and we had plenty of work for them.

In addition to the four Beetles, one for each member of the family, there were a couple of extra engines in the garage (the chassis frequently died before the engine in those New England winters).

Bob and Paul put into practice an interesting concept.

Rather than tow the disabled cars to a garage for repairs, they would drive the garage to the disabled car, on the road or at home.

They had outfitted an old Railway Express van with most of the equipment and tools that would be required for both minor and many major repairs.

By the time I became a customer, they had a going business, but Bob did confide to me after replacing one engine for a very reasonable charge that he was very pleased to do business with customers who paid fully and on time.

I was equally as pleased for the reliable and quality work.

Three years after the knock on my door, Bob Muir died suddenly of a massive aneurism.

Doctors told his widow Carol that the aneurism was so deep in the brain that it would have been almost impossible to diagnose.

Bob had been an active, loving and provident husband and father of five up to his dying moment.

It was an honor to be asked by his wife to write his obituary.

CHAPTER 41

RUPPRECHT R. SCHERFF
OWNED 'FORT' RESTAURANT

By Ray Kelly

Not many of his restaurant patrons knew that the native German behind all the Bavarian cooking and beer steins had been awarded the Bronze Star for heroism during World War II by the U. S. Army.

SPRINGFIELD – Rupprecht R. Scherff, owner of the landmark downtown Springfield restaurant The Fort and Student Prince, died yesterday at home. He was 81.

Born in Langenholzen, Germany, on Sept. 27, 1914, Scherff served in the German army before emigrating to the United States in 1936.

He enlisted in the U.S. Army in October 1941 and was awarded the Croix de Guerre avec Palms from the French government and the Bronze Star from the U.S. for heroism during World War II.

Scherff's restaurant experience dated back to his childhood, when he worked at his family's restaurant, Gasthaus, in Hanover.

"I helped my mother in the kitchen," he said in a 1994 interview. "The restaurant business drew me like a magnet."

Scherff apprenticed in European restaurants before coming to Springfield, where he worked as a banquet manager for the Highland Hotel in the late 1930s. He began working at the Student Prince in 1949. He became co-owner in 1961 and sole owner a decade later.

James Shriver, president of the Greater Springfield Chamber of Commerce, described Scherff as an integral part of the city.

"In his own way, Rupprecht was the biggest booster of downtown and the most supportive businessman to work with in the city," Shriver said. "He loved the city and was an integral part of it. He will be sorely missed."

Stuart Hurwitz, owner of Pizzeria Uno at Columbus Center and vice president of the Greater Springfield Convention and Visitors Bureau, said that Scherff was a "consummate" restaurateur.

"He built an institution. He was looked up to by everyone," Hurwitz said. "It's going to be a real challenge for (his son) Rudi and the family, but I'm sure they will be up to it."

The restaurant is a favorite gathering place of businessmen and politicians.

U.S. Rep. Richard E. Neal, D-Springfield, said the restaurant's "reputation came from Rupprecht's sense of quality and dedication.

"When Maureen (Neal's wife) and I were first dating more than 20 years ago, this was one of our favorite stops and it still is," the congressman said.

Springfield Mayor Michael J. Albano said, "No matter where people came from, they knew the Fort and they knew Rupprecht. He will be sadly missed."

Judge Mary Hurley-Marks, a lifelong friend of Scherff, recalled the quiet donations he made to charities and his work to improve the city.

"He was a tough cookie with a marshmallow center," Hurley-Marks said. "There was nobody tougher or more demanding...but by the same token, he had a heart of gold."

Scherff, who lived at 24 Oak Hollow Road in Springfield, often spoke of the downtown restaurant as his home and its customers and staff as his family.

His family is active in the day-to-day operation of the restaurant.

Employees have described Scherff as not only a precise and demanding workaholic, but a charitable boss who was willing to see his employee through any hardship.

Until February 1994, Scherff worked a staggering 114 hours a week at the restaurant. He reduced his weekly work schedule to 45 hours by early last year, but illness had kept him from work in recent months.

Scherff was saluted as an outstanding American at a banquet in his honor in September 1994.

He leaves his wife, the former Mary C. Schaffer; two sons, Rudi R. and Peter H., both of Springfield, a daughter, Barbara B. Meunier of Springfield, and seven grandchildren.

The funeral will be Friday morning at Sampson Chapel of the Acres Funeral Home, and at St. Michael's Cathedral, with burial at the convenience of the family.

Calling hours are tomorrow afternoon and evening. Memorial contributions may be made to Shriners Hospital for Children, 516 Carew St., Springfield, 01104, Brightside for Families and Children, 2112 Riverdale St., West Springfield, 01089, or the Jewish Nursing Home of Western Massachusetts, 770 Converse St., Longmeadow, 01106.

Died July 23, 1996   **Union-News** (Springfield, Mass.) *July 24, 1996*

⤳

RUPPRECHT R. SCHERFF

1914 – 1996

The Fort and Student Prince Restaurant in downtown Springfield, Mass. fulfilled all the dreams of the American expatriate who had come home.

He felt right at ease, as though he was again abroad.

Bratwurst, sauerkraut, Wiener schnitzel, kalbsripperl, goulash (with a nod to Budapest) and fluessiges Brot (liquid bread), that means Beer.

It wasn't home away from home.

It was away from home at home.

My first meal there was in the late winter, 1961.

I just hope I haven't had my last.

Rupprecht Scherff was not the soup Nazi of Seinfeld.

But he was close.

He ran a very tight ship, but those who remained on board were well rewarded financially and professionally.

Some who took advantage early of his generous profit-sharing scheme took some of this largesse and tried to branch off on their own, with few successes.

As a result, Rupprecht tightened up on those provisions, and made it less easy to bail.

During one of my earlier conversations with Rupprecht at the Fort's gleaming bar surrounded by beer mugs at every eye level, I asked him about the favorite beer I had discovered during my four years in Bavaria.

It was Geiselhoeringer, named for a small town in Niederbayern (Lower Bavaria) that had its own brewery.

He immediately whipped out a little black book, and started leafing through the pages.

There it was.

Geiselhoering, and the fact that I was not the only beer connoisseur in the continental United States.

Rupprecht showed me the figures.

Three hundred cases of Geiselhoering had been imported into the United States in the past year.

Geiselhoering had become the official beer of our regimental basketball team at Straubing, Germany five years earlier.

It had been a fine team, led by former Furman scoring machine Frank Selvy, who later went on to an NBA career with the Los Angeles Lakers.

The team, consisting of mostly former college players, applied to play in the European military tournament, but was turned down because it was not at divisional level.

We argued that we had Selvy and too good a team for the big boys to tackle.

So we were forced to beat up on all the local teams.

Several members of the team took turns driving out to Geiselhoering to pick up a case or two of the lager, for 12 marks (a mark then was 24 cents) a case.

It still ranks in my beer computer memory right up with Franziskaner, Paulaner and Pschorr from Munich, Czechvar or Budvar from Ĉeskė Budějovice in Bohemia, Harp lager in Britain (because I could drink it at my favorite temperature) and Yuengling from Pottsville, Pa. as my favorite brews.

The Fort had a number of drafts, including Spaten and Franziskaner.

Spaten was a nostalgic favorite because when I cycled into Munich to classes at the university, I pedaled right by the Spaten brewery, and if one inhaled deeply enough for long enough, it gave you a leg up* on your classmates during the first couple of lectures or seminars.

And the Fort had Franziskaner weis, or weizen, or wheat beer, which became both a winter and summer favorite after I tasted my first dark Weizen which my brother-in-law brought into the country in the summer of 1978.

I wanted to show off The Fort to the brother-in-law, Xaver Hofauer, during his first visit to the United States that year.

It eventually resulted in a blip in my patronage.

* A soccer term comparable to a bye or home field advantage in American professional football

That, unfortunately, is a long story, and what is more unfortunate, one that I am going to insist on telling.

Xaver and I were speaking German at the bar that August night in 1978 when a gentleman to my left nudged me and queried brusquely, "Wo seid Ihr her?"

I would translate his query into an equally brusque, "Where the hell are you two from?"

I informed him that my brother-in-law was from Munich and that I came from Massachusetts.

You're not from Massachusetts, he snarled, and insisted on proof.

I immediately produced a Massachusetts driver's license which revealed my very un-German name and birthdate and place as Whitinsville, Mass., Nov. 17, 1932.

He had actually complimented me with his assurance that I was a native German and fluent speaker of his language. That assurance may have been buttressed by the fact that I frequently slipped into the Bavarian dialect that I had been exposed to for nearly four years of military service and academic study.

He introduced himself as a brewery owner from Karlsruhe, and introduced us to his son-in-law, a resident of nearby Enfield, Conn., who was on the next barstool.

We started buying rounds and the first time it was the turn of the Karlsruhe brewery owner, there was an unfamiliar small glass sitting beside my tall Pilsener glass of Franziskaner.

It turned out to be Kirschwasser, a potent potion indeed.

The Kirschwasser loosened the tongue, and eventually the vocal cords.

The Karlsruhe native and my brother-in-law, a Passauer turned Muenchener, proceeded to put the Fort through a critical historical and cultural analysis.

They picked out clues and evidence that the Fort was not the pure Bavarian institution that it purported to be. It was obvious to them that Rupprecht was not a native Bavarian. He, a native of Hanover and therefore regarded by some southern Germans as a Prussian, had in fact taken over the restaurant as a loyal employee from a Bavarian couple.

Everything was exposed to their drillmaster inspection.

The menu, the steins, the glassware, the artwork, the garb of the bartenders and wait staff.

By the time the fourth Kirschwasser and accompanying beers had been consumed, voices had been raised, and the conversation was being eavesdropped on by other customers – and Rupprecht.

I plead innocent to initiating the next outburst of exuberance.

A quartet two booths over from the bar suddenly, as if on cue, burst into song. They had heard the loud German-language exchange and decided to sing some German on their own.

A certain measure of decorum evaporated.

When the chorus had ended, it was agreed that the members of the two German-linked families would gather the following Sunday for dinner at the Fort, 15 members in all.

Reservations were made, and the new friends then gathered themselves for the retreat homeward.

Chapter 41

We were met at the door by Peter Wolf.

Peter was a friend, and the head chef at The Fort.

He advised us that his boss had decreed that we would not be welcome on Sunday at the restaurant.

In our state, we could not comprehend the reason.

In retrospect, it is clear as a sobering summer breeze.

The cancellation had a double effect.

For me, resentment built up to induce a self-imposed boycott of The Fort that lasted longer than two years, as close a brush with masochism as I have ever allowed myself.

It was also the last time that I became intoxicated in public.

Peter, a sensitive Saxon who escaped Communist rule to the West in 1949 and came to the United States in 1957 after a two-year sojourn in Colombia, was distraught.

He loved his job, but had chafed under the autocratic rule of Rupprecht.

When we chatted later at the bus station bar between Fort Street and the newspaper on Cypress Street, he said he had been solicited to submit an application for an opening as command chief chef of the 8th Air Force headquarters in Omaha, Nev.

That was the headquarters for the B-52s and KC-135 tankers that were based at Westover Air Force Base in nearby Chicopee Falls.

Top-ranked officers of the 8th had been attracted to Westover for years.

It was a great place to fly to get in your flying time, pick up golf clubs at nearby Spalding, test them at the fine base golf course, and get fine dining at The Fort, Gayda's and other restaurants in the Connecticut Valley.

The Fort ranked high with the brass, and Peter was induced to apply.

He was one of more than 60 applicants.

And Peter was the one chosen.

I hesitate to take any great measure of credit for Peter's later career, but I do know he was very upset at being ordered to be the messenger of bad tidings to us that August evening, no matter the boorishness of our behavior.

Peter went on from Omaha to become command chef at the U.S. Marine Corps headquarters four years later and shortly thereafter joined the U. S. Army Community & Family Support Cener Europe in Frankfurt, Germany. He joined as a military club program analyst and was eventually promoted to food and beverage directer.

A decade after his departure from The Fort, I arranged to visit him and his American wife, Karen Gilfoil, a German major at the University of Massachusetts in Amherst, and a former Fort waitress, in Aschaffenburg, near Frankfurt.

After enjoying two wonderful meals at their home, cooked by Peter, I offered to take them out to a restaurant of their choice.

They picked a small restaurant up the Neckar River in the only section of Germany which produces wine made from red grapes.

It was obvious only in the opening greeting that Peter and Karen were well known.

The rest of the evening was the finest of fine dining.

The wait staff were always there just as you wanted them to be, and never when you didn't.

The meal was superb.

The company excellent.

Peter and Karen enjoyed a fine career, and after Peter's parents had passed away in the Black Forest, Peter retired and they returned to the United States for a well-earned retirement in Maine.

The staff at the fort would indicate to me over the years that Peter would occasionally visit, with no hard feelings on either side.

After Rupprecht's passing, his son Rudi did something that was long overdue.

He gained access to adjacent property and expanded the restaurant, creating an extra bar and an alcove which accommodated the throngs that frequently gathered on weekends and especially holiday occasions when the Fort alumni from all over the globe would return home.

Look forward to doing so again myself.

DONALD NEWHOUSE
CORONARY VICTIM

Funeral services will be held Sunday for Donald R. Newhouse, 54, Springfield Newspapers general manager, who died Thursday night during heart surgery at Massachusetts General Hospital, Boston.

The services will be at 8 p.m. at Harold R. Ascher and Son memorial chapel at 44 Sumner Avenue, Springfield, with Rabbi Jordan Ofseyer and Cantor Morton Shames officiating.

Burial will be in Beth El Cemetery, West Springfield. Memorial week will be at the Newhouse home, 65 Colony Road, Springfield.

Mr. Newhouse died at 10:32 p.m., after more than four hours in surgery as doctors attempted unsuccessfully to open blocked arteries and repair damaged heart valves. An autopsy was to be performed today.

Mr. Newhouse felt chest pains Wednesday morning and immediately drove to Springfield Hospital Medical Center where he was admitted.

He was transferred to the Phillips House cardiac intensive care unit of Massachusetts General Hospital Wednesday night.

Mr. Newhouse was recognized as an expert in newspaper automation. He had been a consultant to newspapers making changes in mechanical departments.

When he came to Springfield in September 1967, from Portland, Ore., his first task was to supervise the design and construction of the new Springfield Newspapers building and plant.

The move was completed on Labor Day weekend 1969 without missing an edition.

He was a 1950 graduate of Massachusetts Institute of Technology with a degree in electrical engineering, and his engineering skills were called on frequently. It was not uncommon to see him, sleeves rolled up elbow-deep in a press unit or other piece of machinery with problems.

While his major concern in recent years was with the mechanical end of newspapers, Newhouse was experienced in virtually all areas.

His career began as a copy boy with the Long Island Press in New York, where he worked for seven years, advancing to assistant Sunday editor before enlisting in the Signal Corps for four years during World War II.

Following graduation from MIT, Mr. Newhouse became production manager of the Portland Oregonian. In 1965, he was named business manager of that newspaper with responsibility for the mechanical, purchasing, data processing, credit and properties departments.

Mr. Newhouse was the target of a gunman during a bitter strike of the stereotyper's union at the Oregonian which began in 1959. While working in his basement workshop he was shot and seriously wounded in October, 1960, by a blast from a 12-gauge shotgun fired by a man hiding in nearby bushes. He was struck in his right leg and hip and walked on crutches for some time. His assailant was never caught.

Mr. Newhouse was known for civic involvement both in Portland and Springfield.

He was a trustee of Springfield Hospital Medical Center, a member of the Chamber of Commerce Task Force, a trustee of Hampshire College and Springfield Technical Community College and a member of the executive committee of the Pioneer Valley United Way.

He was chairman of the finance committee of the Metropolitan Springfield YMCA, a member of the Zoological Society board, and publicity chairman of the Springfield Rotary Club. He led the Chamber of Commerce's "Operation Washington" tour to the nation's capital earlier this month.

Early this week, Massachusetts Welfare Commissioner Steven A. Minter asked Newhouse to serve on the State Welfare Advisory Board.

Newhouse served on the boards of Beth El Temple and the Springfield Jewish Federation last year, and was active in other organizations.

In Portland, he was vice-president and chairman of the board of education of Neveh Shalom Synagogue, a Junior Achievement adviser for four years and president and chairman of the board of the Oregon Museum of Science and Industry

Newhouse was one of the founders of the museum, considered a model for children's museums around the country, and was active in a number of other youth-connected activities in the Portland area.

He was the founder of the auction which raised more than $500,000 for the Portland Zoo and the Science Museum there, and president of the Oregon Inventors Council which advised inventors on marketing and improving their inventions.

He was active in the American Newspaper Publishers Association for more than a decade, serving as chairman of the group's computerization committee last year and on the production management committee.

Born March 1, 1919, in Avon, Conn., he was the son of the late Joseph and Margaret Ann (Connolly) Newhouse.

He is survived by his wife, the former Leila Kirshen; five children; Mrs. Rosalyn Fenik of Boston; Jo, a student at Syracuse University; Melanie Beth, Wendy and David, all at home; two brothers, Raymond of Loman, N.Y.; and Harold of Harrisburg; and a sister, Mrs. Florence Pye of New Jersey.

Died Oct. 18, 1973   ***Springfield Daily News,*** *Oct. 19, 1973*

DONALD R. NEWHOUSE
1919 – 1973

The first time I met Donald Newhouse, he was climbing down the backstairs from the composing room of the old Springfield (Mass.) Newspapers building on Cypress Street.

I had arrived from Belgrade, Yugoslavia in March.

He had arrived from Portland, Ore., in September of 1967.

I introduced myself, and noted that I was also a comparatively recent arrival. I explained that I was a new addition to the copy desk. He politely acknowledged that he did not involve himself much with the editorial side of the paper, and continued down the stairs.

That was certainly the case, because I didn't see him again for five years.

During that period, Newhouse managed the monumental task of building a new newspaper complex in downtown Springfield, part of an ongoing urban renewal project that transformed the city center from the 19th to the 21st century without sacrificing treasures of the 17th, 18th, 19th and 20th.

The families of Samuel and Sherman Bowles had expanded the newspaper enterprise in a patchwork manner over the years so that departments were spread throughout the city, requiring messengers and couriers to convey data, photos, metal cuts and news stories back and forth over several city blocks.

If one took a map of Greater Springfield and outlined major property owners in the region, two would stand out.

The Bowles and the Bishops.

When I asked a local assessor who the Bishops were, he pointed to the initials. They were R. C. and stood for Roman Catholic Bishop, the head of the Archdiocese of Springfield.

It was Newhouse's job to bring in all the disparate properties that the Bowles family had accumulated over the years and establish a modern newpaper plant on the full city block fronting on Main Street.

This he achieved masterfully in two years, and I was one of the willing staff members who was told to carry his own typewriter over to the new facilities when they were completed in 1969. The daily paper was put out without interruption.

We then watched the rats desert the sinking ship as the ancient three-story brick structure next door was razed weeks later.

Newhouse can hardly be faulted for not having anticipated the bane of builders that would surface a few years later, the asbestos scare.

But the owners did perhaps anticipate the invasion and avarice of the trial lawyers, and a lengthy and disruptive purging of the building of asbestos was executed in the 1970s.

My next meeting with Donald Newhouse took place in Boston, at a newspaper awards banquet in 1972. The then managing editor Joe Mooney had invited me and my wife to attend, and we sat opposite Mr. and Mrs. Newhouse at the festivities.

It was a heady experience for the lowly copyreader who had risen to news editor in less than five years, and perhaps was being groomed for better things.

As we drove home to Wilbraham on the Massachusetts Turnpike that night, I asked my wife her opinion on things in general and Mr. Newhouse in particular.

She, true to her Bavarian bluntness, suggested that he would be dead in two years.

Actually, it took fewer than 18 months.

I, a professional newsman for most of my last 20 years, should have been so prescient.

I asked her at the time of her amazing prophecy why she thought so.

She had observed during only one evening and meal together that he was overweight, overwrought and undersocialized.

The death of Donald R. Newhouse, in retrospect, was hardly propitious for The Springfield Newspapers, the City of Springfield, the Connecticut River Valley, or the four-county region of Western Massachusetts.

Newhouse, in channeling all his prodigious energy into the mechanical end of the newspapers, had allowed the editorial autonomy that newsmen, for good or ill, love.

The Springfield Daily News, an afternoon creation of seemingly near socialist policies inherited from the Bellamy family founders (Looking Backward by Edward Bellamy), loyally served the working class immigrants dominated by Irish Roman Catholics who wittily referred to their growing domain as "Hungry Hill."

It primarily served the city of Springfield, which hardly had suburbs during The Daily News' heyday.

The Morning Union, founded to preserve the same during the Civil War, eventually spread its tentacles up and down the Connecticut Valley and into the Berkshires. It stopped and started its presses for as many as 11 editions sent on a fleet of trucks throughout the region, which was more agricultural, less urban and much more conservative than working class Springfield.

Donald Newhouse's hands-off policy allowed the editorial give and take between the Daily News and Union to continue, a confrontation that had existed long before when they were under separate ownership,

The staffs, and their policies, were separate and distinct.

And the reader could choose to adopt one or the other, or both.

I am not sure that the frequent reader surveys conducted by all the managements of The Springfield Newspapers ever focused on that latter group, the readers, who always, frequently, occasionally or rarely bought both papers.

And if they didn't know how many there were, they certainly did not know who they were, and what they actually thought.

Newspaper autonomy is not always fortunate.

The loss of Donald Newhouse was proof in point.

He was not the only new arrival in Springfield in the autumn of 1967. The Newhouses were preparing for the eventual clearout of those who had stonewalled them in the seven years of litigation that followed the purchase of the stock owned by disgruntled Bowles heirs in the late 1950s.

The suit in equity filed and fought out in Hampden County Superior Court in Springfield was not resolved until that same year, 1967.

The former owner, Sherman Bowles, had created a fiction that the newspaper was owned by its employees, beneficiaries of a promised pension of full wage or salary at the time of retirement.

Few of the employees had the actuarial awareness that few of them would stay at the paper for the 30 or more years required to qualify for the pension, or that they would survive to collect it.

Meanwhile, the monies put aside to fund the pension waxed while the few family stockholders, most of whom went on to other pursuits, received pittances of profits for their investment or inheritance.

The Newhouses, in all their sagacity, had purchased for a very small price, stock in the company and a pension fund which eventually paid for the construction of its new modern plant.

The death of Donald Newhouse left a void which was never properly filled.

Newhouse family members had directed news operations successfully in Cleveland (The Plain Dealer), Portland (The Oregonian) and New Orleans (The Picayune and Times-Item).

The Star-Ledger in Newark, directed by the husband of Donald Newhouse's sister, had grown into a statewide paper and allowed the family corporation to revive the ailing Jersey Journal.

Springfield was allowed to fall under the purview of a branch of the family which had allowed the Long Island Star Journal to fail and had failed to follow the readers of the Long Island Press out to Suffolk and Nassau counties.

The Long Island Press thus also failed, leaving the temporarily lucrative field to Newsday.

Management of the failed Long Island enterprises were promoted to Springfield, leading to cutbacks in circulation area, bureaus, coverage and eventual amalgamation.

The declining circulation of the afternoon Daily News cannot be attributed entirely to management, because the afternoon paper was under attack nationally due to the expansion of evening and late television news and the decline of newspaper readership in general.

But decline soon set in in the morning newspaper as well, as Berkshire County was turned over gratis to The Berkshire Eagle (which the Miller brothers, the then owners, gratefully acknowledged to me one day in Boston).

Eventually, northern Connecticut, whose economic, cultural and residential umbilical cord was attached to Springfield, not Hartford, was yielded to the Hartford Courant.

Eventually the Daily News and The Morning Union were merged

into one morning daily, with the management of the declining News taking over key positions instead of that of the still growing Union.

The Sunday Republican, the strongest circulation growth paper of the three and the one with the broadest reach, continued to grow until all three papers were absorbed into it as one daily The Republican.

It cannot be determined how any of these policies would have been affected had Donald R. Newhouse lived. But it is likely that under his benevolent stewardship, all of the editors who were in place or who would have been promoted or hired would have exercised a more aggressive campaign to respond to readers, offer rival editorial viewpoints, build circulation and thus increase both advertising and revenues.

It is a fact of newspaper, magazine and cable television life that the Newhouses know what to do with the latter.

PAUL A. DONOGHUE

1932 – 1991

WEST YARMOUTH – Paul A. Donoghue, 59, assistant sports editor of The Springfield Union-News, died Monday night at his 164 Wendward Way summer home.

Donoghue, who lived at 2 River Terrace, Holyoke, had worked for The Springfield Newspapers for 38 years. He was sports editor of the former Daily News from 1977 until the newspaper's merger with The Morning Union in 1987.

"Paul Donoghue was the ultimate professional," said Editor Arnold S. Friedman yesterday.

"He did whatever had to be done quietly and efficiently, without fanfare, without commotion, without ever getting upset. He tied up every loose end, and did it all with a smile."

"Whether it was dealing with the public, the sports staff, or his colleagues in other departments, Paul went out of his way to be helpful.

"Our profession has lost a fine journalist. Those who knew him have lost a friend. He will be missed."

Carroll F. Robbins, executive editor of the papers and former editor of The Daily News, said Donoghue had a special talent for caring, and was especially helpful to staffers needing advice and counsel.

"It was as though he was everybody's friend," Robbins said.

"I can honestly say that I've never met a man who enjoyed doing so much for other people as Paul Donoghue," said Executive Sports Editor Richard Osgood. "When you asked him about himself, he had a knack of shifting the focus back on someone else. It was part of his nature.

"Paul was a special member of our department. He handled most of the behind-the-scenes work, and was a professional in every aspect. As an assistant sports editor, we might be able to replace the title, but never the man. There was only one Paul Donoghue."

A native of Holyoke, Donoghue was a graduate of Holyoke High School and New York University. He managed athletic teams at both institutions.

He was active in amateur sports for many years, and managed the Highland Vols, which represented Holyoke in national junior baseball competition.

During his career at the newspapers, he became a personal friend to a number of umpires, referees and professional and amateur athletes in all sports. Rarely did he miss baseball spring training in Florida or the World Series.

In addition to his interests in baseball and other professional sports, he never overlooked sports programs and athletes on the local level.

For eight years before his promotion to sports editor of The Daily News, he served as assistant editor of The Sunday Republican.

He was a member of the Baseball Writers Association and the National Association of Sports Writers and Sportscasters.

He leaves a brother, Richard E. Of Holyoke, a sister, Helen Keith of South Carolina, his fiancée, Eleanor A. Hepburn of Holyoke, an aunt, Gertrude Smyth of Holyoke, and several nieces and nephews.

The funeral will be Friday at 9:15 a.m. at James P. Hobert & Sons Funeral Home, with a Mass of Christian burial at 10 in St. Patrick's Chapel of St. Jerome's Church, both in Holyoke. Burial will be at St. Jerome's Cemetery in Holyoke.

Calling hours at the funeral home are 2 to 9 p.m. Thursday.

Memorial contributions may be made to Save School Sports Etc., 378 High St., Holyoke, 01040 in care of Park West Bank & Trust Co..

Died July 22, 1991   **Union-News** (Springfield, Mass.) *Wednesday, July 24, 1991*

PAUL A. DONOGHUE
1932 – 1991

You could always tell when Paul was going to ask you a question.

It was written all over his face.

The raised eyebrows were the major tipoff.

But it was never a question that caused much concern.

If you had the answer, it would resolve both your problems. If you didn't he would go find the person who did.

We didn't meet face to face at first.

When I joined the suburban copy desk, he was in Holyoke, a key member of a full-time staff of three that covered the Paper City, a declining industrial metropolis on the Connecticut River in Western Massachusetts.

Most of the early contact was by phone.

But the copy that came from Holyoke was, as we said in the craft, clean, that it didn't require much editing.

Holyoke, always a tough, brawling city of immigrant Irish and French-Canadians, was undergoing a difficult transformation as blacks moved up from the South and Puerto Ricans recruited to work the Connecticut River Valley tobacco fields, decided, or were forced to decide, to stay.

The tenement blocks along the canals utilized by the paper mills began to fill with larger and larger families, and absentee landlords were the norm.

Holyoke was infamous for fires.

And Paul covered them all.

We were very flexible in those years.

The editorial floors, the composing room and the press room all cooperated to get the breaking news to the right place.

If Paul called in that he was going to a fire, arrangements were made to roll pages from later editions to the stereotype machines first, and ask circulation to rearrange the truck routes.

When Paul moved from the Holyoke office to the Sunday Republican staff, all editions begin to benefit from his professionalism.

At his death, his editor, Arnie Friedman, concluded, "He tied up every loose end, and did it all with a smile."

I must concur.

I ran Page 1 at the Sunday Republican for several years, and one thing one could be certain of when one reported for work late Saturday afternoon, that Paul Donoghue and Horace Hill, an editorial institution who worked at the papers for more than 50 years, had all the early pages in. Rarely did they have to go back for correction after the paper came out, and the local and wire service features used would not have to be updated, revised or rehandled.

When he moved from The Republican to sports, we all benefited yet again.

Paul had cultivated his love of baseball through the years, and gained many friends in the sport. One of them was Ed Hurley, a Major League umpire.

Paul became a fixture at spring training, taking his vacations down South when he was not on assignment.

He and Garry Brown, The (Springfield) Morning Union sports editor, were tight with the Boston Red Sox, and helped provide detailed coverage, at home and away, of the Sox games.

But I was really surprised, and pleasantly so, when Paul approached me in the city room in the fall of 1975 and asked me whether I would be interested in tickets to a World Series game.

I was the news editor, and I had been sent to a news editor and managing editors seminar at Columbia that year. But even under those circumstances I would not have considered asking either Garry or Paul whether there was any chance of getting World Series tickets.

It had been a great baseball season. The Yankees were gone. And the Red Sox would be playing The Big Red Machine from Cincinnati, one of the greatest teams of all time.

"I've got two tickets for the second and sixth games," Paul offered. "Two are for you and two are for Jean."

Jean O'Connell was head of the women's department and she and Paul had worked closely for several years on the Sunday section.

"Which would you like, the second or the sixth?" Paul asked.

"I don't want to be greedy," I answered. I was still recovering from the offer. "I'll take the sixth."

They are 10 bucks each, Paul added.

Baseball fans have seen the image hundreds of times, Pudge Fisk waving the ball fair as it went down the left field line.

My vantage point was a little different.

I was down the right field line, and had no assurance it was fair until Fenway Park erupted.

It was the baseball thrill of the 20th century.

Even bigger than that of the 21st.

You had to be there to experience it.

I was, thanks to Paul Donoghue.

CHAPTER 44

HORACE B. HILL, 93; 50 YEARS A JOURNALIST

SPRINGFIELD – Horace B. Hill, a reporter, critic and editor at The Springfield Newspapers for more than half a century, died on Wednesday in a local nursing home after a short illness. He was 93. He joined the old Springfield Union as a reporter on Jan. 24, 1924. "I didn't think I'd make it a second year," he said when he retired more than 50 years later.

When Hill retired, then-publisher Sidney R. Cook called him "one of the most intensely devoted and dedicated men in the newspaper business."

Hill proved it by continuing to work after retirement.

It was not uncommon to find him toiling 12 to14 hours a day.

"His family"

"The newspaper was his family," said James R. Crowe, retired personnel director, counsel, and a longtime friend. "He was a quiet, hard-working man who just loved working for a newspaper. It was his life."

In the 1920s, Hill wrote six to eight stories a day. Bylines were given sparingly in those days, and reporters' names only went on to pieces of exceptional work.

In two years as a reporter, Hill received two bylines. One was for covering an eclipse of the sun, and the other for the 1925 flood.

Hill transferred to the copy desk two years later because copy editors received $5 more a week. He was named assistant night editor in 1928. In those days, there was a big rivalry between The Sunday Republican and The Union, which were owned by different companies.

In 1932, Hill became night editor, and he held the post for 20 years. He served as managing editor in 1940-45 while then-editor Paul F. Craig was in the armed forces.

Hill recalled that the most exciting story he was a part of was the Great Flood of 1936.

Since most of downtown Springfield was underwater and without electricity, he helped put out the paper by candlelight, and published a hand-printed newspaper that night.

"We didn't want to let a natural disaster get in the way of publishing," he said.

Hill was transferred to The Sunday Republican as editorial writer in 1952, and added the book page to his duties in 1959. He became Sunday editor in 1966.

He was a native of New Haven, Conn., and lived here from 1907. He attended Springfield schools, and graduated from Central High School.

'Editor's editor'

Richard C. Garvey, associate publisher of the Union-News, recalled Hill yesterday as an "editor's editor."

"When I came to work for the Daily News in 1944, Horace Hill was acting as managing editor of The Union, substituting for Paul Craig, who was in the Army," Garvey said. "Well-versed in history and well-read in current events, Horace was an editor's editor, wisely supervising editorial writers.

"Even after his retirement, he would come into the office next to mine every week and supervise the makeup of the Sunday Republican. I asked him once whether he did that because he enjoyed the work or the people, and he answered, 'Both.'"

Hill leaves no known relatives.

A graveside service will be conducted on Thursday morning at Center Cemetery in Southampton. There are no calling hours.

Dickinson-Streeter Funeral Home is in charge.

Died Dec . 7, 1994   ***Union-News*** (Springfield, Mass.) *Dec. 7, 1994*

HORACE B. HILL
1901 – 1994

There were no known relatives when Horace Hill died.

But he did have family, although he had outlived most of them.

The newspaper was his family.

He worked for The Springfield Newspapers, under a series of flags and ownerships, for more than 50 years for money, and several more for love.

And after he died, he left a gift in perpetuity to the children and grandchildren of its employees.

An editor is tempted, when reading the obituary of another editor, to delete all the platitudes uttered by those outside the newspaper world, regarding them as fatuous, uninformed or self-serving.

That was unnecessary in reading Horace's obit.

There weren't any such quotes.

They were all from fellow news people, and to the point.

Horace worked for decades in the bowels of the newspaper world, rarely visited or understood outside.

For the last eight years of his professional life, he and Paul Donoghue put out the early pages of The Springfield Sunday Republican.

This tandem was a combination of diligence and efficiency that made one grateful to see them when one reported late Saturday afternoon to put out the front pages of the paper.

Rarely did one of their pages have to be sent back because of error or because the stories chosen had been overtaken by events.

Horace was of the old school, copy desk visor, black armband and all.

I had heard the stories about the young editor darting about Springfield in his red MG convertible, but it remained difficult to imagine.

Horace had come into the stable of Sherman Bowles and the Bowles family that had run the Springfield Republican since the early part of the 19th century when Bowles took over The Union, a progeny of the Civil War.

As such, he became one of the few beneficiaries of the The Springfield Newspapers pension fund to beat the actuaries at their own game.

When the Newhouse family took over the papers finally in 1967, Horace was one of a number who received a generous cash payout in addition to his fixed-income pension at retirement, which was stipulated to be full pay at retirement with 30 years service.

Perhaps Horace felt this was overgenerous.

Because at his actual retirement, he kept working, if at a reduced number of hours and less demanding tasks.

Management was wise enough to allow him to do so.

And there were numerous longtime associates of Horace who were very happy to have him.

For several years, deep into his 80s, he assisted Paul and Sax Fletcher, the managing editor, in putting together the editorial and book review pages in which he retained a deep interest.

When he was finally unable to take care of himself adequately, and moved into a Springfield nursing home, Paul and his brother Richard kept up the watch over Horace.

Whenever Paul was at the Cape, and Richard was unable to check on Horace, Paul was kind enough to ask me to check on his needs.

The principal one was that he had his newspapers.

He lived to be 93, and there were only a few colleagues at his graveside service.

But there will be many who will remember the name.

For Horace had a trust fund of $50,000 established to provide scholarships in his name for descendants of his colleagues at The Springfield Newspapers.

The first ones were awarded in 1999 and five years later, a total of 28 bequests had been made, under his stipulations, from the non-profit charitable trust he had established, through the Community Foundation in Springfield.

BELOVED JOURNALIST RICHARD GARVEY DIES

By Chris Hamel

Tributes to Richard C. Garvey rolled through the Pioneer Valley yesterday as word slowly spread of the death of the beloved journalist, historian and community volunteer.

Garvey, 81, a Northampton native and past editor of the former Daily News in Springfield, died yesterday at his home here.

The funeral will be 10 a.m. Monday at Blessed Sacrament Church on Elm Street. Calling hours will be 2 – 4 p.m. and 7 – 9 p.m. Sunday at Ahearn Funeral Home on Bridge Street.

Garvey, who spent 57 years in journalism, was recalled repeatedly by those who knew and worked with him as an "institution" in journalism, an "encyclopedia" of Western Massachusetts history, a tireless community servant and a skilled toastmaster. But he also was remembered for his lively intellect and wit, storytelling talent and deep, caring soul.

Carroll F. Robbins, the retired executive editor of the former Union-News, worked alongside Garvey for nearly 50 years.

"I was always impressed by his command of language and his willingness always to tell a story," Robbins said. "He had incurable optimism about the way things in this world would turn out, which he communicated to the community and his staff. Not only do I feel a great sense of personal loss, but I know that Springfield has lost a powerful voice for good in his death."

Upon retirement in 1999, Garvey was a columnist and associate publisher of the Sunday Republican and Union-News, the predecessor to The Republican. His presence at the newspapers, as well as in the community, provided a bridge between the region's rich past and its unfolding present events.

"Dick represented a very important link between the newspaper and the community it serves," said David Starr, president of The Republican and the former publisher of the newspapers, where Garvey built his legacy. "He was, in so many ways, an embodiment of the papers. His role as editor-historian and his role as a speaker at civic and social events has made people see us in human terms, not institutional terms."

... Born in Northampton May 23, 1923, Garvey's career in journalism began in the midst of World War II when he was 19 years old and a sophomore at the Amherst institution then known as the Massachusetts State College, now the University of Massachusetts. Because a heart murmur kept him from enlisting in the Army, he took a reporting job with the Daily Hampshire Gazette to give him a break from college. For $20 a week, he covered the police, fire, court and school beats.

A year later, he was working for the Springfield Daily News, where his first assignment was to cover West Springfield. The move meant he had to commute by railroad on a 40-minute trip that would draw $16 a month from his $35-per-week salary. He later said it was a small price to pay.

In 1951, he was named assistant managing editor of the Daily News, moving on to become the paper's managing editor in 1966. Two years later, he was named editor. In 1986, he became associate publisher. In 1974, the University of Massachusetts awarded him an honorary degree.

He was the author of "Oliver Smith, Esq." And "St. Mary's of Haydenville" and the co-author of "The Northampton Book" and "Bringing Home the News: 175-Year History of the Springfield Newspapers."

Wayne E. Phaneuf, co-author of the latter book and executive editor of The Republican, echoed many yesterday as he recalled the breadth of Garvey's influence.

"Dick Garvey touched the lives of thousands of people over the years with his frequent speaking engagements and his attention to community involvement," he said. "He was an institution that will never be duplicated."

... Joseph Carvalho III, president and executive director of the Springfield Museums, said Garvey was an invaluable resource to him when Carvalho was serving from 1986 to 1994 as director of the Connecticut Valley Historical Museum. Carvalho said he tapped Garvey's "font of knowledge" regularly as the museum pursued history projects....

Garvey's contributions to the community extended far beyond the newsrooms where he worked into the board rooms where he served and the halls where he was renowned for his public speaking.

Alfred A. LaRiviere of Ludlow, retired president and chief executive officer of what is now Freedom Credit Union in Springfield, recalled Garvey's service with the Springfield Rotary Club. LaRiviere and Garvey each served terms as the club's president.

LaRiviere, a Rotarian for nearly 40 years and a friend of Garvey for a longer time, said they worked together as Rotarians to build ties between Springfield's business community and lawmakers in Boston and Washington....

In 1980, when Garvey ended four years as chairman of the Springfield College board of trustees, the college wrote a citation for him. In part, it read: "Where there was ignorance, he provided enlightenment; where there was strife, he sounded the reassuring voice of reason; where there was timidity, he prompted action; and where there was narrow-mindedness, he fostered vision."

In addition to his work on behalf of the college and the Springfield Rotary Club, Garvey's service included stints as a former trustee and board chairman of the Pioneer Valley Chapter American Red Cross and the Community Council of Greater Springfield. He was a trustee of the former Springfield Institution for Savings, the former Mercy Hospital, the former Springfield City Library and Museums Association, and the Forbes Library here. He was a director of the Springfield Area Development Corp. He was past president of Our Lady of Providence Children's Center and the New England Society of Newspaper Editors. In 1968, he was general campaign chairman of the former United Fund.

His humanitarian and community contributions were honored with the Pynchon Award in 1977, the Jewish War Veterans Outstanding Citizen Award also in 1977 and the former National Conference of Christians and Jews Humanitarian Award in 1988. In 1981, he received the Yankee Quill Award for his lifetime commitment to journalism in New England.

He served four years as the New England layman on the U.S. Catholic Bishops Advisory Council. Pope John Paul II designated him in 1989 as a Knight of the Holy Sepulcher.

Garvey, who leaves his widow, Northampton historian Allison Lockwood, also was a well-known aficionado of Calvin Coolidge, the Northampton mayor who would become the country's 30th president. With his first wife, Anne E. Garvey, who died in 1988, Garvey had four children – Philip M. of Westfield, John B. of Chester, Mary A. of Huntingdon, Pa., and Margaret A. Robitaille of Ludlow. He also leaves a sister, Helen D. Bevan, of Holyoke, and eight grandchildren. He was predeceased by two brothers, Edward B. and James T.

Staff writer Diane Lederman contributed to this report

Died September 9, 2004   *The* (Springfield, Mass.) ***Republican,*** *Sept. 10, 2004*

DICK GARVEY
1923 – 2004

Dick Garvey was one of my three favorite Catholics.

The other two were Frank Murphy, another newsman who hired me at The Worcester Telegram and who is chronicled elsewhere in this volume, and Jack Driscoll, a longtime Massachusetts state representative and family friend.

One anecdote characterizes Dick Garvey, as newsman, historian, loyal layman and friend.

Dick ran across me one day in the morgue, newspaper argot for the library.

I was in the process of writing about Bishop Josip Strossmayer, a Croatian cardinal whose bishopric I had once visited in Djakovo, Croatia.

Strossmayer had been the glue that kept the Serbs and Croats together in their united confrontation with the Habsburg and Ottoman empires during the 19th century. The 20th century unionist, Josip Broz Tito, had been able to stitch this unlikely pair of Slavic adversaries together for another half century with the thread of Socialist solidarity, first Stalinist and then Titoist.

Whether Serb and Croat will ever achieve the comity of Jew and Greek in the early Christian church of Paul's gospels may be a triumph of hope over experience.

But my research on Strossmayer had also revealed the interesting role he had played in an important turning point of the papacy, the doctrine on the infallibility of the Pope.

It turned out that the 19th Century Vatican Council session had been anything but unanimous and pacific. Some reports said some of the exchanges before the final voting led to red-capped fisticuffs.

I had only mentioned Strossmayer's role in this session, but Dick immediately provided additional details and elucidation.

Three other cardinals had been adamantly opposed to the adoption of the doctrine, a German, an Englishman and an Irishman from the American southwest.

We discussed the details we knew of the encounter, the personalities of the participants, and totally avoided arguments on the pros and cons of the matter at issue.

Well, not entirely.

Dick did get to the core of the matter, and in a way that typified both his intellect and his personality.

He asked me if I knew what Pope John 23rd had said when he was asked about the infallibility of the pope.

I conceded I did not.

The gentle pope had explained that the pontiff was only infallible when he spoke as the head of the church, or "ex cathedra."

Pope John then concluded, "I never speak ex cathedra."

End of lesson, and doctrine.

It pained me to see Dick Garvey lose his loyal and lovely first wife in death.

It pained me that he had to suffer the exposure of sexual abuse in the clergy of a church being scourged for nearly a millennium of clerical celibacy.

It pained me to see him skip certain church functions because his new wife, although having converted to Catholicism before being wed, had not been invited, as had his first.

It pleased me that he regarded this as an oversight.

It pained me that the church no longer regarded him as the principal conduit for important breaking stories, ostensibly because he was either unwilling or unable to stem the tide of breaking news stories regarding the church and its blossoming scandal.

I was very pleased, as a onetime news editor whose views were frequently opposed to those of Dick Garvey's Daily News, to have been invited to a tasteful retirement reception that he arranged himself for the Oak Room of Springfield City Hall.

Longtime Springfield Newspapers Publisher David Starr was correct in saying that night that the Newhouse family had no intention of cleaning house at The Daily News when they finally took over the newspapers in 1967 after years of litigation.

He gave one of the reasons.

Anyone who worked as hard as The Daily News had to keep the Newhouse family out would be valuable news executives to keep on if they would work as hard for the new owners.

It was a partial truth.

Dick Garvey was highly revered in his Irish Roman Catholic community and in tune with its Massachusetts Democratic politics. As such, it would have been an unwise tie for the new ownership to cut, inasmuch as the politics fit in so well with the International Ladies Garment Workers Union mentality of the former guardians of the now defunct Long Island Star Journal and Long Island Press..

It was a convenient, if not ideal political marriage.

CHAPTER 46

MRS. DOLORES (UTOVICH) PERKINS

UPTON – Mrs. Dolores (Utovich) Perkins, 72, of 134 Main St., a teacher and preacher of the good news of God's Kingdom as one of Jehovah's Witnesses for more than half a century, died Saturday at Christopher House in Worcester.

She was born in Redstone, Pa., and graduated from Brownsville (Pa.) High School. Before that she had been enrolled in freedom schools set up by Jehovah's Witnesses after their children had been suspended from public schools for refusing to salute the American flag. This freedom to extend such honor only to her God was ultimately upheld in the Gobitis vs. Minersville (Pa.) decision of the U.S. Supreme Court written by Justice Robert H. Jackson and issued on Flag Day, June 14, 1943.

After graduation from high school, she served as a waitress in the Stouffer's restaurant chain in the Cleveland area before her marriage to Laurence L. Perkins, currently an elder at the Northbridge Congregation of Jehovah's Witnesses..

She subsequently lived in seven states as her husband accepted assignments as a field office manager for several manufacturing corporations and later for home construction and hardwood flooring companies.

During that period, she served in congregations of Jehovah's Witnesses at Chesterton, Ind., Cleveland (East Side and West Side), Ohio, Waterloo and Davenport, Ia., Birmingham (North) Ala., Oswego, N.Y., Bangor, Me., and in Milford (now Hopedale) and Northbridge (Douglas) Mass.

From 1981 to 1989, the Perkins served as live-in caretakers at the Natick (Mass.) Assembly Hall of Jehovah's Witnesses. Mrs. Perkins assisted in the domestic needs of the hall, a facility where congregations from throughout New England and beyond gather at circuit and district level.

She leaves, beside her husband, two sons, Wayne D. of Oakland, Calif., and Brian I. Perkins of East Brookfield; a daughter, Darla P. Rust of Morden, Surrey, England; two brothers, Lawrence of Cleveland and William Utovich of North Fort Myers, Fla., and 12 grandchildren. She was predeceased by one sister, Marguerite Schmidt of Shaker Heights, Ohio.

A memorial service will be Saturday at the Kingdom Hall of Jehovah's Witnesses at 164 Davis St. in Douglas, which serves both the Douglas and Northbridge congregations.

(Larry Perkins, the widow of Mrs. Dolores Perkins, requested that I write an obituary of his wife. I did so and it was subsequently published in the Worcester (Mass.)Telegram. This is the obituary I wish I had written after I learned more about her)

Died Feb. 1, 2003

⌒

MRS. DOLORES (UTOVICH) PERKINS
1931 – 2003

"Train up a child in the way he should go,
And even when he is old he will not depart from it.

Proverbs 22:6
American Standard Version

Dolores Perkins certainly didn't depart from it.

She spent her adolescent and adult lifetime exercising the faith she had been taught as a child in the hills of southwestern Pennsylvania.

I gained a measure of appreciation of that when I accepted her husband Laurence L. (Larry) Perkins' invitation to prepare her obituary.

And after writing the obit after several interviews with Larry in the couple's Upton, Ma. apartment, I thought I had done a creditable job. He had made several corrections and emendations, and we both felt it was ready to be submitted to The Worcester Telegram upon her death.

It was not until the memorial service on the Saturday after her death on Feb. 1, 2003 that I realized what an incomplete job I had done.

Among the photos on display for friends, relatives and fellow congregants to observe were those showing her attending the Freedom Schools forced on Jehovah's Witnesses just prior to and during the early years of World War II.

I was unaware until that moment that Dolores Perkins was among the thousands of schoolchildren who had been expelled from public schools in several states for the failure to salute the flag, which soon became a federal case leading to one of the most significant Supreme Court decisions of the 20th Century.

This glorious constitutional story had its genesis on the opposite side of the state, in the anthracite coal region of east-central Pennsylvania.

It began when the board from Minersville, Pa. School District voted to expel William and Lillian Gobitas from school for insubordination, and threatened to send them to reform school if they did not receive qualified instruction.

The Watch Tower Society decided to challenge the expulsions and while suits were filed, decided and appealed to higher state and federal courts over the next five years, Jehovah's Witnesses were forced to organize and finance private institutions called "Freedom Schools" in Pennsylvania, Massachusetts, New Jersey, Maryland and Georgia.

Worse was to come.

On June 3, 1940, the Supreme Court ruled 8 to 1 against the Witnesses. Justice Harlan F. Stone was the lone dissenter.

The decision unleashed a spread of mob violence across the country.

So brutal was the immediate violence that it evoked a statement conveyed by radio by the solicitor general of the United States, Francis Biddle.

An excerpt:

"... Jehovah's Witnesses have been repeatedly set upon and beaten. They had committed no crime; but the mob adjudged they had, and meted out mob punishment. The Attorney General has ordered an immediate investigation of these outrages. The people must be alert and watchful, and above all cool and sane. Since mob violence will make the government's task infinitely more difficult, it will not be tolerated. We shall not defeat the Nazi evil by emulating its methods."

Although this mob violence peaked in the spring and summer of 1940, the American Civil Liberties Union catalogued a series of abuses and reported on them in a brief entitled "The Persecution of Jehovah's Witnesses" published in January of 1941.

"Not since the persecution of the Mormons years ago has any religious minority been so bitterly and generally attacked...." the ACLU report said.

Lillian Gobitas Klose, whose late husband was one of the first Jehovah's Witnesses imprisoned in Nazi Germany, a story unto itself, acknowledges in her recollection of those difficult years that these children and her parents were not alone.

Among them was Dolores Utovich. .

In addition to the solicitor general, the First Lady of the United States, Eleanor Roosevelt, pleaded for the cause of the Witnesses in her newspaper column "My Day."

And in Mrs. Klose's account of that period published by the Watchtower Bible and Tract Society in its Awake magazine of July 22, 1993, she wrote, "Throughout all this fanatical violence, the press was highly favorable to us. At least 171 leading newspapers condemned the 1940 flag-salute decision. Only a handful approved."

After the outbreak of violence against Jehovah's Witnesses across the country, and a succession of 19 Supreme Court decisions against the Witnesses, the attitude of several sitting justices and the addition of two new ones moved the pendulum in the opposite direction.

A minority dissent in the case of Jones v. Opelika stated that its members not only disagreed with the majority's approval of a license tax on the distribution of religious literature in Alabama, but felt that a wrongful decision in the Gobitas case had laid the foundation for it.

This opened the door to the Witnesses to challenge both Jones v. Opelika and Minersville v. Gobitis(sic).

Jones v. Opelika was overturned on May 3, 1943 and six weeks later, the Supreme Court ruled 6 to 3 in favor of the Witnesses in the case of West Virginia State Board of Education v. Barnette.

The reversals by Justices Hugo Black, William O. Douglas and William F. (Frank) Murphy and the addition of two new appointees, Robert H. Jackson and Wiley B. Rutledge , created the majority of six, including Stone, which ended eight years of legalized persecution in schools across the United States.

The majority opinion was written by Jackson, a confidant of President Franklin D. Roosevelt. Jackson's inside portrait of the nation's 33rd president was found in the attic of his late son's home in 1999.

That portrait, published under the title "That Man," described Jackson as follows in an introduction by John Q. Bartlett, professor of law at St. John's University in Brooklyn, N.Y.

"In 1941, Roosevelt nominated Jackson to serve as an Associate Justice of the Supreme Court of the United States. Jackson's appointment was swiftly confirmed, and, as a "Roosevelt Court" took shape in the early 1940s, Jackson established his reputation as a brilliant yet independent and hard-to-categorize judge. In one of his famous early opinions for the Court, he authored the ringing invalidation of a public school compulsory flag salute because it violated the First Amendment right of schoolchildren who were Jehovah's Witnesses."

William E. Leuchtenburg, author of " Franklin D. Roosevelt and the New Deal, 1932-1940" and a historian who has been awarded both the Bancroft and Francis Parkinson prizes, wrote in a foreward to "That Man" as follows:

"'If there were no other justification for holding Jackson in high esteem as a jurist," Henry Abraham has written, "his magnificent prose – second in beauty and clarity perhaps only to that of (Justice Benjamin) Cardozo – has earned him a high regard. Who could ever forget the haunting beauty of his phrases? A prominent British jurist wrote, 'Here was a man who had read (British jurist William) Blackstone and was obviously a man of law; but here also was a man who had read and loved King James Bible, and was also obviously a man of letters.' "

My first draft of this vignette stated that dozens of children had been forced out of public school and into "Freedom Schools" as a result of Minersville v. Gobitis (Author's note: Gobitas was misspelled in the brief) More research revealed that there had been thousands, a number of whose accounts are recorded in Witness literature.

In Dolores' case, it was the Gates Freedom School near Brownsville, Pa.

She reminisced about her youth in an 818-word memoir she left behind at her death.

There was a notable lack of bitterness in her memory of a youth spent during the difficult times of the depression, the long trips to public school which included a lengthy walk, a river crossing and long trucks and bus rides, and expulsion from schools it was so difficult to get to.

The memory of her parents, emigrants from Croatia, including tales of her parents' youth, which usually wove a moral lesson for her and her siblings.

She recalls hearing her father, a railroad car shop worker who had managed to obtain his own small farm, turn down a neighbor's plea for help.

"Gosh, Joe, I wish I could help you but I just don't have it,." she heard him say.

Her mother came out to the field at that time and asked what the neighbor wanted.

She quoted her father as saying, "He wanted to borrow a dollar because they were going to foreclose on his house and that's all he needs to keep it."

His mother responded, "Well, call him back; I've got a dollar he can have."

The neighbor saved his house, soon found work again, and eventually paid off his mortgage.

"From where I sit," concluded Dolores (Utovich) Perkins, "it doesn't take formal education to raise children who respect life, other people's property and the right of others to pursue their life and happiness within the bounds of accepted mores..."

JOE MORELLO, DRUMMER
WITH DAVE BRUBECK QUARTET, DIES AT 82

By Steve Smith

Joe Morello, a jazz drummer whose elegant, economical playing in the Dave Brubeck Quartet sounded natural and effortless even in unusual time signatures, died on Saturday (March 12) at his home in Irvington, N.J. He was 82.

His death was announced on his Web site, joemorello.net. No cause was given.

Mr. Morello was most famous for his tenure in Mr. Brubeck's band, in which he was engaged initially for a brief tour in 1955. He became a member in late 1956, and remained until the group disbanded at the end of 1967.

Already popular for its work on college campuses during the 1950s, Mr. Brubeck's group reached new heights with Mr. Morello, who handled with disarming ease the odd meters that Mr. Brubeck began to favor. In June 1959, Mr. Morello participated in a recording session with the quartet – completed by the alto saxophonist Paul Desmond and the bassist Eugene Wright – that yielded "Kathy's Waltz" and: "Three to Get Ready," both of which intermingled 3/4 and 4/4 time signatures.

Less than a week later the quartet recorded Mr. Desmond's "Take

Five," a breezy composition in 5/4, with an airy solo by Mr. Morello over a rigid vamp on piano and bass. The track became one of the most recognizable themes and most successful singles in jazz, selling more than a million copies and reaching No. 25 on Billboard magazine's Hot 100 chart in 1962. Those pieces, and others like "Blue Rondo à la Turk" and "Strange Meadowlark," were features on Mr. Brubeck's most famous album, "Time Out."

Before working with Mr. Brubeck, Mr. Morello had played with the guitarist Johnny Smith, the saxophonist Gil Melle and, briefly, Stan Kenton's big band. From 1953 to 1956 he played in the pianist Marian McPartland's trio, which worked frequently at the Hickory House nightclub in New York.

During Mr. Morello's engagement with Ms. McPartland, Mr. Desmond urged Mr. Brubeck to hear the drummer, Mr. Brubeck said in an oral history recorded for the Smithsonian Institution in 2007.

"He was playing brushes," Mr. Brubeck recalled in the interview," and Paul just loved somebody that played brushes and didn't interrupt with some hard licks with sticks and clashing cymbals." In need of a substitute drummer, Mr. Brubeck approached Mr. Morello.

Mr. Morello's reply, according to Mr. Brubeck: "I'm interested in your group, but your drummer's out to lunch. I want to be featured." By this, Mr. Brubeck said, Mr. Morello meant that he wanted to be allowed to play solos and experiment.

After the quartet disbanded, Mr. Morello primarily worked as a drum clinician and teacher. His students included Jerry Granelli and Danny Gottlieb, both notable jazz drummers, and Max Weinberg, the longtime drummer for Bruce Springsteen and the former bandleader for "Late Night with Conan O'Brien."

But Mr. Morello yearned for the bandstand. "I'm tired of saying to some student, 'This is a stick.'" He told The New York Times in 1973. "I want to get out and play again."

Play again Mr. Morello did. He performed sporadically in the 1970s and '80s, including reunions with Mr. Brubeck in 1976 and 1985. During the 1990s Mr. Morello led his own group, which featured the saxophonist Ralph Lalama.

Joseph A. Morello was born in Springfield, Mass., on July 17, 1928. Sight-impaired from an early age, he took up the violin at 6 and performed Mendelssohn's Violin Concerto in E minor with the Boston Symphony Orchestra three years later. According to a biography on his Web site, Mr. Morello gave up the violin for drums at 15, after meeting his idol, the violinist Jascha Heifetz.

Information on survivors was not immediately available.

Died March 12, 2011   **The New York Times,** *March 13, 2011*

TAKE FIVE

My introduction to Joe Morello came via Willis Conover.

Conover was for a period the most famous American in the world.

Yet he was unknown to most Americans.

That was because he was the impresario of the Voice of America's Jazz Hour, which was broadcast only overseas. That program established one of the most influential presences in the hearts and minds of people all over the world in the middle of the 20th Century.

The Dave Brubeck Quartet was just one of the many jazz groups introduced to a world audience over the Voice.

And the jazz groups followed the Voice, playing gigs first in Europe and then beyond, to Asia, Africa and South America.

Before my return to the United States in 1960 after four years in the U.S. Army and studying at the University of Munich. I had attended performances by Jack Teagarden and his group in such out-of-the-way stops such as Straubing in Lower Bavaria on the Danube and Thelonius Monk to a much larger audience in Munich.

But it wasn't until being assigned to Springfield, Mass by United Press International in early 1961 that I found out that that was the hometown of the drummer in one of my favorite groups, the Dave Brubeck Quartet.

It was a thrill to attend that first performance in Springfield.

The group, Brubeck, alto saxophonist Paul Desmond, bassist Eugene Wright and Morello, had been together already for six years, and were to remain so for six more before disbanding in 1968.

After the performance, several of us, news reporters and aficionados, gathered around Morello for interviews and a general discussion with the hometown boy who had done well.

I believe it was Joe himself who suggested we repair to Handy's Lunch downtown for a bite to eat and to continue our conversations.

Handy's, no longer in existence, was one of those diner-like all-night restaurants (no booze, beer or wine) that attracted a fascinating heterogeneous mix of people on any given very early morning.

At Handy's, the crowd had thinned to seminar size.

And that is what Joe did over bacon and eggs, conducted a magnificent seminar on percussion.

Drums were the means of communication over distances in tribal societies, he reminded us, and then like most great teachers, he went on to describe what he had learned about percussion in those societies around the world.

This learning is conveyed most tellingly on the records and in the albums he cut both with and after Brubeck.

The one that sticks in my memory most succinctly is Caravan, a product distilled from the percussive artistry of the varied peoples of Afghanistan.

The Dave Brubeck Quartet broke up about the time of my return to the Connecticut Valley in the late 1960s, and opportunities to hear the group in live concert were few, for instance at reunions in 1976 and 1985.

But Joe Morello did return to Springfield in November, 1978 for a Welcome Home tribute at the Springfield Civic Center with fellow native and jazz artist, alto saxophonist Phil Woods.

Morello, who was nearly blind since early childhood, became a benefactor of the Fidelco Guide Dog Foundation in Bloomfield, Conn. in his later years, and this relationship produced one more memorable concert.

At FAC Hall at the University of Masschusetts in Amherst, the Dave Brubeck Quartet gave a "Grand Union" benefit performance for the guide dog foundation on Dec. 12, 1993.

Three of the original performers participated, Brubeck, Morello and Wright with flutist and alto sax player Bobby Millitello replacing the late Paul Desmond.

Brubeck conducted a seminar of his own that night in Amherst. It was almost a confessional.

He conceded that he had resisted for some time the imprecations of Desmond, with the support of the rhythm section of Morello and Wright, to experiment more with the timing of their jazz pieces.

That his players were right all along was proved when "Take Five" became, as described in the Morello obituary in The York Times, as "one of the most recognizable themes and most successful singles" of all time in jazz.

Resurrections...

Heaven's in vogue.

Mitch Albom's "The Five People You Meet in Heaven" has been a best seller.

Barbara Walters weighed in with a television special on ABC: "Heaven – Where Is It? How Do We Get There? "

But there is a widely unrecognized alternative.

And it isn't hell or Hades.

There are millions of people on this earth who avoid the morbidity of death by hoping for a resurrection to earth.

And they have instructive antecedents.

How about Job?

The ancient Midianite, Moses informs us, had very earthly hopes.

"His flesh shall be fresher than a child's;"
"He returneth to the days of his youth."—Job 33:25

This quotation is from the venerable American Standard Version of the Bible. But each reader is invited to turn to the original or to his or her favorite translation.

Job's understanding, both in these two lines and in the context of the full chapter, is a resurrection to earth and a spiritual and eventual physical paradise.

More than half a millennium later, King David recorded a similar prophecy.

"But the meek shall inherit the earth; And shall delight themselves in the abundance of peace." Psalm 37:11 (KJ)

How about Daniel?

After a generation in Babylonian, Medean and Persian captivity, he concludes his stirring account by being dutifully acquiescent to his Maker's command:

"But go thou thy way till the end be; for thou shalt rest, and shalt stand in thy lot, at the end of the days." Daniel 12:13

Although Daniel provided many clues to the future in the Messianic prophecy of the 70 weeks of years, of the four superpower beasts of world history and the great shifting conflict of north and south, the issue was still clouded more than six centuries later.

The disciples of Jesus of Nazareth were still confused shortly before his death despite having undergone three and one-half years of training and sacrifice.

Matthew recorded the session.

"Tell us, When will these things be, and what will be the sign of your presence and of the conclusion of the system of things?" Matthew 24:3.

I cite the Kingdom Interlinear Translation of the Greek Scriptures here expressly for its accurate translation of the Greek words parousias (presence) and synteleias tou aionos (conclusion of the system of things).

Mistranslations such as coming, instead of presence, and world, instead of system or age, have misled sincere students of the Scriptures for centuries.

Jesus listed dozens of signs in the chapters recorded by Matthew (24), Mark, (13) and Luke (21), and they had various fulfillments in the first century until the Revelation given to John.

As a Jehovah's Witness, I try to share, with all those who will read or listen, my belief that only 144,000 human beings (Revelation 7:4 and 14:1) in history will rule in the kingdom of the heavens and that millions of others, their DNA securely in God's memory (Psalm 139:16) will be resurrected to a paradise earth after Armageddon.

"Thine eyes did see my substance, yet being unperfect; and in thy book all my members were written, which in continuance were fashioned, when as yet there was none of them." (KJ)

It is fascinating that this verse was written nearly two thousand years before the evolution of the science of genetics or the invention of computers.

And I pray that during Armageddon, God's war on the wicked, I shall maintain my integrity and strength to survive it, and if I were to die before that time, that I would be prepared for my own resurrection.

I feel the same way about heaven as comedian Groucho Marx felt about the Friars Club in Los Angeles.

"Please accept my resignation," he wrote. "I don't want to belong to any club that will accept me as a member."

Why?

I was a middle class kid raised by lower middle class parents who were children of poor immigrants who landed in the Blackstone Valley mill town of Whitinsville, Mass. at the end of the 19th and beginning of the 20th centuries.

So I never rose higher than what some sociologists call upper middle class, and frequently felt uncomfortable there.

What does the 6th verse of the 20th chapter of the book of Revelation say about those who are going to heaven.

"Blessed and holy is he that hath part in the first resurrection; on such the second death hath no power, but they shall be priests of God and of Christ, and shall reign with him a thousand years." (KJ) Some people are destined, if not predestined, to rule, and some to be ruled over.

Given the choice, I choose the latter.

I make another choice, not to recognize an earthly process of establishing sainthood which usurps Jesus' role in choosing who his fellow kings and priests might be.

My question to each reader is "How many saints have you met in your lifetime?"

My honest answer is fewer than half a dozen, and only two, who will remain unnamed, who I think will make the heavenly cut, if I may use a golf cliché.

I have also met one person who has been described as a "saint" on this earth by someone whom I highly respect, and another, a physician, who was called saintly by a patient. But I expect both to be resurrected to this earth, not elevated to heaven.

Anthropologists estimate the number of human beings who have existed on this earth at between 20 and 60 billion.

As a pre-teen, I can still recall staring out past the street light into the woodland beyond, and while listening to tree toads, katydids, and other assorted creatures, wondering what was going to happen to all those dead heathen Chinese that the missionaries had failed to reach.

What a relief, decades later, to learn from the same Scriptures that all were not lost.

"Do not marvel at this," Jesus was quoted as saying in John 5:28,29, "because the hour is coming in which all those in the memorial tombs will hear his voice and come out, those who did good things to a resurrection of life, those who practiced vile things to a resurrection of judgment."

That the latter will not immediately be judged and dispatched early in that

1,000-year reign is testified to by Paul's letter to the Romans, the 6th Chapter, 7th verse: "For he who has died has been acquitted from his sin."

So millions, if not billions, who remain in God's memory, will be resurrected to earth, and have the opportunity to choose whether they will live forever on earth under God's heavenly kingdom rule.

You only live once, they say.

Not necessarily, according to Scripture.

If you only live once, you can't die twice.

The last surviving Apostle, John, makes four references to the second death.

In Revelation 2:11, Revelation 20:6, Revelation 20:14 and Revelation 21:8.5

Let's read them:

"He that hath an ear, let him hear what the Spirit saith to the churches. He that overcometh shall not be hurt of the second death." Revelation 2:11 (ASV).

Are you listening?

"Blessed and holy is he that hath part in the first resurrection: over these the second death hath no power; but they shall be priests of God and of Christ, and shall reign with him a thousand years." Revelation 20:6

Are you expecting to be part of this first resurrection – of the 144,000 who are not quite yet sealed – or the second?

"And death and Hades were cast into the lake of fire. This is the second death, even the lake of fire." Revelation 20:14

Will you still be alive at the end of the thousand years, when the above will happen?

"But for the fearful, and unbelieving, and abominable, and murderers, and fornicators, and sorcerers, and idolators, and all liars, their part shall be in the lake that burneth with fire and brimstone; which is the second death." Revelation 21:8

Not if you are still one of the above.

Hundreds of survivors, relatives, friends and colleagues of the nearly four dozen persons chosen for inclusion in the following pages may not share these expectations regarding the fate of their loved ones.

But I ask forbearance, and an open mind.

How many, I ask, have attended a funeral service and heard a priest, minister, rector, rabbi or imam intone that the most recently deceased would be, or already has been accepted in the kingdom of the heavens.

And how many, I ask, may have rolled their eyes, not wishing to be in the same club.

Having faith in the hope of the resurrection to earth of the 47 individuals who either were the most influential or the most memorable in my lifetime, I felt it incumbent to be prepared for the reunions.

Being either unaware of their deaths or separated from them by thousands of miles when they expired, I attended very few of their funeral or memorial services.

Actor Sterling Hayden once remarked how significant it was to pay one's respects to those one respects.

He cited Yugoslav President Josip Broz Tito as a leader whose funeral he would make it a point to attend. I believe he did.

I had hoped at the time that he would have preferred to attend the rites for Milovan Djilas, the man Tito jailed twice.

As it was, I was unable to attend the funeral of Djilas, when he died, and always regretted it.

But I do hope to experience his resurrection.

I doubt Hayden shared my expectation of experiencing Tito's resurrection.

Strangely, Tito and Djilas discussed the prospect.

It was recorded by Djilas in his memoir, "Rise and Fall," published by Harcourt Brace Jovanovich in 1983.

The occasion was the death of Boris Kidrič, a Slovenian Partisan fighter during World War II and the first member of the Yugoslav Politburo to die after the war, in 1953.

Djilas described the effect the news of Kidrič's terminal illness, leukemia, had on the leadership of the maverick Socialist nation.

"Kidrič's would be the first unavoidable peacetime death in the uppermost ranks of our leadership; somber knowledge, a dull sense of foreboding, penetrated our circle, weighing upon each man individually," Djilas wrote.

Djilas proceeded to explain Kidrič's significance, political and personal, to the Socialist leadership of Yugoslavia, as the head of the newly developing economy independent of Moscow.

During his treatment, Kidrič went into shock after a blood transfusion (a doctor acknowledged to Djilas that a blood subgroup had not been checked.).

Djilas, Edvard Kardelj, a fellow Slovenian and closest colleague of Kidrič, Aleksandr Ranković, another Yugoslav vice-president with Kardelj, and President Tito all arrived.

Although Kidrić survived that crisis, his condition gradually worsened.

During one of his conversations with Zelenka Kidrič, his wife, Djilas interpreted a remark conveyed by Mrs. Kidrič that her husband had thoughts of an afterlife shortly before his death.

Djilas later acknowledged that he had been reproached by Kidrič's widow for imparting " 'comforting' materialist rationalizations" to Kidrič which persuaded him only of death's imminence.

He died on April 12, 1953.

The coffin and the official mourners were subsequently transported by Tito's personal train from Belgrade to Ljubljana, the capital of the Slovenian republic, where the funeral was to be held.

En route, Djilas expounded his materialistic beliefs about the indestructibility of matter.

Djilas described Tito's response as half facetious.

The Yugoslav leader observed that "one ought not to talk about life beyond the grave, inasmuch as no one knew anything about it."

There is no need for such ignorance.

The Apostle Paul said as much in a letter to the Thessalonians.

"Moreover, brothers, we do not want YOU to be ignorant concerning those who are sleeping (in death); that you may not sorrow just as the rest also do who have no hope."   1st Thessalonians 4:13 (NW)

His fellow apostle, John, agreed. Wrote he, in his Gospel:

"This means everlasting life, their taking in knowledge of you, the only true God, and of the one whom you sent forth, Jesus Christ." John 17:3 (NW)

This leads to my favorite Scripture, in Paul's statement to the Hebrews.

"Faith is the substance of things hoped for, the evidence of things unseen." Hebrews 11:1 (KJ).

Or, in a more precise, if less poetic translation: "Faith is the assured expectation of things hoped for, the evident demonstration of things though not beheld." Hebrews 11:1 (NW).

The substance of things hoped for follows in the rest of this work.

...of an Obituary Writer

I started on obits.

Everybody on The Worcester (Mass.) Telegram started on obits.

It was the training ground.

The bereaved may be the most sensitive of newspaper readers.

And the editors who trained us at The Telegram knew it.

That is why each obituary written on the City side went through either a city editor or an assistant city editor and then to the copy desk where it went through both a rim man and a slot man. The same procedure maintained on the State, or County side.

Although members of some families came into the newsroom personally with obituaries and information, most obituaries came in via the funeral homes, and these varied in their thoroughness and accuracy.

It was the responsibility of the obituary writer to filter the information they provided into an accurate obituary that would raise no questions on the various desks. It was also his (there were no hers yet) responsibility to check the newspaper library, or morgue, for any supplemental information.

Reporting and writing obituaries required immediate mastery of the Style Manual that had been published by the Worcester Telegram and The Evening Gazette in 1950.

These 93 pages established the rules for Abbreviations (12 categories), Authorities (encyclopedic and lexicographic), Capitalization (12 categories), Controversial stories, Courts, Cut Lines,* Date Lines, Figures (10 categories),

Local Usage, News Sources, News Writing (6 categories), Obituaries, Office Rules, Police News, Preparation of Copy, Punctuation (9 categories), Sports, Women's Organizations, and Word Usage.

The sooner these 93 pages were mastered, the sooner one gained the respect of members of both the city and copy desks.

*Cut lines were the lines that were written to explain a photograph. The typeset lines were placed just under the metal piece that was cut out of an engraving of photographs and put on a metal block on the turtle which carried the metal type. Stereotyped mats were then rolled and turned into the rounded metal page that was placed on the press.

Obituaries were particularly newsworthy in mid-June, 1953.

A tornado had swept through Central Massachusetts in an east-south-east direction on June 9, wreaking destruction on a northeastern section of the industrial city of Worcester, then the third largest in New England with a population of 200,000.

I was still in New Wilmington, Pa. at the end of my junior year at Westminster College, scheduled to start as a reporter on the city staff of The Telegram the following week.

My mother called from Whitinsville, 14 miles south of the disaster area, telling me that Managing Editor Francis Murphy of The Telegram had called and asked if I could start work immediately. He had earlier agreed to hire me as a summer reporter, an upgrade from the copy boy role I had played at The (afternoon) Evening Gazette the previous summer.

I immediately flew home from Youngstown, Ohio via Newark (my first flight) and reported for work as soon as I could.

The tornado had cut a 46-mile swath through Central Massachusetts, and a lesser parallel companion twister had skipped across the hilltops to the south, causing much property damage (including my Uncle Bill Crawford's chicken farm in Northbridge).

But death, injury and destruction centered on the populous city of Worcester.

The final tally, recorded in the 50th anniversary special published by the Sunday Telegram on June 8, 2003, was 94 dead, 1,288 injured, 4,000 buildings leveled or damaged, 10,000 to 15,000 people left homeless.

"Insurers estimated damage at $53 million." The Telegram reported. "That was in 1953 dollars. It would be $1.3 billion today."

For a long time I believed that the final death toll was 93.

That was because I had established that a woman who died in early September had succumbed to lingering injuries from the tornado, the 93rd victim of the storm. I wrote her obituary shortly before returning for my senior year in college.

She was No. 93.

Apparently, one more victim died later, making the final official tally of 94.

I didn't stay on obits for long after my return following graduation a year later. First was the day police beat and finally the night police, from four in the afternoon until four in the morning.

That is another story.

I didn't write another obituary for nearly a decade.

The interim consisted of 39 months in the U.S. Army, a couple of years at the University of Munich, and a short period of junior high teaching at Shrewsbury, Mass. before catching on with United Press International in Boston.

But not until my transfer from Springfield, Mass., to London, England did I write another obituary.

There I wrote two.

The first was of the Orthodox Patriarch of Istanbul, Archbishop Bishop Athenagoras; the second of Marshal Josip Broz Tito of Yugoslavia.

Both were updates of previously written obituaries filed for immediate use.

The second was probably assigned to allow me to dig into the background and prepare to cover the maverick Socialist leader before my assignment to Belgrade in late 1965.

I'm not sure how many times it was updated before Tito died in 1980.

My acquaintance with obituaries beyond that of an avid reader awaited repatriation to the United States and my joining the staff of The Springfield Union and Sunday Republican in Massachusetts' third largest city in 1967.

A number of years ensued of being an editor of and direct and indirect supervisor of several competent obituary editors and writers.

Fortunately, early retirement preceded the death of the newspaper obituary as such in several middle-size newspapers in New England and elsewhere.

New York Times writer Felicity Barringer addressed this trend of paid obituaries in a thorough article on the issue in The Times on Jan. 14, 2002.

She noted that the policy was established by a few small newspapers and accelerated with more newspapers with substantial circulations, and more healthy balance sheets, adopting the practice.

Among the first was The Portland Press Herald in Maine, which then reported a circulation of 77,000 daily and 123,000 on Sunday.

Barringer noted that newspapers in large cities had largely been given a pass when it came to printing many obituaries, considering the size of their populations and readership.

But, she reported, "In smaller communities, where people know one another and each death has more resonance, obituaries, like wedding and birth notices, mark important moments in community life and have been allotted space and resources accordingly."

The Portland Press Herald was closely followed by The Springfield Newspapers and The Worcester Telegram.

The publisher of The Telegram felt constrained to explain, rationalize and perhaps justify the policy change in an article beside his byline and photo on Thursday, Aug. 7, 2003.

Bruce S. Bennett gave two principal reasons.

"The first," he wrote, "is part of society's changing approach in the observance of a death."

The gist of this argument was that since family members were participating in funeral services and eulogies to a greater degree and were transforming an ages-old institution from mourning to celebrating, the newspaper should reflect this development in its news columns.

The second reason, Bennett reasoned, was : "financial."

It cited cost pressures, noting the recent changes in policy at both Portland and Springfield.

It is honest of Mr. Bennett, and perhaps other publishers and editors as well, to acknowledge that most funeral directors would have preferred that the newspapers not change their practice.

One of their objections was that clients who had prepaid for funeral services had not anticipated a new cost.

What is not generally known is the staggering increase in the costs, which are borne entirely by the bereaved, and not shared by either the newspaper or the funeral industry, which will be addressed later.

Felicity Barringer of The New York Times was prescient enough to interview the president of the Poynter Institute in Florida, a highly respected organization that studies newspapers, to get his take on the changes.

James Naughton told her:

"Newspapers have for many years had the ability to sell death notices to funeral homes and individuals and to publish obituaries. Combining the two or confusing the two is taking advantage of the families" of the deceased.

He added that if newspapers cede to outsiders control over the content of articles, "They might as well abandon the entire staff and let people write whatever they want and then it wouldn't be a newspaper and we wouldn't worry about it.'

This report was written before the proliferation of The Internet, web sites, blogging and twittering, and may be regarded as prophetic.

The editor of the Portland (Me.) Press Herald acknowledged pangs regarding the change in policy.

Jeannine A. Guttman was quoted by Barringer as follows:

"Because of the very difficult economic situations newspapers are in, they are turning to a very painful choice; And it is painful. It's one that no one relishes or jumps into with glee. We decided, rather than cut our news staff, or our news hole, or other resources, we would do this instead."

This explanation is disingenuous, at best.

What the Press Herald did was reduce the news hole and turn it over to advertising.

Newspapers vary in their interpretations as to what constitutes a news hole.

Many count the comic section as part of the news hole. Others include columns, such as bridge and astrology. Cartoons, illustrations and photos eat up other parts of what is regarded in total as the news hole.

My first confrontation with the cost to the newspaper subscriber of this new policy came with a call from a retired colleague.

He had learned of the death in New Bedford, Mass. of a former colleague at The Springfield Newspapers.

The former husband of this colleague took it upon himself to write the obituary of this woman for submission to the newspaper. He waxed on for about 500 words, until he was advised by the paper, under the new policy, of the cost of the obituary.

It was about $500.

The writer, a former managing editor at one of the dailies, then exercised some self-discipline and reduced the size of the obituary by half without doing the deceased or the various readers of the obituary any appreciable disservice.

It must be acknowledged here that newspapers tend to embroider the obituaries of their late editors and publishers.

Among the longest obituaries in this book are those of such editors and news executives, despite efforts by this author and subsequent editors to reduce their size (Please note the ellipses as you read them).

The new paid obituary policy became personal on Aug. 14, 2005, with the death of my mother at the age of 96.

My mother was a wise woman, and wife of a prudent and thrifty husband, who had taught their children frugality.

One of the later prudential acts was to pay for the funeral in advance. This took place during a period of rational exuberance when interest rates were low. One institution continued to pay higher rates, the funeral home. Its rate was 5 per cent, and remained so despite the less generous provisions of the banks.

My mother, who was still reinvesting dividends in her utility stock into her mid 80s, despite our failed efforts to induce her to become a more avid consumer, continued to make money into her 90s.

By the time of her death, the interest on her prepaid funeral had accumulated to an amount that more than compensated for the inflationary costs of the Worcester Telegram's classified advertising department.

The funeral home, whose owner remained unhappy with the policy as many cited in earlier articles, agreed to provide an accounting of the specific costs.

I personally wrote the obituary submitted to the funeral home and the newspaper and had it vetted by relatives.

It was not lengthy, about seven column inches.

A second paid notice was submitted to The Springfield Newspapers, the circulation area where my two children lived at the time.

The bill for the Worcester Telegram obit, without a picture, came to $452.50.

The Republican in Springfield ran the paid notice separately and reworked a short obituary from the material, which was to my taste. The charge, which was less so, was $88.35.

To put this all in perspective, I decided to take the Sunday Telegram of Oct. 16, 2005, the day before this writing, and tally the number of obituaries.

There were 20 of them filling nine column inches over two pages in a six column per page format.

A casual accounting would indicate that the Sunday Telegram received upward of $10,000 that day for a news service that once was free.

There was another half column of advertising from the National Funeral Directors Association promoting advanced planning of funerals, which I heartily endorse, and remarked upon earlier.

There was also another third of a column of larger ads placed by families in memoriam of their loved ones and about a third of a column of house ads by the newspaper, including a box explaining the Death Notice Policy of the Telegram & Gazette.

Another 2½ columns contained agate size notices of Recent Deaths and Funerals Today which formerly constituted the paid death notices.

Several columnists have expressed their views since the new policies in their respective papers that the bereaved now do have the opportunity to personalize the life stories of their loved ones and avoid the formulaic obituaries of the past.

I choose the accounts of professionals, not the misspelled, inaccurate, banal offerings of the amateur.

There are suggestions for the newspapers to get out of this cul-de-sac.

The first is be honest.

Mark the obituary pages as advertisements, just as the doctored up ads that businesses design to look like news pages.

That would remove the hypocrisy.

Secondly, the newspapers could revise their policy and run obituaries as shorter news stories and include all the funeral matter in paid death notices which families would be only too willing to pay for, and there if they wish include more mundane facts clearly recognizable as paid eulogies.

This would also reduce the repetition of printing the funeral information in the obituary for a price and then also giving it away free in the unpaid death notices.

May this diatribe now rest in peace.

And on to a paean to the true hero, the classic obituary writer.

A dean was Alden Whitman, described by former NBC News president

Michael Gartner in a eulogy in The Wall Street Journal of Oct. 11, 1990 as "the best writer of obituaries ever."

The headline over Gartner's eulogy said, "The Man Who Put Life Into Obituaries."

And Gartner cited The Times' own obituary of Whitman as calling him the "pioneer" in the use of interviews of notables to "personalize and energize their obituaries."

But he chided The Times for not having interviewed Whitman before his death at 76 on Sept. 4, 1999 in order to have provided an even more "fact-filled and quote-filled and detail-filled" biography.

Fortunately, Whitman had given his own account of his period on the "obit desk" in the monthly "More," in September of 1977.

The magazine headlined the piece:

ALDEN WHITMAN: 11 YEARS ON THE DEATH WATCH

The first deck, or drop head, read:

The Ultimate Status Game: Deciding Who Dies in 'Advance at The 'Times'

The bottom deck was lifted from the final paragraph of Whitman's own piece, the ultimate tribute by a head writer unable or unwilling to improve on the writer's own gift.

It read:

"A happy oarsman on the Styx."

Whitman describes how he had been a rim man for nearly a quarter of a century, the first decade at the Buffalo Evening News, and another 13 years at the Times, when Harrison Salisbury plucked him from the desk to put the Sir Winston Churchill obituary into shape in the fall of 1964.

The Times had decided to put out a 16-page section on Churchill and had assigned two former London correspondents to write the piece under Salisbury's direction.

Former Timesman Gay Talese has provided a delightful account in "The Kingdom and the Power" how Salisbury climbed the slippery totem pole of Metropolitan Desk success in New York after returning from Moscow as an esteemed foreign correspondent and expert Kremlinologist.

Salisbury was immediately assigned on his return to New York to do a piece on trash pickup in Gotham, an assignment the Metropolitan Desk routinely gave to returning bigwigs from abroad as a sop to Iphigene Sulzberger, the wife of the publisher. Most gave the assignment perfunctory treatment.

Salisbury turned his into a crusade which attracted the attention not only of the city fathers, but the newspaper's hierarchy, via a very appreciative publisher's wife.

It also shoved Salisbury into the news hierarchy, where he was in a position to command such projects as the Churchill obituary.

"One afternoon," Whitman wrote, "Salisbury detached me from the desk with instructions to try to put the Churchill obit into printable shape, to handle the two writers with tact, but to rewrite when I thought it necessary."

Whitman called it a formidable task, but the great British statesman was cooperative to the extreme.

Whitman was given the assignment in the fall of 1964, but Churchill held on until the task was complete.

I can personally attest to that because I was put on the Death Watch in London by United Press International, which had reassigned several of its best writers from the continent to London to perform the same obit writing assignment.

During the next to last week of January, 1965, this assignment led to Hyde Park Gate, Sir Winston's London home, where Britons from throughout the isles and the commonwealth were gathering in homage day and night.

There, the parade of dignitaries, Randolph, Sarah, young Winston, Sir Anthony Eden, and other members of the family passed daily through the portals on what must have been Alden Whitman's most important death watch.

Sir Winston expired on Jan. 25, 1965.

Alden Whitman's career on the rim was already dead.

A.M. (Abe) Rosenthal, another successful foreign correspondent (Warsaw), had been named city editor, had noted Whitman's gifts, and offered him the post of advance obit writer before the Churchill obituary even appeared.

He asked Whitman to write several samples, of which Whitman submitted four, all to Rosenthal's satisfaction.

Then, shortly before Churchill's demise, Whitman was called in on his day off in early January to do another London obit, of poet T. S. Eliot, who had died that afternoon.

Whitman cited this as the first obituary he had written from a standing start, and the result pleased his superiors.

Whitman wrote himself that "Abe's laying on of hands was then official."

Thus began an obituary writing career that brought both The Times and Whitman great notoriety.

Whitman was given wide autonomy.

First he submitted a list of his own choosing to work on, got the list approved, and submitted the finished products.

There was enough material, Whitman noted, for a lifetime job.

His formula was to avoid the formulaic.

"The ideal that animated me," he wrote in the More piece," was to write a self-contained, biographical essay, one that was subtly judgmental, that could be set in type for instant use. The writing problems were obvious: to avoid banality, formulas, and the hackney of laudation. Above all, to escape the trap of repetition. So I ventured various structures and combinations of structures, fresh ways of presenting anecdotes and quotes, and inventive devices in phrasing sentences or clothing common thoughts in uncommon words. If they worked, they were policy."

"The object," he concluded, "was to fashion a true and honest portrait, one that would be valid and readable and go beyond a once-over-lightly that characterizes so many newspaper obits. If the response of readers who knew my subjects is any measure, I think I did fairly well over ten years."

One line in his essay epitomizes his success.

He cited his goal on the Churchill obituary was to produce an intimate portrait, "oozing blood, sweat, and tears (and brandy, too)."

After a year in his new job, he expanded his assignment to interviews with living celebrities to, so to speak, enliven the future obituaries.

Although he masked his purpose, his subjects, among the first, former President Harry S Truman, found delight in ripping the mask off.

"I know why you're here," Truman said in his office at Independence, Mo., "and I want to help you all I can."

These assignments brought travel, and finally, in 1967, acknowledgement, when the Times gave him his first byline on an obituary, on the former U.S. Ambassador to the Soviet Union, Williams C. Bullitt.

Whitman accepted the bylines with pleasure, and even more the resultant travel to Europe, the Far East and West Coast, to interview his future subjects.

At the end of his piece in More magazine, he assumes the well-deserved moniker of name-dropper.

The names dropped include those of poet John Masefield, writer C. P. Snow, the aforementioned Sir Anthony Eden, Churchill's foreign minister and a successor as British prime minister, French literary figures François Mauriac and Andrè Maurois, authors Graham Greene and Vladimir Nabokov, former Nationalist Chinese President Chiang Kai-shek and Madame Chiang, and three dictators, Spain's Francisco Franco, Argentina's Juan Domingo Peron and Yugoslavia's Josip Broz Tito.

At the close, Whitman drops several names of those he enjoyed interviewing the most, either for their historic roles, their traits or their challenging elusiveness.

Among them were Vietnam's Ho Chi Minh, artist Pablo Picasso, British philosopher Lord Bertrand Russell, American labor leader John L. Lewis, atomic scientist J. Robert Oppenheimer, humorist Frank Sullivan and Ethiopia's Haile Selassie, the latter cited for having spit in Italian leader Benito Mussolini's eye in 1936.

"I was a happy oarsman on the Styx," Whitman concluded, alluding to that river in the underworld of Greek mythology.

Briefly, I was transfigured by the Times from being a copy editor into being an obit writer. It was damned nice while it lasted."

Whitman retired in 1976, but he had established a legacy.

A sidebar to Whitman's piece in More magazine described how TV Guide publisher Walter Annenberg envisioned a magazine that would print only obituaries.

Annenberg's idea resulted from his frustrations at the paucity of death notices in the local papers produced at his desert retreat in Palm Springs, Calif.

But despite contacting Whitman on the idea, and obtaining his view that it was feasible, the project was shelved.

Many others took up Whitman's legacy on his retirement in 1976.

Several of them even had the distinction of having their own obituaries published in The Times, as did Whitman.

Among them were Albin Krebs, who died in June of 1992, and whose subjects included author Eudora Welty, cowboy Gene Autry, writer Truman Capote and food authority James Beard.

Another was Robert McGill Thomas, whose obituary on Jan. 8, 2000 was headlined the "Chronicler of Unsung Lives."

The Times gave him credit in the lead paragraph of his obituary of having "extended the possibilities of the conventional obituary form."

Thomas had, The Times reported, developed a fresh approach to the genre, looking for telling details to illuminate lives that might otherwise have been overlooked or underreported.

The Times described him as the sympathetic stranger at the wake, alert for the memorable tale that might not make its way into Who's Who, but would nevertheless graphically define a life.

Among those lives was that of Douglas Corrigan, one of the better known of his subjects. Wrong Way Corrigan piloted his Curtiss-Robin monoplane in 1938 from Floyd Bennett Field on Long Island to Dublin, Ireland instead of his purported destination, California. Thomas pointed out that Corrigan had made repeated requests to make the Transatlantic flight, and had been turned down because his craft had been deemed unworthy.

Others whose memory was resurrected for the Times obit page included Johnny Sylvester. Thomas defined as cynics those who doubted that little Johnny, bedridden at the time, was as sick as portrayed when Babe Ruth promised to hit a home run for him in the fourth game of the 1926 World Series. In the same category were those who doubted that the 11-year-old boy was dying, or that the Babe even promised to hit a homer for him, or that the three home runs he did hit saved the youngster's life.

"Any representations to the contrary, these people will tell you, were simply embellishments of a trivial incident by an oversentimental press in a hypersentimental age," Thomas wrote.

The Thomas obituary also noted that little Johnny Sylvester had died in 1990 at the age of 75.

Others included Chicago clothier Howard C. Fox, who claimed fame for naming the zoot suit, Russell Colley, the "Calvin Klein of space" as the father of the space suit, Rose Hamburger, the 105-year-old racing handicapper and Marion Tinsley, the showgirl turned checker champion,.

Thomas had his own favorite.

It was Edward Lowe, a sawdust merchant from Cassopolis, Mich.

Thomas first established the historical significance of Mr. Lowe's achievement.

He wrote:

"Cats have been domesticated since ancient Egypt, but until a fateful January day in 1947, those who kept them indoors fulltime paid a heavy price. For all their vaunted obsession with paw-licking cleanliness, cats, whose constitutions were adapted for arid desert climes, make such an efficient use of water that they produce a highly concentrated urine that is one of the most noxious effluences of the animal kingdom. Boxes filled with sand, sawdust or wood shavings provided a measure of relief from the resulting stench, but not enough to make cats particularly welcome in discriminating homes."

Thomas thus elevated Mr. Lowe's invention, kiln-dried granulated clay used for grease spills at industrial plants, and found a new million dollar market—KITTY LITTER.

Three years before Mr. Thomas' death, The Times had paid its obit writer the ultimate compliment by including 31 of his pieces in "The New York Times Book of Obituaries and Farewells."

"The Last Word," published by William Morrow in 1997 under the Quill imprint, contains 138 obituaries with a second subtitle "A Celebration of Unusual Lives."

I would agree with retired Times columnist Russell Baker in his foreword to "The Last Word" that "Obituaries these days often provide the only pleasure to be had from the daily newspaper."

And I also agree that they "should be savored slowly."

But I reject his advice that they should be saved for leisurely reading over the last cup of breakfast coffee."

"To plunge into them first thing," Baker argues, "before having endured the rest of the day's news, is like eating the dessert before tackling a fried-liver dinner."

Perhaps so, but in assisting my mother eat her meals in the nursing home in the last days of her 96-year life, I noticed she refused to punish herself with the main dish and insisted on the dessert, and who was I to argue.

Let the reader have the free will to read his newspaper as he or she will.

Millions of essays could be written by readers explaining how people read their newspapers.

"The Last Word" filled the need Walter Annenberg had foreseen two decades earlier when he contemplated a monthly magazine of obituaries.

"The Last Word" is a book full of highly readable obituaries, and I am grateful to my family funeral director for having called my attention to it.

Russell Baker's foreword is also worth reading, as is the introduction by its editor, Marvin Siegel.

Near its conclusion, he salutes the then obituary staff of The Times as follows:

"Fortunately, there is a talented pool of reporters who recognize the creative challenges and pleasures of capturing a life in a thousand words, of writing a story with a beginning, middle, and end. For these reporters the joy of writing obits is one of the best-kept secrets in journalism. The Times has a rich number of such obituarists and it is good to be able to acknowledge the contributions of a staff that produces quality work day in and day out, often without the recognition it deserves: Marilyn Berger, David Binder, Panny King, Enid Nemy, Holcomb B. Noble, Eric Pace, Wolfgang Saxon, Richard Severo, Norma Sosa and Robert McG. Thomas, Jr.

So be it.

In the nearly four dozen essays in this volume, I have sought to celebrate the most influential and memorable lives of my own. I pray to have done them justice, and am prepared to ask forgiveness face to face if I have not done so.

Dates of Death

"A good name is better than precious oil; and the day of death, than the day of one's birth." Ecclesiastes 7:1 ASV

Charles (Chick) Mantell	June 8, 1944
Elizabeth Nixon	Jan. 17, 1956
Richard H. Davis	May 8, 1962
Kenneth LeMere	June 27, 1965
Dr. Franz Schnabel	Feb. 25, 1966
Dr. W. Edward Balmer	Mar. 17, 1966
Henry(Hank)Minott	June 6, 1972
Francis P. Murphy	July 4, 1973
Donald R. Newhouse	Oct. 18, 1973
Mary (Martin) Ryan	Nov. 26, 1973
Robert W. Muir	June 9, 1981
George Merwin	Sept. 14, 1981
Georg Graf von Einsiedel	Oct. 26, 1983
Harry Charkoudian	Aug. 26, 1984

Dr. Georg Stadtmueller	Jan. 11, 1985
Joseph Cotton	June 12, 1986
Pavle Lukač	1988
Daniel F. Gilmore	Aug. 8, 1988
Roger Sylvester	June 27, 1989
Hal T. Boyd	Feb. 10, 1990
Paul Donoghue	July 22, 1991
Arnold Banning	Oct. 5, 1991
Dr. William Vander Lugt	June 9, 1992
Horace Hill	Dec. 7, 1994
Franz Cyrus	(?) Feb. 9, 1995
Milovan Djilas	Apr. 20, 1995
Charles (Buzz) Ridl	Apr. 28, 1995
Alan B. Wade	Sept. 2, 1995
Vernon (Vic) Wanty	June 3, 1996
Rupprecht Scherff	July 23, 1996
Karol C. Thaler	Aug. 12, 1996
George H. Pipal	Nov. 20, 1996
John Donati	Sept. 23, 1999

Freda Clark	Nov. 20, 2002
Dolores Perkins	Feb. 1, 2003
Judge Frank Freedman	Aug. 21, 2003
Sir Peter Ustinov	Mar. 28, 2004
Albert Veronesi	Aug. 16, 2004
Richard Garvey	Sept. 9, 2004
Lawrence R. Pitzer	Sept. 10, 2004
Sadik Duda	May 30, 2007
Boris Alexander	July 18, 2007
Jerome C. Neff.	Oct. 2, 2007
Douglas E. Kneeland	Dec. 15, 2007
Joe Morello	March 12 2011

Acknowledgments

As mentioned elsewhere in this work, an impetus was provided by Mr. (Fred) Rogers when he asked members of his audience when he was inducted into the Television Hall of Fame in 1999 to pause and think about someone who had had a good influence on them.

Those reflected upon in this volume are the tip of that human iceberg. After publication, I shall begin reflecting on the dozens of persons who are not included in this work.

In the meantime, I wish to acknowledge those who assisted me to collect the biographical information on those who are.

* * *

It begins with Eleanor Balmer Orsini, who was 95 when I called on her at her home on Whitin Avenue in Whitinsville, Mass. She was one of Doc Balmer's two daughters, both of whom had attended grade and grammar school with my mother.

Her father's birth book, which we dug out of a maze of material, allowed me to draw a fuller picture of the doctor who became a legend in the Blackstone Valley of Massachusetts.

This legend was celebrated by the Blackstone Valley Tribune in Whitinsville both at the observance of his half century of medical service to the community and in a tribute published in the same community weekly by Peter Hackett, a local historian.

The introduction to those sources were provided by personnel at the Tribune and at the Whitinsville Social Library.

* * *

Harold Banning, one of Arnold Banning's three children, and his oldest son, graduated in our Class of 1950 from Northbridge High School in Whitinsville, Ma., and provided more than what I was asking from him. He gave me a copy of the monograph his father had written about his difficult emigration from The Netherlands and more clippings of his artistic and other interests. That information and conversations with his brother Wil provided a fuller understanding of my own appreciation for their father.

* * *

It was only after I had finished the research on the above two subjects that I began to delve into the background of my Uncle Charles (Chick) Mantell, whose torpedo bomber crashed into the Pacific on June 8, 1944, killing him and his two crewmates.

Only after the death of my mother, his older sister, in 2005 did I find letters that he had sent, including one a few days before his death. There in the desk file also were copies of V-mail letters I had sent as part of a Grammar School project. One was particularly poignant. It was marked deceased. My mother had never shown me the letter that had been returned to me at his death. Research, including contact with survivors of his TBF crewmates on the U.S.S. Cabot, a small carrier, continued. It eventually resulted in the establishment of a memorial to Uncle Chick at Fletcher Street and Country Club Drive in Whitinsville. The idea was initiated by my brother Jack Crawford, who never knew Chick, and took place June 10, 2006 with the cooperation of state and town officials, including high school friend Spaulding Ross (Sonny) Aldrich.. Town Manager Michael Coughlin was particularly diligent in establishing that the article on World War II carrier duty written by war correspondent Ernie Pyle and included in this volume had been based on a visit to the Cabot.

* * *

More persons assisted in providing information about Professor Elizabeth Nixon than any other subject in the United States. I was persuaded to write a composite obituary because none of the three provided by kind library staff members at the Omaha (Neb.) World-Herald, The Sioux City (Iowa) Journal, or The (Youngstown, Ohio) Vindicator provided the complete story. The gaps were ably filled in by Dr.

Dewey DeWitt, archivist at Westminster (Pa.) College, Mary Cooley James, the Director of Alumni Relations at the college, and James A. Perkins, chairman of the Department of English. They alsoprovided me with a copy of Dr. Amy Charles' eulogy and information leading to the University of North Carolina at Greensboro. Mr. Herman Trojanowski, archivist there, kindly provided background information on Dr. Charles. Mary M. McCracken of Carnegie, Pa., a former trustee of the Elizabeth Nixon Memorial Scholarship, provided important insight.

* * *

Westminster College officials are also to be acknowledged in the gathering of information about Westminster and Pitt basketball coach Charles (Buzz) Ridl. Both The (Pittsburgh) Post Gazette and The (Youngstown, Ohio) Vindicator served as sources. The Post-Gazette added a column by sports staffer Bob Smizik, which provided added insight.

* * *

Alumni office records also led to the background on Vernon (Vic) Wanty, the college classmate and native Englishman encountered on the grounds of Canterbury Cathedral a decade after graduation. That led to the Lancaster (Pa.) Newspapers, whose library staff provided a copy of his obituary printed in the Lancaster Intelligencer on June 3 of 1996.

* * *

Greg Olgers, director of Information Services at Hope College in Holland, Mich., was kind enough to provide not only guidance to obtain obituaries of Dr. William Vander Lugt from the Grand Rapids Press and Holland Sentinel, but also included the copy of an interview the late college chancellor had given to a campus publication and a copy of his address at the college's 1972 commencement, the year of his retirement.

* * *

I called Larry Pitzer on Sunday, Sept. 12, 2004 to find out whether he and his wife Phyl had booked the same hotel in Sharon, Pa. for the 50th reunion of Westminster (Pa.) College's Class of 1954, of which both I and Phyl were members. Phyl answered the phone and immediately surmised that I did not know her husband of 50 years and four days had died fewer than 48 hours before. My condolences to the widow of my best college friend, for whom I'd served as an usher at their wedding at Great Neck, L.I., N.Y., were not very articulate. Shortly after hanging up the phone, I called the Sun-Sentinel at Fort Lauderdale, Fla., and received details of the funeral arrangements from the Kraeer Funeral Home at nearby Boca Raton. The Pitzer children lived in upstate New York and New Hampshire, which delayed the funeral and also provided time for me to drive down from Massachusetts for the services the following weekend.

* * *

I, a native New Englander, was caught in a New England trap seeking the place of birth and death of Richard Davis, one of my first editors at The Worcester (Mass.) Telegram. My memory was of driving Dick home to Oakham after the last edition of the paper in the early morning hours. That memory was faulty. Dick was a native of the Oakdale section of West Boylston, just northeast of Worcester, and it was the cooperative officials of that town which provided me the date of his death. Native New Englanders sometimes get great pleasure confounding outsiders by informing them of the village of their birth or residence rather than the corporate town. But after establishing that Dick Davis was from the Oakdale section of West Boylston rather than Oakham, the staff of the morgue (library) of The Telegram provided me all the material I needed on both Dick and Frank Murphy, the legendary managing editor of the paper.

* * *

I am indebted to Barbara Chamberlain of the Harrison Memorial Library in Carmel, Ca., and Victor Henry, reference librarian at the Monterey Public Library for the obituary of Hal Boyd, our landlord at Carmel Highlands. Bill Reedy and Tom DeBettencourt, both Army Language School graduates and former Highlands residents, were also helpful with information over the years.

* * *

One can hardly blame The Monterey (Calif.) County Herald" for not providing an obituary of Boris Alexandrovsky, the retired Russian and Ukrainian language teacher at the Army Language School, later Defense Language Institute, at the Presidio of Monterey. He wasn't dead. Natela Cutter of the Alumni Affairs Office of the D.L.I. bailed me out with the good news. She confirmed for me that the 95-year-old immigrant from the Ukraine was still living at his Monterey home where I had visited him in 1979. I wrote to him and learned that he was not only lucid in the midst of his 10th decade, but able and willing to read and correct the vignette I had written about him. We corresponded several times before his passing. Once again, as in the case of Hal Boyd, Mr. Henry provided me a copy of the obituary.

* * *

Klaus Budesheim, a native of Offenbach, Germany and a fellow congregant in the Northbridge Congregation of Jehovah's Witnesses in Massachusetts, edited my letters and emails to Straubing, Germany to learn of the fate of Georg Graf von Einsiedel. Bernd Hielscher, the Redaktionsleiter, and Evi Fleischmann of the Readers Service of the Straubinger Tagblatt traced his whereabouts to Wilhelmshaven. Ulrich Räcker-Wellnäz of the archives section of that northern German city provided the date of Graf von Einsiedel's death as Oct. 26, 1983. He was born on Jan. 26, 1910.

* * *

Two sources provided background on University of Munich historian Franz Schnabel. Thanks go to Anne Blauth of the Dokumentations- und Informations Zentrum of the Sueddeutsche-Zeitung, who provided a copy of the eulogy written by Rudolf Goldschmit. This supplemented the material I had obtained on the Internet with the cooperation of Klaus Budesheim of Uxbridge, Ma., a native of Oppenbach in Hessia and a willing researcher. Conrad Fuchs's work was published in the Biographisch-Bibliographisches KIRCHENLEXIKON. Herr Guenter Heuberger of the Stiftung Maximilianeum in Munich supplemented that material with a copy of an obituary-eulogy published by the Fakultaet fuer Geistes- und Sozialwissenschaften of the Universitaet Karlsruhe, Herr Herberger dug even more deeply to come up with a eulogy on Dr. Georg Stadtmueller, also of the University of Munich. That work was written by Helmut Schaller and published in the Zeitschrift fuer Ostforschung in 1986.

* * *

Wall Street Journal bureau chief Ian Johnson in Berlin and Garip Sultan of Munich provided leads concerning Misbach Miftofoglu and Sadik Duda.

* * *

Bill Ketter, editor-in-chief of the Eagle-Tribune Publishing Co. in North Andover, Mass., was the bird dog that helped me track down Hank Minott. Ketter, also a former Unipresser who headed the Boston Bureau before moving on to the Quincy Patriot-Ledger and the Eagle-Tribune, led me to the Woburn Times, Hank's hometown newspaper. There, Jim Haggerty did the rest.

* * *

An expression of gratitude goes to Frank Callahan of Worcester (Mass.) Academy, who not only provided details as to Alan Wade's death, but of one of the last important gestures of his life. That was his spearheading a drive to rename the Waltham, Mass. Federal Center the Frederick C. Murphy Federal Center after a fellow member of the 65th Infantry Division killed in France in 1945. Murphy's name had slipped into obscurity with the closing , three decades after World War II, of the Waltham Army Hospital that had been named after him. "They just kind of walked away from the name and forgot it," Al told a reporter for States News Service in Washington in an article published in The Boston Globe. "That may not seem like a big deal to a lot of the public, but to the people in the division and to the family, it's important," Al told the reporter. Callahan's efforts eased the task of obtaining obituaries of Al from both The Washington Post and the Globe.

* * *

Durham Caldwell, a retired television newsman for WHYN, Channel 40 in Springfield, Mass., was instrumental in pinning down the date of death of his colleague Ken LeMere, and providing additional insights into Ken's career. The research led to the morgue (library) of The Republican Co., publisher of the former Springfield Daily News, The Springfield Union and the current merged survivors The (Springfield) Republican and (Springfield) Sunday Republican. Laurie Vanasse and Jeannie Anderson were generously cooperative in providing background material on Ken, and a succession of former colleagues at the relevant newspapers, and several former neighbors. These included material on Joe Cotton, George Merwin, Judge Frank Freedman, the Clarks, John Donati, Al Veronesi, Mary Ryan, Roger Sylvester, Harry Charkoudian, Bob Muir, Rupprecht Scherff, Donald Newhouse, Paul Donoghue, Horace Hill and Dick Garvey. Laurie and Jeannie saved me hours, if not days.

* * *

Joe Cotton himself provided me with much of the material on his fascinating life, and additional material was provided by his widow Vivian. The staff of Farrar, Strauss and Giroux president Jonathan Galassi was kind enough to enable me to contact writer Tom Wolfe. The latter agreed to read the piece and did so with a discerning eye and a kind response.

* * *

Mrs. Marilyn Hughes of Wilbraham, Mass., helped by providing the date of death of her father, George Merwin.

* * *

I am indebted to Pamela Harris, then of Monson, Mass., for added information on her grandparents, Henry and Freda Clark, late of Wilbraham. My daughter Rebecca Dorsey informed me of Freda's death, at the age of 97, in November of 2002. I was living out of the circulation area of the Springfield newspapers at the time. I felt obligated to augment the paid death notice of nine lines which appeared in The (Springfield, Mass.) Union-News at that time, and am obliged to Pamela for helping me do so.

* * *

The Washington Post and Ancestry.com must be credited for coming up with the needed information on Dan Gilmore. Correspondence to several purported sources on this most collegial and competent of bosses came to dead ends before reaching out on the Internet.

* * *

The primary source to locate George Pipal was the United Press International Directory of 1966, although I was surprised to learn that neither George, nor Paul Allerup, who had been in London, were listed there. Both had transferred to New York, where George was now general sales executive and a resident of Old Greenwich, Conn. Bob Carter, the computer guru-geek at my recreational haven, Blissful Meadows Golf Club in Uxbridge, Mass., came to the rescue via Ancestry.com, which produced the information that George had moved. The Napa Valley (Calif.) Register and The Press Democrat of Santa Rosa provided the obituaries that showed that George had replanted his journalistic vineyards to the California wine country, and very successfully. Testimony to that was his listing in a succession of editions of Who's Who in America.

* * *

The obituary of Sir Peter Ustinov is from the premium archive of The New York Times.

* * *

Bob Carter is again credited for assistance in establishing the date and place of the death of Karol Charles Thaler. This information was provided willingly and expeditiously by the Royal Borough of Kensington and Chelsea in London, where Karol lived and died. The certified copy of his death certificate, did not, however, provide the place of his birth. Like so many obituaries of Eastern Europeans who died far from their homelands in the latter part of the 20th and early part of the 21st centuries, the birth places were inaccurate. In Karol's case, it was listed as May 22, 1906, in Poland. Unfortunately, an independent Poland did not exist at the time. I was left under the impression by my many conversations with Karol, that he had been born in the Sudetenland, Bohemia or Moravia, all now part of the Czech republic. I shall sometime revisit this question.

* * *

Die Presse, which describes itself as the Independent Daily for Austria, not only provided a brief obituary of Franz Cyrus, but returned my money order for the information uncashed. The handwritten note in German expressed the hope that the enclosure was of service. The payment by check, in a postscript, was described as unnecessary.

* * *

Acknowledgement for the obituary of Milovan Djilas goes both to The New York Times, which published it, and its author, Serge Schmemann, who first came into sharp focus as a newsman for me with his reports on the eschatological effects of the Chernobyl nuclear disaster in Ukraine. My appreciation also goes to the late publisher, William Jovanovich, who helped us maintain contact with the Djilases, when they visited Princeton University, and Milovan's son Alexa, whom I first met as a teen-age boy in Belgrade and next encountered at Harvard Yard in Cambridge, Mass.

* * *

The Lazovic family of Hilton Head Island, refugees from the Bosnian wars, confirmed that my Belgrade news colleague Pavle Lukač and the Sarajevo Olympics director were one and the same.

* * *

The Department of Athletic Communications at Syracuse University helped pin down the timing of John Donati's football career with roster information. Also received was a page of photos. The picture of J. A. Donati revealed that the marvelous personality that was to attract his future wife Gloria was coupled with remarkable good looks.

* * *

Paul Rigali, Al Veronesi's best and nearly lifelong friend, paid me the honor of reading the piece on Al. He also sent me copies of material that was read at his funeral, of which one defined Al's legacy. It read:
"I set out to find a friend but couldn't find one.
I set out to be a friend and friends were everywhere."

* * *

Bill Fitzgerald of Longmeadow, Mass., a friend of the Ryan family, was helpful in refocusing the memory of Mary Ryan, and pinpointing the date of her death. Judith Reuter of Byron-Hafey-Ratell Funeral Homes provided the obituary.

* * *

Thanks go to Ms. Arax Charkoudian of Chicopee, Mass., for the kind invitation to attend one of the summer weekend gatherings of the Charkoudian clan on top of Minnechaug Mountain in Wilbraham. That was one of her responses to my request for verification of certain facts regarding her Uncle Harry.

* * *

Carol Muir paid me the supreme compliment. She asked that I write the obituary of her husband Bob, a father of five who died at the age of 40 of a cerebral aneurism. Carol was a Jehovah's Witness, and I was not at the time, but she had confidence that I would do my professional best as an editor at The Springfield Newspapers. It was the first time I had experienced Jehovah's Witnesses in the grieving process. It also greatly strengthened my perception that this was Bob's first death, and it was highly unlikely, God willing, that there would be a second.

* * *

Dave Evans, treasurer and controller of The Republican Co., publisher of The (Springfield, Mass.) Republican, kindly forwarded me information on Horace Hill and the scholarship he set up for descendants of employees at the newspaper. Jean Parent and staff members at the Community Foundation of Springfield added to my appreciation of both Horace and his generosity with the information they provided.

I am grateful to the late Dolores Perkins not only for her life example, but for a copy of her 818-word memoir which she gave to me before her death. These gave me added incentive to delve more deeply into the First Amendment issues that attended her childhood, and to the influence, ever more appreciated, of U.S. Supreme Court Justice Robert H. Jackson in aiding those striving to achieve and maintain freedom of religious expression and freedom of the press.

Bibliography

ALEXANDROVSKY, Boris
  • Peninsula Herlod, July 20, 2007

BALMER, Dr. W. Edward
  • The Blackstone Valleys News Tribune, March 23, 1966

BANNING, Arnold
  • Worcester Telegram & Gazette, July 7, 1991
  • The (Worcester, Mass.) Evening Gazette, Bannings still bloom at the 60-year
  • Mark, Aug. 27, 1987
  • Worcester Telegram & Gazette, VALLEY ART FESTIVAL WINNERS ANNOUNCED, April 25, 1990
  • Friesian Emigration to the United States, by Arnold Banning, March 11, 1991
  • "Summer of '49" By David Halberstam, William Morrow and Co. Inc.

BOYD, Thomas Hal
  • The (Monterey, Calif.) Sunday Herald, Feb. 11,1990

THE BIBLE, American Standard Version , 1ST Peter 3:1 (MUIR)
  • American Standard Version, Leviticus 11:32-40 (BALMER)
  • American Standard Version, Numbers 19:11-19 (BALMER)
  • American Standard Version, Hebrews 5:12-14 (VANDER LUGT)
  • New World Translation of the Holy Scriptures, Galatians 3:28,29 (VANDER LUGT)
  • American Standard Version, Psalm 111:10 (VANDER LUGT)
  • King James, Hebrews 11:1 (VANDER LUGT)
  • New World Translation of the Holy Scriptures, Hebrews 11:1 (VANDER LUGT)
  • KJ, ASV, NW, 1st Corinthians 2:10 (VANDER LUGT)

- American Standard Version, Matthew 25: 31-33 (DJILAS)
- American Standard Version, Matthew 25: 46 (DJILAS)
- American Standard Version, Psalm 139:16 (VERONESI)
- American Standard Version, Acts. 24:15 (VERONESI)
- American Standard Version, Proverbs 22:6 (PERKINS)
- King James, Revelation 20:6 (RESURRECTIONS...)
- New World Translation, John 5:28,29 (RESURRECTIONS...)
- New World Translation, Romans 6:7 (RESURRECTIONS...)
- New World Translation, Revelation 2:11; 20:6; 20:14; 21:8 (RESURRECTIONS...)
- New World Translation, Revelation 7:P4; 14:1,3 (RESURRECTIONS...)
- King James, Hebrews 11:1 (RESURRECTIONS...)
- American Standard Version Revelation 2:11 (RESURRECTIONS...)
- New World Translation Revelation 20:14 (RESURRECTIONS...)
- American Standard Version, Revelation 21:8 (RESURRECTIONS...)
- New World Translation 1st Thessalonians 4:13 (RESURRECTIONS...)
- New World Translation, John 17:3 (RESURRECTIONS...)
- King James, John 17:3 (RESURRECTIONS...}

CHANDLER, Charlotte, "Groucho & His Friends", Doubleday & Company, Inc. Garden City, N.Y., 1978

CHARKOUDIAN, Harry
- The (Springfield, Mass.) Daily News, August 28, 1984
- From Marash to Massachusetts, a memoir, by Tom Crawford, Jr.
- The New York Times, Yerevan Journal, Page A4, December 9, 2004

CLARK, Freda
- The (Springfield, Mass.) Union-News, November 22, 2002

CLARK, Henry J.
- The (Springfield, Mass.) Union, July 29, 1966

COTTON, Joseph S.
- The (Springfield, Mass.) Morning Union, June 13, 1986

- The (Springfield, Mass.) Morning Union, June 18, 1986, Harvard Freshman in 1936 Earns Degree 30 Years Later
- HARVARD CLASS of 1936, Fiftieth Anniversary Report, CAMBRIDGE, Printed for the Class, 1986

CYRUS, Franz
- Die Presse (Vienna), Feb. 9, 1995

DAVIS, Richard (Dick) Davis
- Worcester (Mass.) Telegram, May 9, 1962

DJILAS, Milovan
- The New York Times, April 21, 1995
- The New York Times, An Insider's Critique of Stalin and Communism, From 'The New Class', April 21, 1995
- "The New Class," By Milovan Djilas, 1957
- "Conversations With Stalin," By Milovan Djilas
- "Wartime," By Milovan Djilas
- "Land Without Justice," By Milovan Djilas
- "Black Lamb and Grey Falcon," by Rebecca West
- "The Road to Sarajevo," by Vladimir Dedijer
- "Rise and Fall" by Milovan Djilas
- "Rise and Fall" by Milovan Djilas, Harcourt Brace Jovanovich, San Diego, New York, London, 1985

DONATI, John A.
- The (Springfield, Mass.) Union-News, Sept. 25, 1999

DONOGHUE, Paul A.
- The (Springfield, Mass.) Union-News, July 24, 1991

DUDA, Sadik
- The (Durham, N.C.) Herald-Sun, June 7, 2007

EINSIEDEL, Georg Graf von
- Straubinger Tagblatt, Straubing, Germany

FREEDMAN, U.S. Judge Frank H.
 • The (Springfield, Mass.) Republican, Aug. 22, 2003

GARVEY, Richard C.
 • The (Springfield, Mass.) Republican, Sept. 10, 2004
 • "Bringing Home the News: 175-Year History of the Springfield Newspapers, by Richard C. Garvey and Wayne E. Phaneuf

GILMORE, Daniel F.
 • The Washington Post, Aug. 9, 1988

HACKETT, Peter, "Historic Sidelights," Blackstone Valley Tribune Advertiser, March 11, March 25, 1981

HENIG, Robin Marantz, The Monk in the Garden, The Lost and Found Genius of Gregor Mendel, the Father of Genetics, Houghton Mifflin Company, Boston, New York, 2000

HILL, Horace B.
 • The (Springfield, Mass.) Union-News, Dec. 7, 1994

KNEELAND, Douglas E.
 • Bangor (Me.) Daily News, Dec. 19, 2007
 • Chicago Tribune, Dec. 18, 2007
 • The New York Times, Dec. 19, 2007

LeMERE, Kenneth F.
 • The Springfield (Mass.) Daily News, June 8, 1965

MANTELL, Charles (Chick)
 • The (Worcester, Mass.) Evening Gazette, July 4, 1944
 • Ernie Pyle Says:

MERWIN, George
 • The (Springfield, Mass.) Morning Union, September 15, 1981

MIFTAFOGLU, Misbak
- Genghis Khan and the Making of the Modern World, By Jack Weatherford, Crown Publishers, N.Y.

MILLER, Lee G.
- "The Story of Ernie Pyle" Viking Press, 1950

MINOTT, Henry (Hank)
- Daily Times, Woburn, Mass. June 7, June 12, 1972

MUIR, Robert W.
- The (Springfield, Mass.) Morning Union, June 19, 1981

MURPHY, Francis (Frank) P.
- Worcester (Mass.) Telegram, July 5, 1973
- Worcester Telegram The Evening Gazette, Tornado June 18, 1953
- Telegram & Gazette, STORM for the AGES, June 6, 2003
- Sunday Telegram, TORNADO, June 8, 2003

NEWHOUSE, Donald R.
- The Springfield (Mass.) Daily News, Oct. 19, 1973

NEFF, Jerome (Jerry)
- The Island Packet, Hilton Head, S.C., Oct. 4, 2007

NIXON, Elizabeth
- Columbia Missourian, January 18, 1956
- Eulogy, Dr. Amy Charles, Westminster College Archives, New Wilmington, Pa., June 12, 1962
- The (Westminster College) Holcad, January 6, 1956
- Omaha (Nebraska) World-Herald, January 18, 1956
- Sioux City (Iowa) Journal, January 18, 1956
- Sioux City (Iowa) Journal, January 19, 1956
- The (Youngstown, Ohio) Vindicator, January 18, 1956

...OF AN OBITUARY WRITER
- The Kingdom and the Power, by Gay Talese, The World Publishing Company, New
- York and Cleveland, May 1969
- The Last Word, The New York Times Book of Obituaries and Farewell, Quill
- Morrow, New York, 1997
- More, ALDEN WHITMAN: 11 YEARS ON THE DEATH WATCH, September, 1977
- More, OBIT FOR A MAGAZINE, FOOTPRINTS (Deceased), September, 1977
- More, THE GHOUL POOL, September, 1977
- The New York Times, Concerns on Space and Revenue Growth of Paid Obituaries, by Felicity Barringer, Jan. 14, 2002
- Telegram & Gazette, Social Change, economy drives new T & G policy, by Bruce S. Bennett, Publisher, Aug. 7, 2003
- Worcester Telegram and The Evening Gazette, Style Manual, 1950
- Worcester Telegram & The Evening Gazette, A Record in Pictures of the Catastrophe that Struck Worcester and Central Massachusetts June 9, 1953, June 18, 1953
- Telegram & Gazette, Storm for the Ages, June 6, 2003
- Sunday Telegram, Remembering the Tornado of '53, June 8, 2003
- The Wall Street Journal, Viewpoint, by Michael Gartner, The Man Who Put Life into Obituaries, Oct. 11, 1990

PERKINS, Mrs. Dolores (Utovich)
- Worcester (Mass.) Telegram, Feb. 3, 2003
- Jehovah's Witnesses, Proclaimers of God's Kingdom, West Virginia State Board of Education v. Barnette (1943), Watchtower Bible and Tract Society of New York, Inc., (1993)
- Jehovah's Witnesses, Proclaimers of God's Kingdom, Minersville School District v Gobitis (sic) (1940). Watchtower Bible and Tract Society of New York, Inc., (1993)
- That Man, by Justice Robert H. Jackson,
- Watchtower, 1955, Pp. 427-428, 588-591

- Yearbook of Jehovah's Witnesses, 1975, Pp. 170-71
- Watchtower, June 11, 1987, Pp. 21,22
- Watchtower, Sept. 15, 1993, Pp. 10,11
- Watchtower, Dec. 1, 1995, P. 22
- Awake, July 22, 1993, P. 14

PIPAL, George H.
- The (Santa Rosa, Calif.) Press Democrat, Nov. 22, 1996

RIDL, Charles G. (Buzz)
- The (Youngstown, Ohio) Vindicator, April 29, 1995
- Pittsburgh Post-Gazette, Quiet man's legacy by Bob Smizik, May 3, 1995

ROONEY, Andy, "My War", Times Books, Random House, 1995 (DAVIS)

RUSSELL, Bill,
- The New York Times, Golden Memories, Dec. 5, 1983

RUSSELL, Bill and BRANCH, Taylor; Second Wind, The Memoirs of an Opinionated Man, 1979, Random House, New York

SCHERFF, Rupprecht R.
- The (Springfield, Mass.) Union-News, July 24, 1996

SCHNABEL, Dr. Franz
- Sueddeutsche Zeitung, Abschied von Franz Schnabel, Feb. 28, 1966
- Biographisch-Bibliographisches KIRCHENLEXIKON, Band IX (1995) Pages 519-521, Konrad Fuchs (Biographical Synopsis)
- The Northbridge Service Men's Album, 1941-45, Compiled by Augusta H. Lorenz and Lawrence M. Keeler, Whitinsville, Mass., 1947
- Kurzbiographie, Universitaet Karlsruhe, Fakultaet fuer Geistes- u. Sozialwissenschaften
- Franz Schnabel (1887—1966) Archivische Dokumente zu seinem

Wirken in Muenchen ab 1947

STADTMUELLER, Dr. Georg
- Nachruf George Stadtmueller zum Gedaechtnis von Helmut W. Schaller, Zeitschrift fuer Ostforschung (ZfO) 35, 1986, Pages S. 403-405
- "Michael Choniates, Metropolit von Athen (ca. 1138-1222)
- "Forschungen zur albanischen Fruehgeschichte"
- "Osmanische Reichsgeschichte und balkanische Volksgeschichte"
- "Geschichte Suedosteuropas"
- "Geschichte der habsburgischen Macht"
- "Geschichtliche Ostkunde"
- "Grundfragen der europaeischen Geschichte als Problem"
- "Polen in der europaeischen Geschichte"
- "Wartime" by Milovan Djilas

SYLVESTER, Roger E.
- The (Springfield, Mass.) Union-News, June 28, 1989

THALER, Karol
- Royal Borough of Kensington and Chelsea, London SW3, England

THE HISTORY OF NEW WILMINGTON, PENNSYLVANIA
- 1797-2003
- The Story of a Small Town
- New Horizons Publishing Company,
- New Wilmington, Pa.

THOMPSON, Morton, "The Cry and the Covenant," Doubleday & Co., Inc.
- 1949 (BALMER)

USTINOV, Sir Peter
- The New York Times, March 30, 2004

VANDER LUGT, Dr. William
- The Grand Rapids (Mich.) Press, June 11, 1992
- The Holland (Mich.) Sentinel, June 10, 1992
- "Of Course, Diogenes...", Commencement Address

- William Vander Lugt to the Class of 1972 at Hope College, Holland, Mich. June 5, 1972
- Vander Lugt guides Hope in search for truth, Nov. 16, 1970
- "Hope College anchor", August, 1972

VERONESI, Albert
- The (Springfield, Mass.) Republican, Aug. 17, 2004

WADE, Alan B.
- The Boston Globe, Sept. 8, 1995
- The Washington Post, Sept. 8, 1995
- The Boston Sunday Globe, April 18, 1993

WANTY, Vernon (Vic)
- Lancaster (Pa.) Intelligencer, June 3, 1996
- (Worcester, Mass.) Sunday Telegram, Learning about a better way to honor World War II veterans, By Albert B. Southwick, June 20, 2004
- The New York Times, When Revolutionaries Took On the U.S., by Carol Pogash, Dec. 11, 2004

Made in the USA
Charleston, SC
02 January 2015